ETCHINGS
in an
HOURGLASS

ALSO BY KATE SIMON

A Wider World: Portraits in an Adolescence
Bronx Primitive: Portraits in a Childhood
A Renaissance Tapestry: The Gonzaga of Mantua
New York: Places and Pleasures
New York (with Andreas Feininger)
Fifth Avenue: A Very Social History
Mexico: Places and Pleasures
Italy: The Places in Between
Rome: Places and Pleasures
Kate Simon's Paris
Kate Simon's London
England's Green and Pleasant Land

ETCHINGS
—— in an ——
HOURGLASS

KATE SIMON

1817
HARPER & ROW, PUBLISHERS, New York
Grand Rapids, Philadelphia, St. Louis, San Francisco
London, Singapore, Sydney, Tokyo, Toronto

ETCHINGS IN AN HOURGLASS. Copyright © 1990 by Kate Simon. All rights reserved. Printed in the United States of America. No part of this book may be used or reproduced in any manner whatsoever without written permission except in the case of brief quotations embodied in critical articles and reviews. For information address Harper & Row, Publishers, Inc., 10 East 53rd Street, New York, NY 10022.

FIRST EDITION

Designed by Alma Orenstein

Library of Congress Cataloging-in-Publication Data

Simon, Kate.
    Etchings in an hourglass/Kate Simon.—1st ed.
        p.   cm.
    ISBN 0-06-016219-8
    1. Simon, Kate.   2. New York (N.Y.)—Biography.   3. Jews—New
York (N.Y.)—Biography.   4. Authors, American—20th century—
Biography.   5. Simon, Kate—Health.   I. Title.
F128.9.J5S58   1990
974.7′100492402—dc20
[B]   89-46117

90 91 92 93 94 NK/RRD 10 9 8 7 6 5 4 3 2 1

For those who at many times and in various ways have lightened my life. Since I have no protective saints, no promise of heaven or hell, I have with great thanks chosen the following immortals, among them beloved, durable friends, to walk with me in my own Elysian fields, flowers at our feet, fruit-tree blossoms sweetening our air, as we wander in affectionate communality, as in Giovanni di Paolo's *Paradiso:*

Masaccio (Tommaso Guidi), Risë Stevens, Leo Tolstoy, Irving Berlin, Leonardo da Vinci, Greta Garbo, Gesualdo, Emily Dickinson, Cole Porter, Antonio Gaudi, Ella Fitzgerald, Thomas Eakins, Donatello, Édouard Vuillard, Charlie Chaplin, Béla Bartok, Edward Lear, Amedeo Modigliani, Quartetto Italiano, Rodgers and Hammerstein, William Shakespeare, ivory Virgin in Cloisters (damaged, very beautiful), Francesco da Laurana, Anton Chekhov, Giacomo Puccini, Nicholas Hawksmoor, Beverly Sills, primitive Catalan art (Barcelona), Rudolph Valentino, Plácido Domingo, Lotte Lehmann, Gloria Swanson, Geoffrey Chaucer, Clyfford Still, Francesco Borromini, Antonio Vivaldi, Caravaggio (Michelangelo Merisi), Charles Dickens, Lotte Lenya, Fyodor Dostoyevski, Budapest String Quartet, Mary Pickford, John Keats, Eugène Boudin, Francisco Goya, Claudio Monteverdi, Dimitri Shostakovich, Woody Allen, Giuseppe Verdi, John Constable

Contents

ETCHINGS
in an
HOURGLASS

This is a true story. However, with the exception of members of my family and public figures, I have not used the real names of living persons.

1

"Golden Lads and Girls All Must . . ."

THERE'S a man goin' roun' takin' names"; the spiritual sings of death, long an acquaintance. Several years before my biblically allotted three score and ten he began to become an intimate, sitting tired and drooping in unlit corners of my rooms; exhausted, senile, he shakily marks down the names of the myriad he must list. I first heard him scratching mine when a vomiting ulcer painted my bathroom walls with blood. A year or two later he put a second check against my name because my heart became tired of me. Now he has made a sharp little third check.

That illness began as uneasiness and instability, no overt sensations of illness, rather malaise. I was with a friend in Yucatán, an area I had enjoyed on many visits: the slight, delicate-featured Mayans and their little wives like clean white pillows, the stark pyramids of Chichén Itzá, the baroque elegance of Uxmal, the superb arrogance of Palenque, and the pretty amiability of park-studded Mérida. However, my skin wasn't fitting properly; the practiced, easy patience and good humor I had earlier acquired in Mexico—to accept sudden changes in schedules and prices, to believe the heartfelt promises not kept; to be charmed by the vagaries of *mañana* and *ahora*—became prickly annoyance. The mangoes in the market lost their pink flush, the vendors their gold-toothed animation. I was also wrapped in vivid nightmare imaginings. When I learned there had been a minor accident in the New York subways, I saw clearly and couldn't dispel the pregnant figure of a girl I was fond of as a victim of that accident, and I was constantly propelled to and from Mérida's telephone and telegraph offices. To whom could I address a telegram inquiring about her condition? To which police station or hospital? I knew it was craziness but couldn't hide from the image of her injured body or from my consuming anxiety. The waking nightmare was gradually washed away by the calming words of my friend, only to give way to another obsession. I had bought an embroidered white Mayan dress—wide, long, a lyrical thing—for this daughter of a close friend. Carrying it back to my hotel, I was beset by an old Jewish superstition I didn't know I knew, convinced that giving her the dress before delivery meant a difficult or tragic birthing. (Checking later, I found that the superstition referred only to baby gifts offered before the baby was born, a reminder of the hazards of childbirth long ago.) Was my translation of the superstition a curse, a flashback to the time I had hated all pregnant women because I had no children and thought I never would have any? My friend took the dress from me as I was about to return it, pushed it deep into my suitcase, and said firmly, "Forget it." I didn't altogether, ultimately presenting the dress with a feeling of dread, as if I were Medea offering Jason's new young wife the robe that would destroy her.

The mental aberrations to a degree assuaged, my body took over the erratic. I was hungry but couldn't eat; I had fleeting stomach pains I treated as ordinary attacks of Montezuma's revenge; the usual trustworthy medication didn't help. I lost weight, energy, and amiability; every small contretemps split my stomach and head open. Realizing that I was dragging down my friend's spirits and enthusiasm, I arranged that we visit Palenque, which she had never seen. It was a long, absorbing drive from Mérida, with stops at lively, curiously contrasting villages interesting enough to dry up my stream of afflictions.

At Palenque we hired a young guide full of arcane mathematical information derived from Mayan codices, his compilation to be published, he hoped, as new revelations concerning the city that was once a great religious and court center. We climbed the small buildings, admired at a distance the white lacework finials of others, examined the masterly plaques of beplumed nobles and corn gods, and were then confronted with the tower that held the burial place of an ancient prince. My friend examined carefully the tall, worn, and irregular steps and refused to climb them. I, still responding to a challenge as if I were my adolescent self, began to make the climb with our guide and a crowd of young Mexicans on holiday. The ascent was slow, steep, and uncertain, but I made it with the help of our guide, who gave me a hand and a pull-up once in a while. The actual tomb, at the top of the tower, was unique in Mexican archaeology. Like royal Egyptian tombs, it had been a repository of jewels and rare artifacts. But they were gone, probably taken to the Archaeological Museum in Mexico City to become part of its rich Mayan collection. It was disappointing but not seriously, since I *had* made the climb and was rather proud of the feat. The descent was trickier. My short legs had difficulty reaching successive deep steps, and my foothold was made unsteady by smooth-soled sandals, which slid on the time-grooved, ancient stones. I slipped and kept on slipping, bruising my back as it bounced off one stone edge to be sharply hit by another. When I stopped, almost paralyzed with pain and terror, several Mexican gentlemen took my arms and tried to guide me down. I couldn't move, shaking with fear and shame. My young guide stepped before me and said, "Grip my shoulders—grip them hard and don't let go." I dug my hands into his meager muscles, and for what seemed to be hours he carried me, my nails mercilessly piercing his flesh, down and down, to the accompaniment of derisive calls from one young group: "Why did you bring your grandmother here if you have to carry her down?" When we reached the last step, the guide walked away quickly, not waiting for the customary tip, not permitting me to thank him. I staggered to a rock under a broad, red-leafed tree, curtly refusing a drink and the use of a fan offered by a couple who had descended with me. My friend had gone off to walk in less demanding places and I was alone, examining the gnarled tree of veins on my hands, listening to my jumping heart, too ashamed and angry with myself to talk to the solicitous couple.

I had observed the proliferation of brown spots on my forearms; I could go to the movies at a reduced rate most afternoons; I paid half fare on the bus; I could not be evicted from my apartment. I was nominally a "senior citizen," a euphemism that I found contemptible as I sat on that Palenque rock. "Senior" was for high school and college students. I was old—plain old and maybe sick unto death, as the aberrations of my mind and body had been trying to tell me.

It is difficult to know what the protective mechanisms were, but, by the time we were back in Mérida I was able to accept the possibility of a mortal disease without terror or even ordinary worry. We continued exploring Yucatán as patience returned, good nature again smiled. The aura didn't hold, though; a dour cloud wrapped itself around me when I returned to New York. Various scales showed a startling loss of weight that launched my medical authorities on probings into places with their own secret and, I imagined, easily humiliated lives. The final diagnosis, more than half expected, was cancer of the stomach.

I awaken in a hospital bed in an ordinary room discreetly cut off from an adjoining area by a wide opaque curtain; no sound, no movement except the white figure of a nurse slipping in and out of the slit in the never-opened curtain. My bed is wide and unbarred, quite different from the surgical intensive-care crib I last remember. Could it have been two days ago, or three or four? Where had I been in those vanished days since a young nurse who introduced herself as a member of the surgical team asked me sweetly to extend my arm for an injection of Valium, or so I think she said? Blank, impenetrable nothing thereafter. Where was the non-I, the any-I whose body was split open? (I see the body of a frog in a high school biology class, lying in a swamp of formaldehyde, splayed wide open, his legs extended and pinned to his gummy bed.) Why was I not present when tubes were put in my nose and mouth; electrodes pasted to my neck; my body, like the frog's, splayed open while the pathologists—unseen, unheard, unknown—took from me tissue that was frozen, examined, reports rushed back to the surgeon, the leader of the troops, the king sending his emissaries to seek out the enemy so that he might destroy it with his terrible swift sword?

I lift my hospital gown, a listless piece of faded cotton with the cleanliness of respectable poverty, and gaze down at my astonished flesh. On my belly, from the bottom rib to the pubic line, I see a small railroad track of staples, my flesh a novel form of stationery. I'm amazed and amused: I had expected stitches concealed by bandages and here I was, raw flesh clamped together as if it were a bundle of papers. I drop the gown, still tiredly amused, as a young doctor walks in. He introduces himself courteously and smiling the bedside smile of solicitude, asks how I feel, if I am comfortable. Yes, I seem to be OK, but could he tell me what had happened to my stomach and its coral-colored cancer, which I had seen as a rather attractive ring in a photograph taken by a camera attached to the end of a long, suffocating tube I had earlier swallowed and disgorged? Was it encapsulated—I had chosen this word as comfort, as an indication of limited size and growth, enemy cells besieged by the sturdy normal? No, he was sorry to say, it had not been encapsulated. I now had one-third or possibly one-quarter of a stomach left, and in the intervals between the dashings back and forth of pathologists, my spleen had been excised, an ovary (benign, the surgeon later told me but better out, and really at my age did I need it?), and assorted other bits and pieces.

I was "riddled," as they say, diminished, reduced; to misuse Lewis Carroll, a subject of "uglification and derision." I began to wonder about what the X rays, the scans, the eellike camera had not picked up. My mother's voice returned to me, telling of someone in Warsaw who had been consumed by the Crab, the zodiac's Cancer. With her remembered voice I returned to childhood visions; myriad tiny crabs burrowing viciously in my flesh, chewing on my cells, spitting out their poison, nesting and feeding in what had been altogether mine, now become theirs. How could I remain friendly with a minute, dwarfed, feeble stomach that could once engulf heaps of pasta arrabiata, the creamy dishes of Normandy, fat bagels draped in Scottish salmon? My straying mind, still somewhat anesthetized (I am convinced that the effects of anesthetics last much longer than medical wisdoms say they do) found itself chanting with Shakespeare, "Golden lads and girls all must, as chimney-sweepers, come to dust." And, more angrily, "Flesh, flesh, how art thou fishified!"

As death, a gigantic crab, stared at me and I at him, I found that I wasn't afraid—furious, but not afraid. My misted mind repeated a vow that I would never again fast on Yom Kippur, a tribal ritual that had long ago been my one piece of obeisance to the God of Israel. For this and earlier cruelties, God owed me many repentant Yom Kippurs, observed in whatever howling Hebrew way he liked. A tribal debt I did pay was a series, in the hospital and later at home, of Holocaust dreams which, whether they so identify them or not, burden many Jews who escaped the extermination camps or, as I did, the horrors of the Warsaw ghetto, where aunts, uncles, and cousins I knew only as a very young child were exterminated. The dream scene was a clean white office, that of a hospital, although there were no beds or medical equipment or nursing personnel about. The room held only a desk behind which sat a small, spare man with a sharp, dry voice and the face of Eichmann-Goebbels. Dressed in a stiffly starched white coat he called the names of a line of Jewish prisoner-patients who stand before him. To the first he said with the uninflected voice of a robot, "You die today." To the second he announced, "You die tomorrow," and so on down the line. In the first dream I was the thirteenth to die. With each successive dream of that icy, pristine room and the ugly, narrow Eichmann-Goebbels face at the desk, I moved up in line until I headed it. "Today you die, Jew Simon." That ended the series; I could not envisage, even in a dream, my actual death.

(At no time in the dreams was I afraid, as I felt no overt fear at the meeting with malignancy, practically no reaction—a return perhaps to the times when my cherished people, the staffs of my life, were judged incurable, on the inexorable path to death. I was determined, at those times, to think no more, to feel no more, to be as alert and helpful as I could while I closed myself into a wall of ice, becoming stylishly thin as I fed only on heaps of frozen terror. But that fuller story is later matter.)

I return to muse long on the three women with whom I had shared another room, a four-bed "cancer" room. I was surrounded by the dying but not feeling at all moribund, possibly because of my coat of ice, possibly because my roommates and their paths to death were so absorbing. Next to me lay an extraordinarily beautiful Latino lady in her eighties. She was blind and haughtily proud of her remembered beauty, insisting on maintaining rituals that graced that beauty. Every day two or three of her grandchildren came, usually during their work lunch hours. They brought no food or sweets or flowers; those were the weekend offerings of their parents. It was the young people's duty and pleasure to kiss her hand, to brush her long white hair and arrange it as she instructed them to, feeling with her graceful fingers the shapes they had devised. This was done by the boys as well as the girls, whoever came earlier. It was left to the girls to put rouge on her cheeks and powder her face and neck, to dress her in a fresh bed jacket and spray her with perfume. The boys plumped her pillows, straightened her slippers evenly at the foot of her bed; she insisted they lie neatly together although she, completely bedridden, never saw or used them. Since I spoke Spanish, I introduced myself to her and asked from time to time whether I could help her in any way. She was pleased to hear my voice in her language and used me, lightly, tactfully, to check on her grandchildren. Had the boys put her slippers side by side neatly at the foot of her bed? Had those careless girls put too much rouge on her or powdered her like a clown? Yes, the slippers were neatly placed, the rouge and powder perfect, lovely. Was her hair well combed and arranged? Yes, very nice. *Por favor,* she had dropped her rosary somewhere on the coverlet, could I help her find it? With pleasure, and I got up, put it in her hand, and watched her pray. Not too often, not too ardently; she seemed to prefer other, more private calmants, a poised old queen looking without agitation at her past, waiting in elegance and grace for death.

The woman opposite me was in a last tortured stage. She whimpered like a child, shrieked noises that, to make them bearable, I translated into raucous jungle bird calls. She howled like a trapped animal, her torment unassuaged by testy nurses who insisted she'd had all the medicine they could give her, untempered by an anxious daughter whose crumpled face and twisted fingers could do nothing for her mother.

My third neighbor was an old Jewish lady who had been in the hospital, one of the nurses told me, a long time and would probably never leave it alive. She wore no wig but like many ultra-Orthodox women in the privacy of their homes, covered her head with a scarf. I never saw her without it. She had a candle, always lit, at the side of her bed and read for long hours in one or two Hebrew books. From time to time she rejected a meal, suspecting that it was not as kosher as she required although the hospital's kitchens were seriously kosher. The rejection came with a sweet, apologetic smile: "Don't worry, nurse, it's not your fault. I don't need much to eat; next time." Occasionally she was visited by one or two Hasidic gentlemen in long black coats and round black hats. Their role, it seemed was not so much to comfort her as to enter with her into discussions of the Law and interpretations, often needle sharp and complex, as put down by rabbinical thinkers. I could make out some of these words from the remnants of Yiddish and Hebrew I had learned in my childhood. I could speak with her, too, a little, and awkwardly. She blessed me when I smoothed her sheets, when I poured her a glass of water. In a low, measured voice she pitied me for being a Jewish daughter who did not live with God as intimately as I should, who would not know the joys of meeting the Holy Ones as she soon would—in God's time, whenever he was ready. On days when she felt enough strength in her dwindling body she became comfort and counselor to coreligionists in other rooms on our hall. The magnificence of the Catholic woman and of the Orthodox Jewish woman acted as balm to my once-in-a-while sense of insult at having been attacked and quite probably induced me to refuse chemotherapy, an assault that had tormented four of my dead friends. No such postponements, thank you. Like my roommate mentors I would take death calmly, when it chose to come, or so I planned and hoped.

The hospital stay was, of course, greatly lightened by the visits, the gifts, and the splendid bouquets of flowers which I received with pleasure and some surprise. Since I was a child, and my father criticized me as ugly, erratic, disobedient, inconsiderate, extravagant (with what money or possessions?), I had found it difficult to believe I was loved and still, somewhat, do. I can · accept evaluations of myself as fairly accomplished, courageous, reasonably intelligent, sympathetic, independent, and durable, but lovable is difficult; my father had seen to that. I still feel a touch of the impostor in me when I accept such tokens of love as attention and deep solicitude. Do I really deserve them? I never know surely. (I have given love and even felt its concomitant burrs of jealousy and longing but am confused, in these latter years, by the fact that a similar degree of love can be evoked by a piece of music or a painting. Or even a place, like Siena or the jeweled tower of the Chrysler Building, or Barcelona—loves free of the tentacles that search for pain.)

At home I was attended to by a three-times-a-week "housekeeper" and had frequent visits from a cheery nurse who told me how and what to eat and described sensations that might be new to me and how to handle them. I listened, more interested in her brisk cheeriness than the unremarkable information that came from her plain, sincere face. The housekeepers were another matter. One waved the vacuum cleaner about and then settled herself in the living room to listen to my conversations with visitors. Another told me that it was part of her job to bathe me and wash my hair. Often dizzy and worried about stepping in and out of the tub alone, I accepted, to regret it almost immediately. Being washed reduced me to helpless infancy or, worse yet, to senile feebleness, for which I was not ready. After a few weeks they left, replaced by an optimistic, energetic friend I had not seen for some years. She apparently carried with her constantly a debt she felt she owed me for help at a crucial time in her life. I had forgotten the events but was pleased with her presence and the fact that bread upon the waters did not always vanish on an indifferent tide.

After she left I felt very much alone. My visitors, except for a few of the very faithful, had dwindled in number and interest when I discarded my new dressing gown and changed into ordinary clothing. Some expected people didn't appear, or call, or write, introducing me to knowledge common among sufferers of cancer: We are often avoided, as AIDS sufferers are avoided, by people fearful of contagion from the clasp of a hand. (My wandering strands of reference bring me the cold, stone hand of the Commendatore who pulls Don Giovanni to his death.) Comfort and escape from a brooding, new sort of loneliness, a particular loneliness of the aging, warmed me in the country houses and flats of cronies in London who comforted, cosseted, and fed me and clothed my new, slimmed shape with fine garments they had outgrown in their wholesome spreads.

Back, reluctantly, to the showers of papers, the claims to fill out, the endless cantankerous dialogues with insurance providers, and, finally, to start on this book. It is a chilling task, this opening of a Pandora's box that might better be left untouched. It must be quite unlike the book about my childhood, the light and the dark of a merry dance with bewildered pauses, marching in a parade of irresistible, unique, immigrant characters. The second book, mainly of my adolescent adventures, experiencing, learning—from teachers, from jobs, from the streets of New York, from neighbors in strange living quarters. And it dealt with the college years, with me as a faithful Fanny Brawne to Keats, as Eleanor of Aquitaine in her circles of courtly love, as substitute for Jane Morris who had been so cruel to my gifted hero, William Morris.

This present book will circle with reluctant memory around glowing passions that faded to dull tatters, years whipped by storms of pain sharpened by madness and illness. And, since I am the agglomeration I am, it will be a recounting of varied pleasures and entertainments, with me standing off, as I frequently do, watching my doppelgänger companion mimicking the twin me.

2

Jerry

I WALK on Fifth Avenue or Madison and glimpse a man who looks like him, and then another and yet another, who folds himself into a line of passing backs. I can't be sure that one of them is or is not Jerry and am horrified by a vision of time's bacteria rotting my memory. How could a man who was the lodestar of all my impulses for five years have been so thoroughly drowned in the black lakes of forgetting? He was, it is true, not particuarly distinguished in his looks—medium height, medium breadth, medium coloring—a "just my Bill" type physically. I had met him one summer evening at the house of friends. He was bright, witty, and fashionably, comfortably, leftish, as we all were. In the course of the evening's conversation someone suggested that Stalin's pact with Hitler might seem odd to those who sat on political fences. It might appear to be a disturbing act, but the general consensus was that Uncle Joe knew what he was doing; he was to be trusted. I had been in this sort of conversation before and was ready to leave early, but the humor and lightness with which Jerry spoke, the little jokes he made, lifting the sentious atmosphere, attracted and kept me. More than that, though, I was caught by the awareness that he found me attractive, lit my cigarettes with alacrity, and kept offering me the stark little cakes that were the usual treats at such gatherings. When midnight arrived he asked if he could walk me home. I consented, tamping down my eagerness and pleasure at having been selected above two other unaccompanied women. My mother and my husband had been dead for some time, my daughter was away in a country school, and I was chilled to the bone with loneliness. There was no promise of spring for me, nor that of a summer ripening; I might as well have been an abandoned old woman in her seventies as a young woman in her early thirties. My vistas were bleak: landscapes of poor-paying jobs, tight apartments, the past and future nurturing of a child too early matured in independence and restraint. No dates, no love, no sex, and none in sight, maybe soon to become altogether unimaginable.

Here was an entertaining, eager admirer to whom I yielded eagerly that first night. He set off fireworks, a great multicolored explosion of sexual fullness. My adolescent experiences had been collages of curiosity, ineptitude, and hopefulness; my marriage had lost sexual strength with Steve's terminal illness. Here, now, were the transports I had read about. (As in Hemingway; as among the heroines of contemporary novels who wait for years to be carried to the bed where their every vein, every artery, every breath flow together as perfumed rivers; where contentment is honeyed, languorous; where hands become flowering branches and hair turns into lustrous ferns.)

I don't know that I ever loved him sentimentally, wreathed him in cozy, expectant illusions and dreams, but I became addicted to him as the creator of a new, delicately receptive being who came to vivid life at the sound of his voice on the telephone or the touch of his hand. He was, of course—my usual luck— married with a watchful wife who, I suspected from a few hints and his confident skill, probably had lived with earlier infidelities. His work, which took him out of his office at irregular times, afforded us erratic hours for meeting. In order not to miss his calls and impromptu visits, I left my job to become fat on bread and potatoes, the only foods I could afford on my meager savings. I left the apartment as rarely as possible to stay ready for him. He was frequently concerned and contrite over the fact that I lived so poorly and equally troubled by an arrangement that made his partner the keeper and dispenser of moneys; he could hide extremely little of his earnings or expenditures. I don't know how, but he did manage to buy me a warm coat that first winter and to pay for an enchanted holiday weekend when his wife was visiting her Chicago sister that first spring. It was during those long, untroubled hours in a small suburban inn that Jerry began to introduce me to variations in which I joined him with enthusiasm. No reluctance, no qualms; where he led I would follow. And we walked some and ate some and danced as we had danced in the jazz and blues clubs of the Village, swaying to the erotic melancholy of the "Tin Roof Blues": "Rock me baby, rock me in your big brass bed," and the saxophone wail of "Sweet Lorraine," both musics never to be erased, still tattooed in me. And drank fair quantities of Tokay wine. I thought of Tokay not as a wine but as a magic elixir and a potent enhancer of the bittersweet Hungarian gypsy music I began to listen to avidly, evoking again and again that transfiguration weekend.

The summers were our time. His wife and children were in their country house, and except for weekends, we were free to spend most of our evenings and nights together. The weekends were worn away in scrubbing laundry and floors and in Sunday— parents' day—visits to Lexie's country school. Not to be seen by friends and acquaintances in commonly frequented places, we sought out obscure restaurants. Our favorite was one on Ninth Avenue, a French bistro that then served sailors off French ships docked at Hudson River piers. The proprietors of the long, dimly lit room of a few tables and a long zinc bar were good cooks of basic, hearty dishes and became quite attached to us and our *"grand amour,"* particularly after I put down my fork in midmeal one evening and said, "Let's go home. Right now." Madame, at her *caisse* near our table, had enough English to understand my words and enough zest for *l'amour* to understand the drive under the words. She beamed and wished us a very happy goodnight, as she did each time we left her establishment. By eavesdropping, she must have learned a good deal about us, although I've often wondered how much she gleaned of a subject Jerry introduced several times. He wanted to watch, and maybe participate, while a woman (some old, willing friend) made love to

me, reaching for a variation of the eternally seductive triangle—
a basic pattern of living it seemed (and still does) to me. I said
OK, why not? Somehow, it never happened.

The months passed, and the last of my savings. I had to find
a job and did, a dizzying job in which I was spy between mistress
and wife, spokeswoman for female personnel, writer of tactful
letters when the boss said, "Tell him to go to hell," a general
slick factotum who would now be paid decent sums of money
for the deft juggling the job entailed. Jerry began to talk divorce,
but I did not press; I could not imagine severing him from his
children, any more than I could leave my daughter. From time
to time I heard from a close friend that the wife knew who I was,
had studied me on the streets near my house. The poor woman—
I was amazed to find myself pitying her—was starving herself, I
was told, to match my comparative slimness, learning to use
makeup as boldly as I sometimes did, shedding her plain-Jane
clothing for the colorful, ethnic, Villagey costumes I then favored
and thought suited me. Knowing my identity, she found my
telephone number and spent her tormented night hours phoning
when she thought we might be together. Jerry persuaded me not
to answer, although I always feared that it might be an emergency
call from Lexie's school.

As jealous as she was of me, I was jealous of her, of her
safeties, of her country house, of her large city apartment, of
living with her children. The jealousy became a strangling rope
around my throat and chest when I saw her enter the ladies' room
of a restaurant I frequented. As I recognized her, I slipped into
a booth and stayed there listening to her describe to a friend the
past weekend: She and Jerry had wandered around the area of
their country house searching out antiques and rugs, obviously
spending a good deal of money. I choked on the thought of the
money she had and used lavishly while I had none. The jealousy
grew to a blinding fury when I thought of the little money and
its potential pleasures, of which she had deprived me. Jerry had
been putting aside inconsequential sums, five dollars here, ten
dollars there, to build up a travel fund for us. What he would
do about wife, children, work he didn't say and I didn't ask. I so

longed for the journey and its dazzling freedoms for both of us that it was no longer a dream; besides Lexie, it was my most solid reality. Jerry had amassed and hidden about one hundred dollars in a so-called secret pocket of his wallet. Looking embarrassed and sickly, he told me on one quick visit that the money had disappeared. The question was unnecessary, the answer too simple; his wife had taken to inspecting his clothing and accessories very carefully, had found and stolen our treasure: my Paris, my Venice, my Istanbul.

Several days each summer we went to some obscure village in the Adirondacks or New England, finding grassy hills and deep-hanging willows for lovemaking under summer suns. The fifth summer, though, approached under an altered sky. The grace notes and trills of sex were a shade less compelling; I found myself more eager to listen to the pages of a book (*War and Peace* and a diaphragm lying side by side in my luggage seemed to tell the prophecy quite wittily, I thought) than listen to his witticisms and his solo recital of the never-never divorce and the never-never trip that would surround me with the glories of Rome and Florence. The toothsome scheme of arranging a *pas de trois* with one of his past lady friends no longer interested me; the utterly obedient enthusiasm had been worn away by repetition. He, too, began to move toward an end in his own way. The finale, for which I was not ready yet, came shockingly, painfully, as I saw him approach a pretty girl, a college-student waitress at our motel, with the becks and smiles, the light touching, and the glowing eyes that for so long had been solely mine. He was back in his hobby of seductions and in that return had created a new triangular pattern, in which I was potentially the woman to be eluded and lied to.

Shortly after those closing chords to five suffering and exalted years, I went off to Mexico on a modest sum of money my mother had left me. Jerry swore that he would come to find me in Mexico. He didn't come; I didn't expect him. It wasn't until I had been remarried for over a year that Jerry invited me to lunch to announce that he had the money for our trip. He didn't care what his wife thought or did, we owed ourselves wandering through

Europe together. His interest in young women was purely fatherly, but he would watch his behavior if it offended me. Please, please. I assumed he had borrowed the money and asked him why he hadn't done that before my marriage. It was too late now; I couldn't and wouldn't leave my husband and especially not my daughter, who was now living at home with us and enjoying the new father whom she looked on as an affectionate older brother. No and again no.

From time to time, over intervals of years, I heard from Jerry, pleading that I spend two or three days with him in one of his country hideaways. I refused to see him and continued to refuse, politely, calmly, until it was necessary, uncontrollable, to explode. One of the last calls, both of us already falling out of the "middle-age" basket into the one marked "aging" repeated a sentence I had always loathed: His wife was going to visit her sister in Chicago and he urged, insisted, that I spend that time with him. The anger stored for many years burst loudly. "Where were you when Lexie was sick and died? Did you help me? Did you console me? When my sister was sick and died, leaving three babies, where were you? When did you share any of my miseries? I am no longer the woman you knew and, for God's sake, never tell me again that your wife is away and I'm to become your lusty lover for a couple of days. Don't call me again, never. I swear I'll hang up on you." I did hang up when I heard his voice once or twice later. Now he is anonymous, almost any walker in the streets. He's gone. I rarely think of him; almost never. Why does the irrepressible little voice in my head sing with Berlioz: "Reviens, reviens, ma bien-aimée"?

Or is it not the love but the essential triangle to which I call? Psychologists, analysts, novelists and playwrights back to the Greeks, have made the love triangle an immortal pattern, betraying, perhaps, an innate human configuration, a concealed basic organ compounded of jealousy and passion. It seems to me that long before I could read anything less simple-minded than the Dutch Twins, I could see the excitements and the universality of triangles, the very stuff of later movies. Ruthie was my best friend, but it gave life a certain painful piquancy to find out that she had gone to the library without me; she had preferred to go with Minnie. It was unjust but I learned early that in the triangle of my mother, my brother, and me, my brother was preferred. And although my father was not affectionate with me, it was my brother, I noticed, who was always severely punished; I, rarely. My second husband was married when he began to court me, one triangle; another was shaped by his angry mother, her son, and me, the new third. (One could go on and on shaping and reshaping, discerning triangles among one's friends' and one's own arrangements.)

The triangle I was never quite capable of sketching accurately was one never seen but frequently heard. It took its angles from voices in a hotel in Nantes, in a room next to that in which Bill and I stayed for several nights. The voices were tenor, bass, and soprano, a trio that alternated heavy breathing and tunes of ecstasy—one voice, two, all three—with shouts of anger nicely laced with obscenities. The last act (for me) of this unseen drama opened with the three voices in their expected concert of squeals and gasps. Suddenly, a door flew open and we heard fast steps running down the hall, the soprano voice shrieking, *"Il m'a mordu!"* Who bit her, the bass or the tenor? And why didn't they stop her from running down the hall and yelling her woe? Since Bill wouldn't let me open the door, I never saw her or where she was bitten, or found out who owned the culprit teeth.

3

Culture Shocks: Indian—and Japanese

W HILE I was living in Rome I received a call from an expatriate acquaintance in Mexico City who was bright and sociable, with an impassioned appreciation of the relationship between the lowly peso and the exalted dollar whose repetitions (chorused by many other expatriates) I found boring and vulgar possibly because I was living the good life on the cheap as well. I didn't like or dislike her especially; I knew nothing but her energetic, talkative surface. She told me during that call that she would like to go to India and would I come along? I had just about finished a book on Rome that I meant to put aside, to distance for a later, fresher view. Furthermore, I had recently been approached by the Indian tourist authorities to do a book for them in collaboration with an American publisher. I had made no promises, sensing that it would be a long and certainly difficult task. Although I had known hovels and hunger in Mexico, I was afraid of staring at Calcutta. Sara's call and my subsequent agreement to travel with her provided an opportunity for exploration before I committed myself.

Our elaborate route from Rome ultimately landed us in Bombay, to settle into an antique waterfront hotel (the Taj Mahal?) hardly changed, I imagined, from the time it served the masters of the Raj: languid fans on the ceiling, beds enshrouded in cheese-cloth, servants in ornate headdresses to bring us startlingly early tea, ready or not. We had driven from the Bombay airport in the early evening and were captivated by the rows of eating stalls in their timid glow of oil lamps, by the children asleep in string beds in the front yards of ramshackle tenements. It was during that ride from the airport that I absorbed my first infusion of the smell of India—a heady melange of perfumed body oils, cow dung, spices, urine, and floral scents—an odor that is not wholly gone from the lumpish sack of memories that shape me.

After breakfast (did they call it tiffin or had I mistaken something on the BBC?) of scones, marmalade, and more black, ironclad tea served by a splendidly dressed waiter all starch, braid, and plumes above bare feet, we walked along the waterfront. Gazing seaward, we stopped, our eyes fixed, incredulous. Yes, without any doubt, a good number of locals were defecating on the beach, obviously the communal morning purge for those who had no toilets. We averted our eyes and walked swiftly on, discussing what the men (there were no women that we could see) used as toilet paper. Leaves? Or nothing, washing their trousers frequently? Did they kick sand over the fecal matter or did they trust the tide to wash it away? As we were animatedly discussing the matter, beginning to move into scatological jokes, a skinny half-naked boy, strolling with his arms behind his back, came toward us. As he spoke the words of a common joke, "Look, Ma, no hands," he pulled his arms forward to poke them into our faces. Both bare arms were handless. He examined our shocked faces intently, then sauntered away leaving us transfixed, ready to leave India immediately, restrained only by the fact that we had booked a boat trip, to leave in an hour, for the bay that held the Elephanta caves, our first *in situ* encounter with the masterly beauties of Indian sculpture, which we had experienced before only in museums and art books.

Later that day we wandered inside the city and came upon a temple into which we were invited by a young acolyte (wrong word, but I don't know the appropriate designation) surrounded by figures of Ganesha, the endearing elephant god; by Nana, the bovine spirit; by Siva of the many arms and third eye, and by chromos of *Mahabharata* events. In exchange for a small donation to his temple he offered a garland of flowers. I put out my left hand to receive it and he politely told me that I must use my right hand; the left was for earthly, vulgar matters. (Such care exerted even on the morning beaches?) We left him with bows and clasped hands at our foreheads in imitation of his farewell gestures and headed for the market, my usual choice of priorities for getting to know something of a town.

It was unlike any market I had ever seen anywhere. Fruits and vegetable areas, so large and radiant in Mexican markets, were comparatively minor matters here. One large space was filled with the busy practice, exercised by gnarled old men in dhotis, of extracting hair from the ears and nostrils of other gnarled old men in dhotis. In a nearby open-air clinic, toenails cracked by the stones and heat of long pilgrimages were cut and oiled. Here a tooth was extracted, there a boil lanced, without the help of an-esthetic balms. Walking deeper into the market past stalls of spices and greens, past lengths of gaudy sari cloth and heaps of sandals, we reached an area of small shanties haphazardly supporting each other, women leaning against the uncertain wood and tin, and ragged children, some of them too young to walk, rolling in their mud of dust and urine.

Although I had seen the "cribs" of pre-Castro Havana— women calling and displaying their charms out of wooden booths like torn boxes—and had heard of the picture windows that made Dutch portraits of prostitutes in Amsterdam, had watched the whores who haunted Mexican hotels and the heartbreaking preg-nant whores—there was apparently a taste for them—who stood outside the main station in Rome, I had never before Bombay seen prostitution as one of the acknowledged service centers of a market. I was told by a Jewish cloth vendor whom I visited when I spotted a Star of David on his window that the women were divided into those who lived in "unnumbered" and "numbered" houses. The women we encountered first, in the unnumbered cabins, received the smallest sums for fifteen or twenty minutes with a market customer. They lived in their makeshift hovels with other women and their many children, all of whom scattered outdoors while one woman attended to a client. A short distance off were the numbered houses, cottages whose several inhabitants earned higher rates—the services more leisured, the children placed outdoors not quite so much rags and bones. The women themselves were less slatternly, neater, with gentler voices than those of the poorer competition. Not far from the numbered houses were the boys, boys as clean-faced boys, boys in heavy makeup, boys in saris, shining with hair oil and circlets of earrings and bangles and neck chains. We saw no rooms or houses. Where did these boys take their men—or women? Possibly they leased time and space from the women in the numbered houses. Or were they taken to customers' houses? I knew something of their like in Rome, but those Italian boys were proud, playful, often magnificently dressed, never of the moods and qualities of these starvelings adorned in bitter pantomime.

It was a long trip that consumed about two months, and we covered a good deal of India and its astonishments of beautiful and hideous sights: the exquisite paintings of Ellora; the fearsome shrouded figures, still or convulsed, on the streets of Calcutta; the gossamer silks of the weavers; the fresh blood of a kid sacrificed to black-faced Kali smeared on the face of a baby; the female delicacy of the Taj Mahal and the masculine pride of the nearby old royal city of Fatehpur Sikri. We were choked by the smell of disks of cow manure drying on the walls of Indian village houses, were attacked by an army of gibbons who would not let us enter their temple in Bangalore.

Although our lives together, our travels, were mutually agreeable, there was one thing I would not do with Sara and that was to sit with her for endless hours in the bars of hotels—where there were bars—to attract male friendship. One drink, two, all right; not more. I could never fathom what she hoped from the Indians who wandered in. They were few, most of them salesmen or tourists, and certainly not interested in two American women settled in the middle of middle age. She, whose longtime lover had died about a year before, praised him loudly and wetly after she had had a few drinks, and, having listened sympathetically to several such drunken dirges, I avoided them. How alluring her tears and sad story might have been to the bar gentlemen I can't tell, except by her ostensible lack of success.

On some of our journeys we had escorts provided by a New Delhi travel agency. Whether they considered it chic or it was done to make us more comfortable, they said their names were Nick—voluble, short, and threatening stoutness—and Jack—slender, older, and more taciturn. Having seen a number of Indian movies and much Indian sculpture, noticed people lying under street eaves masturbating, and caught steamy erotic airs everywhere, I was yet startled by one visit we made with The Boys. They had conducted us to a restaurant beyond the old market of Delhi, a flower-wreathed spread of tables that looked down on the pulsating market. This was the best tandoori restaurant in the area, they assured us. They explained the origins of tandoori cooking and how it was prepared, the perfect informative guides. I was listening and chomping away contentedly at this new, delicious version of chicken when Nick, who was leaning more and more to being my boy (assigning Jack to Sara), took my left hand and held it tight. I didn't mind; I could manage the tender meat with one hand. He pulled my hand into his lap. Still eating, I made no move of resistance or discomfort and waited for developments. They came. He had taken, in a pause between mouthfuls, his penis out of his trousers and pulled my hand down to stroke it, guided by his hand, softly, languidly. My imprisoned hand stroked while I sturdily ate my chicken with my free hand, as he did his. It went on quite awhile, to my perverse amusement. He had no ejaculation in spite of the mounting, though controlled, breathlessness the pleasure gave him. I thought again of often-repeated stories about Indian sexual control: men could go on for hours and not ejaculate; finally having ejaculated, they could draw their semen back. I began to believe the stories, Nick now a corroborating witness. I was too busy observing his phenomenal control and wondering how I would clean my hand if he did spill semen to become aroused myself; not stimulating, too remote, it was an act in which I was an instrument, not a partner. I might have been a glove, a napkin, anything more titillating than his own bare hand.

*   *   *

Still inspired by the certainty that she would meet the not-impossible he in a bar, or maybe on a train or plane, or somewhere, Sara decided with my enthusiastic consent (I was becoming bored with constant Nick and Jack) to visit Khajuraho, the world-famous temples of erotic sculpture in panels of group play, without our escorts. We boarded a small, wavering plane at dawn, and we were met at the end of the flight by several jeeps that carried at each side of the driver a man with a gun at the ready. Whether it was true or served as spice for a long, bumpy journey in dour wilderness, we were warned that there were tigers, like those the rajahs and their guests once hunted, still lurking. And then there were vicious outlaws, who might attack, rob, and kill us. It was a nerve-jangling journey, through shrub and sand under a sun whose heat smothered our open car. When we reached the temples the temperature was about 120. Sara took a quick look around and then retired to a local rest house complete with café and rooms to rent. I was enthralled by the imaginative, graceful chamber music of sexual joinings performed by groups of smoothly fleshed gods and goddesses with soft bellies and fruity breasts. Even more enchanting were the single, sinuous figures of dancers and singers, as sensual in their joyous fleshliness as the "*partouze*" arrangements. When I had exhausted every figure in the large temple complex and my bare head began to take fire, I left for shelter in the rest house.

Sara was waiting for me over a cup of tea accompanied, to my distasteful surprise, by Nick and Jack. After no greeting at all they attacked me: "Why didn't you tell us you were coming here? We had to find out from the airline that arranged your flight and we took the one immediately after. How can two women alone come to Khajuraho? You're not lesbians, we know. Why didn't you arrange to come with us? We would have reserved a room here, studied the sculptures, and then come back here to practice, the four of us, what we had learned. We can still do it. That's what this place is about, that's what it's for, to teach the best sex fun." I said no, thank you, we were not staying; we were returning on the evening jeep and the night plane.

*   *   *

Nick and Jack made the rounds of Indian shops with us, bargaining on our behalf for coral in the old market, introducing us to gold- and silver-coated market sweets, guiding us to sari shops, and helping us buy lovely Indian toys in government crafts shops. We became close companions again, then bored with them again. Sara and I decided to take the long train journey without them to see Mahabalipuram, sculptures worked downward into the rock, not far from Madras. After a stay in a small Madrasi hotel, eating curries that cut through our throats and heads, eased by gentle, peculiar pancakes, and sharing a dormitory with Indian women and myriad large-eyed, passive children, we enquired about a country villa we might rent. A local agent found us a small villa, the former property of a banished rajah, available at a reasonable price. It was built in the French style with bright, fragrant gardens that sported two peacocks and a shy peahen. Our rooms had long windows and broad balconies overlooking the formal gardens; our meals were prepared and served by swift, silent servants; our beds were well-wrapped in the usual white veiling. It was a contented time. Sara was pleased with the modest price; we could easily visit the many attractions of Madras: to watch craftsmen carve the blocks that stamped the designs on the fine cotton saris worn locally, haunt the market for antique versions of those blocks, and return to the cool balm of our villa and discreet servants.

During one languid siesta, after a shopping spree for small bronze figures of Indian gods to carry home as gifts, we half asleep and the servants sleeping in the shade of a backdoor overhang, Nick and Jack burst into our room. As at Khajuraho they began instantly to reproach us. Why hadn't we let the agency office in Delhi know that we had left Madras? They themselves had taken some tourists to the elephant carvings at Mahabalipuram, put them on a train back to Delhi, and had begun to search for us in Madras and then, on some vague information, had been directed to our retreat. We soothed them (easy), invited them to dinner, and shared with them the whiskey they had lifted from the agency office. To the cracked sounds of an ancient phonograph, a relic of the rajah, we began to dance to "After the Ball" and "It's Three O'Clock in the Morning." The whiskey, the fragrant evening breezes, the sentimental tunes, made a soft nest for smooth, slow, amorous play. Jack pulled Sara, still dancing, into her bedroom. Nick pulled several large floor cushions out on a balcony and, under a pale crescent moon and the scent of blossoms, we made love.

The next morning The Boys said they had to return to their office, a long trip that would take all day at least. We thanked them for the pleasure of their company and kissed them on the cheek, like sisters. At the door Nick turned to me and said that I owed him twenty dollars and could he have it right away? I looked at him, stunned and angry. "I don't pay for sex, never have, never will." No, that was not it. We owed him the money for the gas they had used driving around looking for us. The office wouldn't supply it, the money would have to come out of their pockets. But, I said, we had not invited them, there was surely no reason for searching us out except for the night of entertainment and sex they had anticipated, or at least hoped for. OK, true, but we American ladies ought to be grateful for their care of us, and we owed them twenty dollars however we interpreted their visit. I gave him the twenty and said we would never see them again, and that was the way it stayed.

The feet of pilgrims and wanderers, all of them carrying the ubiquitous begging bowl like an extra hand; the disdainful hooves of sacred cattle stirring the hot sandy dust of the roads; and the fatty odor of cowpats drying in the sun to be used as fuel rose to our parched throats while the Indian sun burned through our straw hats. We were approaching Udaipur, mingling with the restless myriad walkers—pilgrims, beggars, the homeless, those in search of a holy place in which to die—as we had before in traversing India. The welcome novelty here was groups of striding women who wore, instead of saris, brilliant wide skirts, great yellow suns on bright red or the reverse, red suns on yellow backgrounds. The broad swing of their skirts, the brisk strong motion of the legs thrusting against the vivid cloth reminded me strongly of gypsies, the gypsies I had come to know during one childhood summer in Coney Island. (I later read that this province, Rajasthan, was actually a root home of the earliest known gypsies). The car that carried our luggage, and the new guide we had found in the area, met us at the edge of the city and drove us to a roomy old hotel: slow-moving ceiling fans, beds wrapped in netting, and the luxury of a bathroom all our own. On to the essential, inevitable local attraction—a ride on an elephant. He was tired, elderly, and gaudily caparisoned, and we, swaying on the old back, tried to look as if we were happy adventurers, waving and smiling stiffly at the photographer, who seemed to belong to the elephant—or was it vice versa?

Toward evening, a long tea session with a jewelry merchant whose blandishments were not only pieces of costly gems exquisitely set, his many obedient servants, his own plump, oily self robed in silks buttoned by many diamonds—genuine, he assured us—but his compliments, a waterfall of them, directed at the taste and shrewd judgment of American women. We bought neither compliments nor jewelry. Our guide then suggested that we visit a famous guru, a seer who lived on the outskirts of town and who was a particularly gifted prophet. With one voice we turned on our guides: no gurus, no jewelry, no shops— not for Sivas or silks or Kali masks and certainly not fortune-tellers. But he wasn't an ordinary fortune-teller, he was truly a holy man, and if we wanted to pay him a few rupees for his food that would do; OK if we gave him nothing. We consented and drove through the dusk of Indian scents until we reached a hut from which three men emerged. One, dressed in a common costume I found singularly ugly—cotton trousers, a long shirt, and a short, Western vest over that—was busily chewing and spitting out the blood red juice that had earlier frightened me on Indian streets: the look of plague. The second man was quite old with soft, floating white hair, wearing a worn dhoti and a cotton cloth on his shoulders. The third, young and princely, wore an embroidered robe and plumed turban, a figure out of a Mogul painting. Like the dignitaries of those Persian-Indian portraits, he had fine, highly arched eyebrows, a delicately etched mouth, and long eyes—a beauty and appropriately haughty. This was the noted seer who conducted Sara and myself, along with a few other visitors, to benches under a great tree. He studied our faces and hands and emerged from his studies uttering the prophecies of a fortune cookie: long, prosperous years and many happy journeys. As we were leaving, he gestured me back, not yet finished with me, possibly because I had been fairly generous in my gift. Returning with him under the tree, I let him examine my hands again. They revealed not only a long lifeline but much emotion and talent. It was my forehead that told him much, an unusual forehead that showed unmistakable signs of the deer, swift, sensitive, curious, and the loveliest of creatures. I refrained from pointing out that in spite of my long lifeline he had appointed me a probably early death; deer were the most frequently hunted and vulnerable of animals. I didn't want to hurt his feelings and his self-assurance, and besides, he was so beautiful.

After the fortune-telling session we retired to a nearby tea stall where we were soon engaged in conversation with a young American who carried a large portfolio. He said he had quit a job in a minor museum and was looking for something better to suit his talents and interests, maybe a curatorship in East Indian arts, which he was studying and gathering. I asked if I might see the works in his portfolio. He showed me a few, some as fine as the best of late Mogul art I had seen, some lumpish copies painted in local ateliers. He asked my opinion of each painting. Not altogether knowledgeable about Indian art, I gave him my opinions in moderate, tentative words.

Before we parted that evening he asked if I would meet him in a nearby palace the next day; there were paintings on display in its great reception hall, preliminary to a sale arranged by the agent of a local rajah. I met him and happily turned painting after painting from piles assembled on a long table in the sacked, torn-up, sadly confused palace. At one point my new friend asked that I put aside the pictures that especially pleased me. I did, and he made his own selections as well. He then took both selected bundles, left them with the agent in one of the vast empty rooms, and escorted me back to my hotel. I knew he was going to buy my selection, pictures I yearned for and none of which—though their prices were then very modest—I could afford. I was furious and loathed my young exploiter. I later heard from museum friends that he had got the job he wanted and had sold at fat prices the pieces I had helped him collect. When I saw the displays of Kangra miniatures on Madison Avenue after my return to New York, each small portrait priced at five and six thousand dollars, I felt cowardly and stupid. How could I have let them go to that greedy lout? Why had I not risked some of my carefully hoarded small moneys to buy a few? Why hadn't I borrowed money from a friend who could and undoubtedly would have staked me? It was nauseating to know that I was still a depression kid, probably always would be, trying to save a nickel tied in my handkerchief, too proud to ask for a loan.

Reluctantly, inevitably, we journeyed to Calcutta, the unbearable city, the city that broke the writer V. S. Naipaul "in half," that tore up my mind and took my accustomed earth from under my feet. Streets lined with shrouded people, some immobile—dead? Some shivering under their wrapping rags with fever, masturbation? One thumb raised and begging, a leper, the rest of his hideous body completely hidden. Among the splendid museums and stately official buildings, streets and streets edged by a stream in which naked babies urinated and wallowed and of which they probably drank. What was called a house along the stream was a tiny shack the size of a small doghouse; for a million others the house was the sidewalk and the runnel of water, water that ran down toward the railroad station that now housed three generations of refugees made homeless by Muslim-Hindu massacres. My unbelieving eyes stared at the large, proud headlines in the papers: so many deaths of elephantiasis, so many of leprosy, so many of tuberculosis, and, in the largest letters of all, many, many of cholera, a plague that ran with the street waters from an old set of British barracks above the city. The streets wore a low cloud of biers being carried where? We did not, could not follow them. I questioned a local physician about this outbreak of cholera and why, in the twentieth century, when there was a known source of pollution and remedies available, weren't appropriate measures taken? He looked at me out of his antiquely sad eyes and said slowly, patiently, as if to a child, "My dear, there are something like one hundred thousand deaths here of starvation alone. Were we to rescue too many from cholera that number would go up to one hundred fifty thousand or two hundred thousand." Brought up in the liberal Western tradition (with enough goodwill, energy, money, intelligence, and dedication, the ills of many societies could be alleviated), I was thrown off my earth, flung into whirling vertigo. I didn't understand anything: this fatalistic response; the resistance to birth control when children were at great risk from disease and starvation; a society that, in spite of established—on paper—regulations, kept its garbage collectors and sewer diggers "untouchable," segregated in hungry villages. I couldn't understand a religion of fatalism that declared this life an unreal interval before the next, authentic life. But mine was my life, my beliefs, and I couldn't allow them to be so shredded. I insisted we leave India immediately. We did. No book, but some lingering regrets that I could no longer smell India or see the swinging skirts of Rajasthani women, that I could no longer wander the temples of goddesses with silkily cushioned flesh and stare into the velvety deer eyes of Indian children.

We went on to Ceylon (Sri Lanka now), into rude, suspicious checking of everything we had: money, jewelry, small alarm clocks, articles of clothing. We forgot the unpleasantness when we later passed bands in enchanting costumes singing quietly into the night, watched slight, pretty women wash their babies in quiet pools, and stood before a gang of work elephants uprooting and carrying away huge trunks of trees. The dignified, orange-robed monks we met everywhere neither addressed us nor asked for alms, an insistent form of address in India. The only disturbance in this two-dimensional (after India's excess of dimensions), lyrical, picture-book place occurred while we were sitting at breakfast in a guesthouse in flowery Kandy. Sara suddenly gasped and whispered, "Look at the big cat sitting under our table." I found myself staring in growing panic at the head of a mongoose. I rose slowly and tiptoed to the door to find the proprietor of our pension. It was indeed a mongoose, he told us, trained not to hurt people but to watch out for snakes, which sometimes slid through the lower gaps of the wooden houses. Many houses, he assured us, trusted their safety to a trained mongoose.

Strolling through the magnificent gardens of Kandy, astonished at the lushness and curious shapes of some of its plants, I felt that I was not quite there. Still battered by India, I became convinced that the most sensible voyage beyond India should be to a place of uneventfulness, of monotony; a rest-cure house in which one could reassemble oneself, the habitual self, feet on familiar ground, the head released from the Indian vertigo, from the incessant music of the duet sung by beauty and death.

An essay, "In Praise of Shadows," written by Junichiro Tanizaki, describes in part the mystery of the geisha as she had once been, a ghostly figure floating like a thin veil of smoke out of a dark corner of the geisha house. As she emerges, her hair a dark shadow lost in darker shadows, one sees a phantom face, dead white, the eyebrows faint, short brushstrokes, the lips not red, the teeth not white, but painted in shades of green and black. She has the allure of being "other," of unknown possibilities of sex among whispers of death.

It was she I went to look for, although knowing she was long gone when I visited Kyoto. I found only a vestige—a woman in magnificent stiff brocades held by layers of obi, tottering on wooden pattens so tall that she was supported through her uncertain steps by two women, one on each side of her. Her face was painted white, touched with faint strokes of eyebrow, her lips lightly rouged to leave two pink blossoms at the center of her mouth; I couldn't see whether her teeth had been darkened as in the Tanizaki picture. I watched her make her halting, dainty way down to a corner of the street where, with elegant flowing gestures like slow waves, she entered a waiting limousine.

Having seen a geisha who appeared almost as treasured and evocative as her forebears, I was satisfied and ready to explore the art treasures of the city. Swinging along a large, long street, stopping now and then to read directions in my guidebook, I had not noticed that a sweater draped on my arm had slipped away from me. As I continued to talk, I felt a tap on my shoulder and turned to see a beautiful young man, much taller than the middle-aged short Japanese to whom I was accustomed. He offered me my sweater, picked up from the street. I smiled and bowed a little as I had seen it done and said thank you, hoping the combination would express my gratitude. But he was not ready to let me go. He put up one long finger, let my eye rest on it, understand it, and then pointed the finger at himself. He was alone, solitary. Understood. Then he pointed his finger at me with a questioning look. Was I solitary too? It is usually my practice to say or gesture no. If I had the language I would explain that my husband was with me, engaged at the moment in business but expecting me back in our hotel very soon. I don't know yet exactly why I nodded to the young man that I was indeed alone. He was attractive, very, but mainly I was interested to see how this little scene would act its way out. Very simply. He made a circle of his left forefinger and thumb and played his right forefinger quickly and lightly in and out of the circle. It was fast, clever, direct, ummistakable, and I was so charmed by its efficient clarity that I began to laugh. The oversensitive youth must have heard derision in my amuse-ment. He strode off, muttering words whose meanings I could only imagine, and I went on to Art, surrounded by school groups, each child hung with cameras, large heavy amulets. Their teach-ers informed them of the importance of the art treasures in hard, quick words roared through megaphones. I soon left kids, mega-phones, and cameras, still amused at the efficient, no-nonsense proposition of my gorgeous young Japanese.

4

Cluster of Enlightenments

AMONG my varieties of education, in a diversity of small jobs and the people who ruled me in them, political enlightenments that were vague and ignorant in detail; the contributions of Hunter College; of concerts, plays, and museums, there was a summer semester at Harvard Medical School. Steve, my husband (not strictly legally) and later my daughter's father, already had his medical degree but lacked one subject that his school had not offered, a significant blank in the record that would earn him an internship. So, we went off to Brookline, where we lived in a pleasant, old-fashioned boardinghouse that kept students, and attended an intensive course in the physiology of the digestive and nervous systems. The crowded classes for this rapid, concentrated course were held in a vast auditorium. Because of Steve's poor hearing, we went to classes early and tried to find front seats together. At first it was difficult; the competition for front seats was keen. After I had explained to a few people that Steve couldn't hear, there was generous understanding from students who saved seats for us. Still, the desk, demonstration tables, and blackboard were rather far from the front rows and, in addition, the course was given by a number of professors—a few, I was told, of great note—who spoke at different levels or muttered or had exotic accents. We agreed that I would take classroom notes; Steve could manage the lab work on his own.

Every morning I entered with my pad and pen and, having no stenography, took notes as rapidly and accurately as I could. Strained, anxious, I was in great measure to be responsible for his pass grade and the subsequent internship, though I was sure that his laboratory demonstrations and experiments would be brilliant enough to carry him through. Gratifyingly, surprisingly, he understood my garbled notes, which he supplemented with matter in his texts. One of the strangest and most disconcerting of those tense days was one on which a famous scientist, the inventor of a remarkable machine—I seem to remember that it was called the Drinker respirator—decided to select for quizzing, at the end of two or three of his sessions, a few of the assembled body. I was one of those he chose to quiz. After answering briefly one or two questions, I went dead, paralyzed, mindless. I wrote the questions for Steve, then explained who I was and why I was there, and could my husband, for whom I had made a note, answer. Yes, of course, and he complimented me for my loyalty and effort and Steve on the full, informed answer he had given. Relief to heights of jubilation.

I remember nothing more about that summer except that the heat was intense, and although I had always thought of myself as a sort of cactus-human who could come to no harm in the sun, I did, much to my shame, pass out several times, and Steve had to put me into cold baths and apply ice to various parts of my boiled body. There was nothing else memorable about that summer, unless events have slipped through the disordered mesh-work of memory. One or two medical students were friendly, but Steve's difficulty in hearing them—he never learned to lip-read well—and his need to study texts more intensively than they did, and my need to be at his side constantly, kept us separate, seg-regated. I saw none of the notable museums of Harvard, nor did I explore Boston. The only deviation from our school-boarding-house-study routine was the celebration of Steve's pass grade. His father must have sent the money—we certainly didn't have it—for a splendid dinner at the Copley Plaza Hotel, where I was dazzled by the lace place mats and a waiter behind each chair:

an aristocratic elegance that I had never before lived except in childhood movies.

When a reluctance that amounted to a passion not to join any political body, to avoid meetings and active commitments, I lived in a climate known in derisive Yiddish as "pity socialism," a diffuse cloud of goodwill and sympathy for all oppressed people and no urge (though there was the guilt) to alleviate or improve their plight—until the Spanish Civil War, which took on for some of my generation the aura of a holy war. A democratic government was being destroyed, its people slaughtered in the thousands by the overwhelming trio of fascist forces—Franco, Hitler, Mussolini. It was a *cause*, a cause for which a number of my young acquaintances would risk their lieves—and many lose them—as members of the Abraham Lincoln Brigade. It was a cause that .marched among sympathetic streets and as it marched, sang, *Die heimat ist weit/Nun sind wir bereit. Wir kämpfen and siegen für dich/FREIHEIT.* ("Our homeland is far, but we are ready. We struggle and fight for you. Freedom!") From my friends and a record I bought, I learned to sing, "Los Quatro Generales," a favorite Loyalist song of defiance. I studied, fully entered Hemingway's *For Whom the Bell Tolls* and kept a private shrine for Jim Lardner, who died in the Loyalist cause.

Before he settled into his residency, Steve decided to go to Spain as a physician and I would go along as some sort of nurse. Although I lacked experience I was strong, energetic, and enthusiastic; surely I could be of some use. After an interview with one of the physicians who examined the young men eager to join the Abraham Lincoln Brigade, Steve was told that his deafness and medical history barred him. Consequently, we became busy with several physicians we knew, collecting medical supplies and shipping them to the Loyalist forces in Spain, not discouraged even when we were told they might be taken by opposing hands. When the war was over, with Franco as the fascist ruler of Spain, we carried for a long time a profound sense of personal loss, as if a close family of friends had died after imprisonment and torture. Spain then moved back slowly into history and behind the heavy curtain of later events: the battering of London; threads of information growing thicker and blacker about the extermination of Jews—and gypsies and homosexuals—in the countries Hitler had conquered and was determined to "purify." (I was almost pleased that my mother died before she knew of the destruction of the Warsaw ghetto, where dozens of her relatives, and mine, had lived.) The Spanish Civil War and the lingering sadness it left came back to me during a visit to Montpellier in France shortly after World War II. There I met many Spanish refugees, poor and melancholy, some of the younger people with no memories of the parents who had sent them into exile when they were three or four years old to save them from the bombs that were destroying Spanish cities and lives. Later during the same trip, talking to people in Granada and Córdoba I found the Civil War still alive—neighbor who had not spoken to neighbor for many years, still on opposite sides of the Civil War fence and spitting venom as they spoke about that fascist neighbor, that communist nun-murderer. It is still difficult for me, at this long remove, to see films that deal with the Spanish Civil War, as difficult as it is to watch films of the Holocaust, both events that have, in some way I cannot precisely define, altered my life. Certainly, in some inner core I feel a guilt that I think all Jews who did not directly experience the Holocaust feel about it, and a sense of failure to help an infant democracy flourish.

The venue and time were unexpected when I was, many years later, plunged into face-to-face reminders of Spanish and Jewish refugees. It was in China, on a railroad train. The first-class tour had put us on an imitation of the old Orient Express: lace antimacassars on the seat arms, freshened antique velvet curtains at the windows, comfortable berths, and warm puffs against the cold night. Supper had been satisfying and more politely served than our usual slapdash group dinners, at which I often ate cold bone and skin ends because I was too snobbish to grab at passing platters. The novelty of being on a near-elegant Chinese train brightened the conversation; it was an animated evening and an unexpectedly comfortable night. The next morning we were told that breakfast was to be served in a car a short distance down the track. Most of the group decided to do the walk out of doors. I wanted to see what and who were in our adjoining cars. Most of them were empty, in the process of being lightly dusted in the absentminded local fashion. One car, however, was crowded, its riders wrapped in a silence of uncomprehending, frightened faces. Crammed on wooden benches, sitting on the floor, were mainly old men and young women with quiet young children on their laps and, spotted through the car, several very young soldiers. All the faces wore the same lost expression of bewilderment, all the bodies resigned, unresistant, all the clothing shabby. There was no one to ask who they were, where they were going (our English-speaking Chinese leader, I knew from experience, would offer an innocuous, optimistic explanation, as he always did with awkward questions), but I knew surely that I was seeing the remnants of a village, maybe all the boys forced into the army—being transported to an unknown place, as Jews, as Spanish children, as English children had been, and for all of them and these displaced Chinese I began to cry from a well of tears that must long have been gathering.

Shortly after my education in physiology in Harvard's Medical School summer session, I enjoyed another short voyage into medical information. These sessions were infinitely more entertaining: no notes to take, no quizzes, no fears of embarrassing or failing Steve. Dr. Paul Schilder, who, I believe, was the head of psychiatry at Bellevue, where Steve was involved in some special study, had invited the wives and families of young medical pesonnel to attend his demonstration lectures (a mission apparently designed to broaden the understanding of a still arcane subject among the general public). He was a short, dark-haired man with two fingers missing from one hand, the hand he used for gesturing as he spoke in a high-pitched, German-accented voice—the near-soprano voice opening each introduction with "Z-i-is patiens-s-s." He brought out patient after patient, pointing out specific characteristics of their conditions and the causes. His technique with those who would not, could not, easily respond to his questions was unique and impressive. He hooked his arm tightly into the arm of the silent, distant patient. Pressing it against his own side, he often elicited responses, whispered in cracked voices. Why could sheer body pressure pull a patient out of his isolation? The voices were slow and reluctant, but they were voices, connections. I've often thought of this phenomenon since: the life-giving touch or hug or kiss, the primitive meetings that could mean so much, their lack such a pit of emptiness.

I envied—not knowing what suffering might have gone on before this stage of their disease—the paretics, exultantly happy madmen whose corrupted brains had given them the gift of supreme success and power. One of them exultantly told Dr. Schilder that he couldn't count all the money he controlled, that it could certainly buy him the next presidential election. He wasn't sure, though, that he wanted it; when would there be time for sailing his big yacht around the world? Maybe he would buy an island instead—Cuba, England, perhaps—and become its king, a good, just king, of course. The less lucky had radios in their heads, bad voices accusing them of crimes and hideous drumming incessantly in their ears. As a girl who had been brought up with the word *meshugge* (crazy) carelessly applied to any deviation of conduct, mostly my own, I continued measuring these new wider boundaries, expanding and contracting them with each successive encounter and personality, and I still do, never quite sure of the firm lines between sanity and insanity— if such exist in an increasingly bewildering world of fanaticism and violence.

A girl I knew whose husband was an intern at Bellevue and who also attended the psychiatric sessions suggested that I take Russian lessons with her from a woman who lived a few streets from Bellevue. They were very cheap, she told me, and I consented to go with her. The teacher was a dumpling with wild gray hair streaked in bands of black dye, the mass of hair carelessly pushed up and out around a swarthy, avid face. Like several older Russian women I knew, she affected the wide colorful skirts and the layers of fringed shawl that recall gypsies or maybe the flamboyant stars of the Yiddish theater, flashing jewels and brilliant lengths of silk in the Café Royale. To me, she looked like a plump Fury with a Medusa head. She was exceedingly talkative, mainly about the high romance of her life as a young woman in Russia, restlessly pacing up and down, swirling her gypsy skirts as she moved around the small room. Not a good teacher but conscientious, she decided that my friend was holding me back and that I should have separate solo lessons. Such an arrangement earned her an extra small sum, but there was other justification in her plan. Having spoken Polish as a child and been forced very early to pick up bits of several other languages, I had a sharper ear than my friend and could more nearly imitate the difficulties and subtleties of Russian sounds. Not in school at the time or working, I had the time for study, soon reaching a stage where I could, with a fair accent, recite a little poem about falling snow and children playing with snowballs.

There my Russian lessons stopped, forever frozen in Russian snow. Steve's program permitted him to call for me at the end of one lesson, and I could see that, after a first glance, my gypsy-Medusa continued to stare at him with a lost, drunken, mesmerized look. He had an appealing smile, was well-mannered and soft-spoken and, what must most have moved her Russian soul, he was a Tatar type, with long green eyes, high cheekbones, and a strong mustache. Our meetings thereafter became hymns in adoration of Steve. "Never I see so byoochiful a men. So byoochiful you husband and so gentlemen. You lucky to hev such *kresavitz* [beauty]. You pretty and smart but is many pretty and smart girls, but not too many so vonderful men." I endured two or three more sessions in praise of Steve and then told Anya? Manya? Natasha? that I had been offered a job that didn't allow for lessons or study time. Long after I left the Russian dumpling, each time I looked at Steve, I saw her black eyes rolled to heaven and the coarse mouth spewing, "Byoochiful, byoochiful. . . ."

When Lexie was a year and a half old I decided to go back to Hunter College to finish out the courses that would earn my B.A. as an English major in classes I could attend in the evening.

That decision shaped what was probably the most balanced time of my life. I was enraptured with Lexie's first few words that quickly, like minute rivulets, began to gather in streams of playful sentences: "Ice cream, nice cream." "The wind is crying because the buildings scratch it." Her feet, fumbling for the ground as she hung on to my hand, steadied to a sure strut to the sandbox. And I derived great pleasure from watching the other babies in the carriages of my young neighbors, who sat with me in the park near our houses, gossiping and exchanging baby lore, each boasting of the progress of her child, no one resenting the pride; it was all justified.

In the evening, after I had put Lexie to bed in the care of her grandparents, bolted down a fast supper or none, I dashed to the subway and down to Sixty-eighth Street. The classes provided their own particular pleasures. They were small, my classmates mainly people who had struggled their way to the end of a demanding English major during several years of attending night school after a full working day; all studious, intelligent, and ardently determined. Almost as joyful as watching the miraculous learnings of my child were my own tentative, then surer, steps into Irish literature beginning with the Ur-hero Cuchulain; reading the biblical stories in Anglo-Saxon that revealed Abraham as a Hebrew earl, the lord of many ceorls. There have been more ecstatic times but none so honeyed and elegantly rhythmed, in a graceful choreography that inept life rarely achieves.

On my first trip to Jerusalem in the early fifties I was the guest of my brother and his family. His job was to collaborate, suggesting medical practicalities, with the architects who were building the new Hadassah Hospital. (The building already on Mount Scopus was unusable, in disputed territory). My sister-in-law's job was to find edible food acceptable to two well-nourished American children. Israelis were then eating mainly bread and an onion—when it could be found—or a shriveled root bought in the market leaning against the barbed wire that then divided the city. The "foreigners' " right to rations gave my sister-in-law long hours on lines to find blue chickens, frozen into baskets in

Eritrea, which had to be boiled first, then roasted, then hacked into fricassee pieces, and finally just barely edible after the long day's effort and the exhaustion of a tank of cooking gas. My two nieces complained about the food, the plethora of tinned tuna fish, and waited for visitors to bring them apples, candy, cookies, and, most important, bubble gum.

One of the sightseeing tours my brother conducted for me left us at the main gate of a large house in a Druse village on Mount Carmel, near Haifa. My brother, who had established strong ties with one of the major powers in an extended farming family, was taken into a meeting room of the wise man (the *chachem*—used in Yiddish, from the Hebrew or Arabic, and, in the habits of that ironic tongue, more often meant to denote a fool). I was conducted to a sort of warehouse where there sat a tall, stout Druse woman and a two-year-old blond child. She was heavily pregnant but still pulled the veil from the front of her ingeniously designed dress to let him try to nurse. Whether he was fed milk or only comfort it was hard to say, but during the two hours or so we spent together he was often at her breast, his snotty little nose pressed into the flowing expanse of flesh. We, she and I, filled the hours with a great deal in our separate languages. I'm convinced that there was continuity of conversation, question and answer, in our speech, some of it accompanied by gestures. I pointed to her belly, made a gesture of big roundness and she put up eight fingers—eight months pregnant. Did I have children?—pointing to the boy and out a window through which I could see other children playing. Yes—I indicated one, since Lexie was still alive then, in college. She made a pantomime of drinking tea and chewing, adding some smiling words that were probably in praise of the special delicacies she offered. I nodded yes, added "Thank you very much," and beamed at her. Heaving her great bulk off her floor cushion she began to clamber up the tall shelves laden with boxes on every side of the room, as swift and sure as a mountain goat. She brought down a box of tea, a basket of mint, boiled English sweets in one gathering, and in another, two or three varieties of English biscuits. She spread them all before me on a low table while in a corner she boiled the tea, the little boy now back in her arms. We talked about tea in her country and in mine, about sweets and biscuits, about how many sweets she allowed the child—an inordinate amount, it seemed from his unsupervised swift grazing. I asked her, with a gesture of pulling at my belly, who would deliver her. She pointed to a door from which, at odd moments, other women stared at us. One of them, I took it, would be the midwife along with the help of the others when her time came. And so it went, for an entertaining and inform-ative time until the dignified old woman who had conducted me to my hostess led me back to my brother's car (which, inciden-tally, earned him a high title among these people, since very few private cars were then owned by Israelis or Druses or Arabs).

I had a number of such conversations in the marketplaces of Tanzania, buying Masai beads and *ketenge* (North African cloth used as body wrap), and at roadside stalls, bartering, everyone quick eyed and good humored; polite "no" shakes of the head, and resigned, nodding "yeses" for the exchanges: a small piece of sculpture for a pair of rubber-soled sandals, a carved letter opener with a delicate bird as handle for a well-used red leather wallet. There was conversation and bargaining in Macedonian dialect in Yugoslavia, and among the mountain peoples of Mex-ico who spoke only Zapotec or Tarascan. The one conversation I was most eager to have never took place. Trailing behind my group, as usual, in a Chinese street, I was confronted by a middle-aged woman in the common peasant costume of black cotton trousers and shirt. My hair was then cut very short; maybe I was a man, she might have thought, maybe a foreign official, because I wore a tweed cape. But I wore earrings and shoes with heels: maybe some sort of odd woman. She came closer, as if smelling me would determine my sex. Just as I was about to open my cloak to show her my shape, my dress and necklace, the voice of our Chinese guide, an overwatchful man, called "Come along, Mrs. Simon, you're holding up the group." In another village not far from Beijing, a girl approached me with welcoming in-terest. She touched my sweater and gloves, and I pointed to the row of shacks from which I had seen her emerge, taking her hand to suggest we were friends, hoping she might conduct me to her house and family. She appeared to understand and was leading me into her alley when the annoying voice came, "Come along, Mrs. Simon; we are waiting for you." No private contact, no matter how brief, was allowed in China or in Leningrad, or in beautiful, bitter Prague. Voluble Budapest welcomed anyone, everyone, in any language. It kept its tourist shops profitably busy and large foreign audiences revelling in old operettas like *The Grand Duchess of Gérolstein*, the casts inhabited by ladies who all had the opulent, pearly, creamy Gabor looks.

While my daughter was ill at home, still able to read and listen to music, I was almost constantly near her, should she call or need me. My domestic duties were few; ironically, this envenomed period of my life was the most prosperous and afforded full-time domestic help. (I have since had a skewed attitude toward money, certainly nor normal, but are there normal attitudes toward money?) Living in a full, dark cloud of anguish (Emily Dickinson called it "lead"), not capable of concentration on reading and impatient with telephone calls that asked the same embarrassed questions about Lexie's condition, I had considerable time to spare. A publishing friend suggested that he might find free-lance editorial work I could do at home. He taught me the rudiments of indexing as his house preferred it. Carefully alphabetizing detailed items proved quite absorbing, and I was looking for neutral, objective, small escapes. In time, still continuing the welcome, cool disciplines of indexing, I began to do rewriting, particularly of translated matter where meanings were dictionary correct but twisted in rhythm or dusted with ambiguity. One book I found a thorough escape was well and smoothly translated. It was the *Makioka Sisters* by Junichiro Tanizaki, a broad portrait of a Japanese family, interesting for its mores, its habits, its thought and most fascinating in its recounting of matters taboo in the novels I knew at the time. Hospital scenes were fully and clinically detailed—he or she had a pustulant extrusion, for example—described carefully in color, size, and smell; the patient excreted two pints of bloody urine; enemas were detailed as if in nursing manuals. These bodies were the whole body, not only superficies covering mysterious unmentionables.

When, in one of her unspoken rages of hatred for me, Lexie moved to her aunt's house—the aunt finally triumphant over my youth and fecundity—I could not stay at home, although I continued to do a few hours of editorial work each week. I needed another occupation, one entirely apart from my world, in some attractive area about which I knew very little. I had looked at paintings, knew the Mexican muralists and the great Italians in Florence, enjoyed them, puzzled by their mystery. How was it derived? I didn't really care too much, but trying to imitate, to re-create it might pull me away from a life of waiting for ultimate disaster, for a further descent into the heavy nothingness of "lead."

I joined a group of pleasant, leisured ladies who were being taught by a good painter out of his time—not political enough, lyrical, heavy with impasto, unfashionable. I began, like the rest, with flower pieces, carefully rounding a petal, pointing a leaf, pleased with the attempts but not the results. I hadn't the patience for drawing or even the slow stroke of a brush and began to paint as if the canvas were an object of vengeful passion, with palette knives and bold colors. At first I attended the usual once-a-week sessions but the need to be away from my apartment grew increasingly demanding. I began to spend much of my time in the studio, painting at first from little black-and-white snapshots I had taken in Mexico, one figure from one picture, one figure from another. Our teacher, apparently determined to make a painter of me, suggested I use an adjoining studio in which I could be alone, in my own hours. Within a couple of months I reached an ambitious stage of large canvases, working for a long time on a scene I had observed and remembered of a synagogue in Israel. It was a Yemenite synagogue, brightly lit with figures of men in furred hats, in dark robes, and in yellow shining robes, praying at the side of a wall hung with strips of gaudy North African cloths and carpets. Outside the windows in the dusk sat the women wrapped in white, maybe silently praying but certainly waiting, faceless white bundles, for their men to conduct them home. I managed to get the women, the pale twilight cluster leaning against the outer wall of the synagogue, but had trouble with the central group of men in their sharp colors and light, their vivid verticality not quite the contrast I wanted with the horizontal spread, like a low bank of clouds, of the women. As I worked on a separate panel of the men and reworked it, I suddenly knew I had what I was reaching for. As poets have said about their recognition of the absolute rightness of a line, my hair stood on end. I went next door to the group room and said to the teacher something I had never said before: "I have a painting." He came running in, stood before the small canvas, and said, "Yes, you have." He later took it from me and submitted it to an A.A.A. show, a large show that drew art from all over the United States, art that had never been publicly displayed before, amateur or professional.

I was told I could retrieve it after a week from the time of submission, and I went with a friend to the gallery on Fifty-seventh Street, a walk marked by the fact that a bolt from a height of skyscraper construction missed my shoulder by a hairsbreadth. What if it had entered my head or fired its way through my shoulder into my lungs? I thought calmly about these possibilities for a few minutes and then, with an accustomed delayed reaction, began to shake: Was it another portent of death? Lexie's maybe soon. Mine sooner, I hoped. I had about recovered when we reached the gallery, I to be dismayed by the fact that the woman at the desk who was to return my painting said I couldn't have it. (They had, of course, misplaced or lost it, the sort of thing that happened to me.) My friend was inappropriately jubilant over the loss and, banging me on the back, repeated and repeated that it wasn't lost; I couldn't have it because it was going to be hung as part of the show that would open the following week. OK, small triumph; there were thousands of entrants, the show would be large and I an "also hung," although that simple fact was surprising.

At 7:00 A.M. on the day after the show opened, the teacher's wife called me, stammering with excitement. "Go buy the *New*

York Times! Read about the show! Go buy it now!" I dressed quickly and ran down for the paper. The *Times* art critic had explored the show, selecting seven or eight paintings for detailed descriptions of their subjects, praising their inventiveness and execution. Mine was among them.

I should have been pleased and burbled delighted responses when friends called to congratulate me, elated because this prestigious critic had launched me as a bona fide painter. But I was dismayed by the notice; the *Times* critic had pushed me into a class for which I knew I was not ready; I was an amateur with an occasional streak of luck, an amateur nevertheless, and not ready for accolades. He had unsettled me. Like the old lady in the folk tale—"This was none of I." I did not paint again, never picked up a palette knife or dab of color, for two years.

Living in London later I learned of an inexpensive art school originally established for poor students in Whitechapel, at the end of a long, many-Londoned bus ride from my apartment near Earl's Court. The fee for one morning per week for the year was twelve pounds, something less than twenty dollars. No one asked me to leave if I stayed on beyond my allotted time, or to pay an additional fee. The two instructors, an elderly courtly man and a young shy man who looked and spoke like a curate in a nine-teenth-century novel, never tried to teach me. The older man stood for a moment and looked at a painting of exsanguinated demonic figures I had translated from the people I had watched at the statue of Eros waiting for the local Boots Pharmacy to open (the place where London had decided to give drug addicts free shots, on the principle that this would diminish the sale of drugs; it didn't, and the practice was abolished a few years later). He looked long and said, "Interesting." The shy curate took a quick look, said, "Interesting," and flew by. I never had any instruction and didn't want it. I loved the day; the painting; the bus ride that once drove me into the very recent, glass-stewn aftermath of an Irish bomb assault on Old Bailey; the ride that pulled me along bridges, into old squares, past Whistler's river sites and the raffish life around the Earl's Court Tube Station—all in their own way, now that I was learning to see with a fresh eye, art lessons.

*   *   *

I have not painted for many years but think a great deal about replanning my small apartment to accommodate painting space or, instead, joining one school or another for locker-room facilities and the use of portrait models. Sometime, maybe, I will release the near-painter that the *Times* critic made of me; with no great expectations but the satisfaction of filling a troubling void, an incompleteness.

It was the period of "open admissions" for New York colleges, which meant guilt and embarrassment in the education community over the obvious lack of quality and concern in high school teaching. The program was meant to satisfy those who complained that minority students—those who had not already dropped out before their senior year—had emerged semiliterate at best. Their definition of *book* was, as often as not, *TV Guide*, and the rest of the skills and knowledges they should have accumulated were a lightly spattered meaningless page. The courses designed for them in Brooklyn College, where I taught for a year in the late seventies (until the program was dropped in a short, fast chop), were remedial in part, while my particular section centered on a broad and fairly intensive course that developed into a variation of a "civilizations" humanities course. My partner's field was visual matter—painting, sculpture, architecture— linked with my discussions of writing, music, and sometimes the dress and mores that colored the history of each period we discussed.

They were an engaging group, a mix of several backgrounds and temperaments. Maria Gomez, a well-read, responsive girl, had been put in the program because of her Latino name, which, according to the heedless gods who ruled these matters, placed her automatically in the underachievers' camp. Dominick— vain, reckless, trying on homosexual stances and dress—was a gifted designer and should have been in an art school. Roberto, a little slow, steady and serious, a fat boy with a naive earnest face, insisted on going to college because he hated his father's butcher shop, his fate to serve and inherit if he couldn't fling a college degree in his father's minor mafioso face. Louise, as light in head and spirits as bright ribbons, and as pretty, was there because her mother warned her that she would break her daughter's head before she let her become the sloppy, ignorant wife of a melting-in-booze retired cop, like her Aunt Kathleen.

José seemed to have no autobiography, no parents, no address. Tall and skinny, angular yet graceful, his young face stiff with the austerity of control and silences, he did not take his lunch breaks with the others—probably no money—and slowly, step by careful step, began to make me his confidant. He would not tell me where he lived or with whom, and it became easy to believe the whispers of his classmates: that his mother was a prostitute who would often bar him from her house, slipping him a couple of dollars under her closed door for his food and keep. He was a wanderer, unlike the others, most of whom had never been to Manhattan or even ventured into a neighborhood a quarter mile from their safe, familiar streets. He knew the financial district, whose massive tight power he admired; he knew the lower East Side, where he could buy cheap food, and he knew Chinatown intimately: this through the guidance and friendship of an old Chinese gentleman with whom he practiced the antique martial art of Tai Chi. He did his homework (a considerable amount of varied reading I assigned) in a Chinatown branch of the public library to which his old friend guided him.

José had the makings of a scholar—curiosity, a passion for research, and lucidity in presenting his information. At one point, between trips to the Frick Collection, the Cloisters, a walk across the Brooklyn Bridge, and classes that introduced Greek temples and Romanesque churches, Héloïse and Abelard, and Shakespeare sonnets, we assigned illustrated lectures for each student to give on some subject of especial interest to him or her. José brought in maps of China, elegant examples of Chinese calligraphy; presented a terse, clear history of China and an explanation of Tai Chi; and then performed a graceful balletic interpretation of the exercises. Even Dominick, who was impressed by little of anyone's achievements but his own, applauded.

Always separate, always remote from his peers and maybe

because he was not distracted by them, José was a pleasure to teach. As gratifying as knowing that nineteen out of twenty students had made their way from deep in Brooklyn to the Cloisters in Washington Heights in subway systems they had never before used (during a flu epidemic, on one of the coldest days of the winter), was hearing José ask as we stood in front of a set of medieval tapestries, "Mrs. Simon, didn't the early Italian painters—like that one who painted the Virgin sitting in a flowered field—copy these mille-fleurs grounds in the tapestries?" I liked talking with him and hearing about his discourses with his Chinese friend, and enjoyed seeing him carry the *Times* (as I did for my long subway rides from my home in Manhattan) and hoped he hadn't had to pay for it, had picked up a discarded copy.

It was when he began to cut classes and telephoned me on those absent days—which became more and more frequent—and later began to ask for directions to my house from wherever he was wandering that I became uncomfortable with him. Other teachers complained of his absences, and one committee was about to expel him, a suggestion I fought successfully but not too happily because of his increasing insistence on intimacy with me while he kept himself stubbornly distant from the rest of the group, deliberately friendless and isolated. One day I invited him to have a cup of coffee with me after school and during our conversation stressed the danger he was running of being expelled and the fact that I did not want him to call my house—that our relationship was to remain that of teacher and student in a classroom atmosphere, and that was all.

He began to attend classes again, stopped phoning me, and offered me a wordless apology that was one of the loveliest acts of homage I have ever experienced. It happened following one of our lessons on the Middle Ages. We had discovered, in spite of the group's shouted skepticism, that Joan Baez had *not* written "Greensleeves," that it had existed centuries before her birth; we had discovered that Marco Polo was a real man, one of several adventuresome merchants of his time. I told them some spicy stories, French *fabliaux*, and read them some Chaucer as I was taught it had sounded in its own time and in a modern version. Then I told them the story of the Juggler of Notre Dame who, having nothing else to offer the Virgin, gave his only gift, his keenness of eye and swiftness of hand, to amuse her. There was a lunch break after I told the story, and José stayed, as frequently, in his seat. I was going over some papers when I looked up to see that he was near my desk, pacing through his Tai Chi movements. But not at his full height. His knees were bent as he went through the smooth gestures, which now had the color of supplication and adoration; using the language of Tai Chi, he was the juggler and I the Virgin to whom he was offering his best gift.

I don't know what happened to José or to Dominick and Maria and Louise, who, slightly giddy with wine at a class party, insisted that I was too attractive and exotic to be a spinster, surely I must have lots of lovers. Like the woman of mystery they wanted, I didn't say yes, I didn't say no. I wonder if Roberto still loves Shakespeare sonnets, a few of which he translated into his own simple but telling, perceptive Bronx words. All I could find out about the group, from which I was suddenly separated by official ukase, was that no one dropped out of college at the end of that year, a distinct triumph for my partner, myself, and mainly for the shiningly eager and undervalued youngsters.

5

"Est-ce Que Vous Êtes Juive?"

I THOUGHT I had been through with it in my early job hunting when I was asked my religion on an application for some exalted job or other—filing, sorting papers: Writing "no religion" was a promise of an overindependent, obstreperous employee, of "Sorry, miss, the job is filled." It later appeared as punctuation marks in subsequent conversations. A man with whom I shared a bed in Mexico expressed surprise at my ineptitude with money; how come, since I came of a money-sharp race? In Paris my street was haunted by a drunken clochard whose muttered litany was *"Les juifs, ces voleurs, ces vieux cons. Nous-avons besoin d'un nouveau 'Itler!"* My neighbors, to their credit, shrugged and sighed resignedly, *"Toujours les juifs. Pourquoi?"* I was welcomed as a Jew in the Marais, still a distinctly Jewish area in the nineteen-sixties and early seventies, and treated to matzo and kosher pâté when I visited a Jewish antiquarian to find an ivory pointer used to trace the phrases of the Torah. One of my closest friends in England, a pillar of the High Church, once described a mob at an airport: "You know, of course, who were the first people to crowd through the line," typically English anti-Semitism and broadly spread. (It tries to be indirect, subtle, not naming names, but makes its hits nevertheless and with shameful persistence.)

The Italians didn't seem to care much. There had been, of

course, bureaucratic delight in selecting Jewish intellectuals and aristocrats—witness Giorgio Bassani's *Five Ferrarese Stories* and his *Garden of the Finzi-Contini* (their names probably still listed on the wall of Ferrara's Jewish center) and a strutting of locals imitating German storm troopers. But by and large there was, in spite of the hapless, cowardly pope, an unusual degree of protection of Jews by Italians. Nuns and priests took care of Jewish children, citizens sheltered Jewish neighbors; Italian soldiers disguised Jews in their own caps and military jackets to make them appear authentically Italian. Although anti-Semitic quips often fouled the air of the antiquarian streets of Babuino and Coronari in Rome, they were muted after Mussolini succumbed to Hitler's directives, when gangs of Jews aged fourteen to ninety-four were taken off to death camps or immediately killed. Such acts were incomprehensible to most Italians. As a crime of jealousy, of thwarted passion, as the imperative of an old vendetta, the extermination of a rival mafioso with a face, a name (met *mano a mano*, so to speak), was acceptable, habitual. But to gather up bundles of unknown bodies on a diabolical political principle was beyond Italian understanding.

My most memorable meeting with my heritage took place in Florence. I had an introduction to the sculptor Bernar Reder, a sculptor who paralleled Marc Chagall in his interpretations of Jewish folklore and cabalistic symbols. (Before the present Museum of Modern Art was built, his figures filled the garden of the small building, and one large gallery was devoted to his unique architectural inventions. He has died since, and gaudier art fashions have shrouded him except in the devotion of a few faithful admirers.) As I had expected, knowing something of the sentinel guard duties and characters of artists' wives, Mrs. Reder answered their phone and coolly invited me to tea on the following afternoon at four o'clock, and please try to be on time. I was on time, having earlier wandered through a garden full of Reder sculptures that led to a tall, narrow villa not far from Santa Maria del Carmine, which held the Masaccios I worshipped; a good omen for my visit, I decided.

An Italian maid opened the door and invited me to sit in a

whitewashed *sala* that held only a table and some chairs and, on one wall, a shelf of sculpture models and sketches. Mrs. Reder appeared after a few minutes, shook my hand, asked news of our mutual friends, and then ordered the maid to bring in tea and *biscotti*. As we were making the usual forced small talk, a monumental figure loomed in the frame of an inner door. He was tall, broad, with a forceful face and a shock of wild, brown-gray hair. The smock he wore, stiff with clay and streaked with charcoal, was bound to his full body by a crude leather belt. The presence that filled the room, the eyes as direct as arrows, the full voice that greeted me in Yiddish was an encounter with biblical colossi, Isaiah, Jeremiah, Moses. He stared at me for a moment or two, then said, "We have met before." I couldn't remember any earlier encounter but to avoid awkwardness said, "Maybe at the Klingers'? Or the Millers'?" "No, no, a much longer time ago. I never forget a Jewish face, and yours is very Jewish." This took me by surprise; blue eyes, blond hair, short nose had translated me into Polish, Swedish, German, Russian in many eyes, rarely stereotypically "Jewish"—except to sixth-sense antennae among members of my tribe. "Yes," Reder repeated, "I know you for a long, long time, maybe as far back as Esther the Queen. I keep all my Jewish faces with me; I always recognize them."

He settled down to drink several cups of tea, no biscuits, which he called *tiniff* (unclean), and asked me what I was doing in Florence. Like every visitor, I was looking at art, I answered. He hoped I hadn't missed the Donatellos on the Church of San Michele. I hadn't and he approved, as he did when I ventured to say in a small voice that the works at the Pitti were less attractive to me—my ignorance, surely—than the works in the Uffizi, particularly the early paintings. Yes, he approved of my enthusiasms again; although they were *goyisch* in design and intent, they had Jewish suffering in them; look at the agony of the Jewish mothers of that apostate Christ. And where was I going after Italy? I hesitated, uneasy, and mumbled something about having stayed out of Franco's Spain for a long time but since he was now an ally of my government, why miss the Goyas and the Velázquezes—particularly the "Meninas"—and that wonderful, ancient "Woman of Elche" and, of course, the Gaudi buildings, the earth-and-blood early Catalan paintings in Barcelona, and the Moorish towns in the south? Reder shot up, immense, bursting the walls, shouting like a furious prophet, "How can you go to that sinkhole, that stinking grave?! How can you?" I whispered something feeble about the Civil War long over, unfortunately lost to the fascists, but I expected my husband, whom I hadn't seen for a long time, to meet me in Madrid, and, and. He broke in, roaring, "Franco, Schmanko, to hell with that little *pisher!* I'm talking of 1492 when those Catholic dogs threw the Jews out of Spain, our great poets and doctors and philosophers forced to become fake Catholics. And drag their bitter ways into other countries, persecuted, denied property and professions, locked up like animals in ghettos. That's what I'll never forgive Spain for: forcing our people out and, incidentally, becoming itself more stupid in the process, losing its minds and arts to become a bunch of sullen, superstitious peasants. I would never go there, even if they gave me the Toledo synagogue and all the El Grecos. How can you, a *Yiddische tochter* [Jewish daughter] with such a Jewish, ancient Jewish, face even *think* of going there?" He stalked out of the room.

I returned several days later. He was still difficult to mollify, his voice full of scorn, until I asked if he would sell me a piece of his sculpture, which remains an important part of my landscape. The price matched exactly the sum of my first book advance. I felt rich and successful for a long time: a published writer on the way to becoming a patron of the arts. And pleased with having been, maybe, a lady in the court of the beautiful, valiant Queen Esther, as Reder had suggested; or as I decided he had.

Certainly not altogether unconsciously I must have been seeking confirmation of my antiquity when I lived for a time in Israel. One of the major museums in Tel Aviv offered a service that traced Jewish names and ancestry. When I submitted my father's name the response was inconsequential; his name was derived from the craft his grandfather followed, nothing more. My mother's name, though ostensibly Polish, was actually a masquerading, a remanipulation of letters, that the scholars, the cabalists, recognized as one of the disguises of "the Rambam"—a familiar name for Maimonides, the twelfth-century rabbi of Cairo, physician to the sultan of Egypt and greatly esteemed philosopher. Separated from him by centuries, by meshworks of genealogy and Polish rape, I yet enjoyed the thought that my most minute capillary might carry a minuscule trace of his blood. A swiftly fleeting thought, easily dispelled, since the likelihood of tracing genealogies through numerous diasporas, and through name changes imposed by monarchs and, later, immigration officials, makes the whole matter a game of uncertain questions and elusive answers.

6

Caves, Gambling Table

O N our first trip abroad my husband, Bill, drove our
sturdy, hired Peugeot, which never succumbed to serious illness (an insignificant cough now and then, nothing more), southward to Nantes of the puzzling night mentioned
elsewhere, then on to Périgueux. There we settled in to feed fatly
on the local pâtés, to explore the ancient houses and church of
Sarlat, to follow the Dordogne River through its naive villages
and lyrical views and mainly to see the cave paintings of Lascaux.
At that time, the late 1940s, the caves were still little known and
open to any rare visitor who cared to see them. As we parked the
car near the caves I realized that I had, right away, to find a
bathroom. There was nothing in sight but a stall that sold cigarettes, a few cakes, and sweets. When I asked the big, bright-
cheeked stallkeeper, a character out of the *Marius* trilogy or *The
Baker's Wife*, where I could find a toilet she burst into a roaring
laugh and, gesturing a wide circle with her plump arm, said,
"*En plein air, Madame.*" I found a tree, managed fairly efficiently, and have since loved the French of the south with their
Italianate attitudes and accents infinitely more than I do the
French of the north.

We were conducted through the caves by a man with a torch,
shedding the same sort of light that illuminated the painters and
their remarkable images of the animals they worshipped and

hunted. Particularly breathtaking was a great bull whose wide, full chest incorporates a protrusion of rock—possibly the earliest use of the sculpturesque in painting. Dazed with the genius in these primitive works, we returned to our hotel to rest and, having rested, planned the next leg of our trip. We decided on Albi, which I thought, mistakenly, had been the site of the Albigensian wars. It was a long ride through whiplike rains that beat down on our windshield and battered our windows. We knew there was a Toulouse-Lautrec museum in Albi, a short distance from the small hotel in which we settled. We left the car and in damp raincoats and under a crippled umbrella sloshed our way to the small, undistinguished museum building. The door was locked; no one answered our knocks and calls. A passerby, cradling his breakfast baguette under his sweater, told us that the caretaker of the museum was the concierge of a house a few streets away. We roused him from his bowl of café au lait and bread and politely requested that he open the door of the museum—after he had finished his breakfast, of course. He replied that he had many things to do in his damned house for its *emmerdeurs* tenants and he hated the damned rain. Why didn't we just take his key—there it was—and let ourselves in?

We did and, totally unaccompanied, unwatched by anyone, we wandered through small paintings, letters, documents, photographs, souvenirs—no great works (those had been taken to Paris and to museums all over the world) but invaluable items that testified to the contorted, tragic life. It wasn't until we were back in the car, having returned the key to the concierge, that we began to question our foolish honesty. Both Bill and I had been equipped with big raincoat pockets in which objects could easily have been stashed, or inside the folded umbrella, or inside his shirt or my blouse. No one saw us go in or out; only the concierge had a key and rarely, we were sure, visited the museum. Certainly he had only the most perfunctory knowledge of its contents. We blamed ourselves lightly for having been fools, deploring the upbringing that exaggerated respect for other people's property, even the disregarded, the neglected.

*   *   *

Up one Corniche and down another, unhampered by traffic—
Europe had not yet restored its automobiles or its sources of
gasoline—we dropped past the closed, disconsolate palaces of
Monte Carlo to reach (as I remember its name) the Hotel de
Paris, the one hotel functioning in the area. Or was it the only
one whose gaming rooms were open? Bill enjoyed gambling, and
I wanted to wander through the fabled gaming halls. Our room
was a travesty of grandeur: the once-heavy Belgian linen curtains
now limp and torn, like big old dishcloths; the once-brocaded
bedcover faded and lifeless; the ornate chairs cracked and wob-
bling. The meals were basic, dull English, culled from what was
meagerly available and cooked by local boys in plain, boiled style,
haute cuisine was thoroughly gone, as if it had never existed.
After our first dinner of something or other accompanied by the
ubiquitous brussels sprouts, we went into the gaming rooms.

Bill bought one hundred dollars' worth of counters while I
began on short voyages to meet the people I expected to see,
mainly out of Dostoyevski's *The Gambler*. And there they were,
as if there had been no revolution, no fall from splendor, no
World War II: tall, thin Russians dreaming themselves princes
and dukes and owners of thousands of serfs working boundless
properties; now threadbare, nervous pacers from table to table,
yet still grand dukes. And there were the other classics: little
ancient ladies dressed in shards of evening wear, each with a
ribbon around her throat (a mode of hiding wrinkles? a substitute
for the lost collar of pearls?). They all carried little books in which
they marked winning numbers at several tables, never placing
bets. I followed, fascinated by them: the clawlike, gnarled hands
clutching the notebook and pencil, the shred of sequins on a
droop of black net, the fake diamond brooch on the neck ribbon.

In time the old ladies and the threadbare dukes became too
repetitious. I bought twenty-five dollars' worth of chips and placed
myself at the side of a table, opposite a blond young man who
was losing small sums consistently. My gambling experience was
practically nil (my bets on horse races often depended on whether
I liked the name of a horse's sire or not), but I knew that a small,
reasonably safe bet might be placed, in roulette, by covering

corners; that is, trying for small winnings on four numbers and a color. I placed five-dollar bets, choosing as I might in a present-day lottery—numbers that felt lucky: my telephone number, Bill's birthday, and so on. On this random system, I won and kept winning, accumulating in a short time something like three hundred dollars. The blond young man, the only other person at our table, began to echo my bets at much higher stakes. He won along with me as the table lost and lost. Exalted, powerful, we kept grinning at each other, coconspirators now against the croupier and the house. After an hour or so the croupier called the manager, who told us politely and firmly that our table was closed; we were welcome to play at any other open table. At that point I became a mad Dostoyevski gambler. I would not, absolutely not, leave my table, arguing my right to stay in furious, stuttering French. What I could not express, but felt with deep, desperate conviction, was that this table held my destiny. It was my new mother, Dame Fortune, who was promising me a lucky, prosperous life. This table loved me and I loved it: I must stay with it. I tried to hang on, my hands grasping the edge of the table, blazing with fury while the croupier ushered—*pushed*— me away.

I've played slot machines since, have won loud silvery splashes of quarters in Atlantic City and Reno, but I had no attachment to these impersonal machines, nor they to me. Should I return to Monte Carlo again and find my table, will it again become my ruling deity? Will I again become a nut out of a distorted memory of Russian fiction?

7

"Pavane for a Dead Princess"

I T was one of my daughter's favorite pieces of music from an early age—a fact that already promised a sophisticated, mature musicianship. At seven she asked for piano lessons and soon played extraordinarily well, with a startling fidelity to the composer's demands. This went on for a promising while until I placed some new, rather simple music before her on the piano. She couldn't play it; with an embarrassed laugh she told me that, really, she didn't know how to read music. Her teacher always played a new piece she had assigned and Lexie caught it all— melody, chords, rhythms, and manner—in the one hearing and could reproduce it perfectly. Her teacher and I were nonplussed but even more astonished by the remarkable musical ear and memory. She learned quickly to read music but was never quite as expert as she might have been. Composition—and they were never childish melodies and simple words—and the cello began to interest her more. We were showered by an eagerness to work with her by professionals we met through musician friends. One young composer, wearing a shabby coat and a large hole in a shoe, offered to teach her for no salary at all after he heard a couple of short compositions. I couldn't accept his offer and paid him a nominal sum—all he would take for the pleasure of working with her, he said. A cellist who was a member of a leading quartet took her on as a pupil for no charge at all—he was making enough money, he said, and this was a rare talent. Practicing the cello, composing at the piano, she also decided to study other instruments. Her goal was to become a conductor. I knew that the field was then—with a few rare exceptions—totally the domain of men, but there was no point in discouraging a ten- or twelve-year-old from an ambition that required so much absorbing work and time, that gave her so much pleasure, before it had to be approached as a problem.

In all learning she seemed to skip the preliminary grades, moving immediately into the advanced. Her first childhood drawings, unlike the spate that many young children produce, were narratives of related characters, rather like the *predelle* that told of saints' lives in a set of miniature paintings under a major church painting. Unlike most other children she did not stop drawing and painting at eight or nine and soon produced pictures that bore sophisticated balances of color and design and sure perspective. One of her great pleasures, at which she spent a long, painstaking time, was to make Christmas cards that were colorful and witty, each designed for the particular enjoyment—with reference to particular characteristics—of the person for whom they were meant: imp-faced angels to a friend with slightly malicious humor; a set of varicolored baby dolls for a social worker friend; a Scrooge-faced Santa Claus to one of our misanthropes. Her reading and writing were in her usual speedy line of achievements. Her first school—the Little Red School House, where she was on scholarship—bored her intensely, except when her class created a large, communal mural. The rest seemed to have been, in the earliest grades (five-year-olds primarily), visits to various places—a stable, a milk-bottling plant—the children to report, when they returned, on what they had seen. Her answer when I asked her about her day and what they had done in school, was often, "They talked and talked, everybody talked, and all about the same thing and the same way." Somehow during that time she had learned to read but I didn't know it. On a visit to

her camp in the summer of her fifth year I offered to read her
the comics in a Sunday paper. She took the pages from me and,
with little hesitation, read the comic strips through, aloud.

Shortly after, she announced that she wanted to write a book.
I brought her some blank books from the printing and binding
company for which a friend worked, and she started on her book.
Large letters, a few words on the page, as she learned (with little
help) to write them, telling short, illustrated stories. In the second
book there was a denser, swifter placement of words, describing
a primitive society of soldiers, wives, children, government, practices, and superstitions, with vivid pen-and-ink illustrations scattered through the pages. Later, she wrote a full book that was
accepted for publication. Her editor asked for a few revisions,
which she was unwilling to make—eager to start another, a better
book—but by then she was sick and shortly after, dead.

The events leading to her death appear elsewhere in this back-
and-forth account—the memory fleeing, reluctant, darting here
and there harried by emotions and attempts to avoid recalled
emotions. She was a solemn baby with long fingers, strawberry
blond hair, and green eyes, a staring baby who studied everyone
and everything around her quietly and intensely. She was a good
child; I didn't ask for obedience; I didn't need to. She was indulged
where I thought she should be, and she asked for little else that
I didn't gladly give. I respected her fancies, which made our lives
adventuresome. One day she decided to be a fairy queen sitting
on a chair lifted by telephone directories and did little all day
but bow and gesture and wave a flower, the wand of a fairy queen.
I addressed her as "Your Royal Highness" and brought her meals
on a tray covered with a lace cloth. She ate daintily, wiped her
mouth carefully, and asked me to compliment the royal cook.
Another day she was a bird and flitted and sang through our
apartment eating bits of food I left in small dishes here and there.
Steve's mother, with whom we then lived, had never, she said,
seen so well-behaved a child and sometimes accused me of slowly
poisoning or hexing my good little girl to keep her so docile and
contented.

As she seemed to have been born with advanced learnings,

she had from the earliest age a pure morality that often made me think of her (and her father as well) as advanced types in the evolution toward an ultimate perfectibility of man. She would not lie and scolded me for lying to her, which I did rarely and only to protect her. It was not that she couldn't, I suppose; it simply never occurred to her to lie, it was not within her, almost as if she were the ultimate human animal who had discarded some useless parts of her body. As I had to grow into sympathy and understanding of others in my late adolescence, she did not. In the country school she attended when she was about ten (with financial help from her grandfather and my mother), she assigned herself the role of comforting children who cried with homesickness; who were disturbed enough to set fire to their beds; the fierce, irrational attackers; the shamed wetters of beds. Once, when I visited her, I found her wearing a torn shirt and a skirt that had become too short and tight for her. I asked her why she hadn't told me that she needed new clothing. Her answer: She knew I worked hard and didn't have much money, and these things were good enough for climbing trees and picking blackberries. Moved and humiliated, I brought her several new articles of clothing, explaining that my earnings were meant for her as well as for me and my obligations. I took her out of the school when she was about twelve, when I knew she could manage her afternoon hours of practice and homework while I worked, and mainly because our separation had somehow caused her to glamorize me and become shy and worshipful, as if I were a distant luminary. That I could not brook and was determined that we live together again.

I first met Steve, my daughter's father, when I was in college. We were never actually married because he was involved in a filthy divorce suit, trying to open a messy knot drenched in Prohibition liquor and young, driven sex. The girl, etched by many rumors as a nymphomaniac and diseased, would not consent to a divorce. She coveted the prosperity of the boy's family and counted on its reluctance to enter scandalous accusations and contests to give her great sums of money as a settlement. The family, in financial decline by then, could not consent either financially or morally. So I lived with him as his wife in his parents' house, even changing my name to his in college records. One of his attractions, other than his strong Tatar face, was his frailty—a trait to which I was always attracted, as witness my love for the consumptives Keats and Chopin and the ascetic, frail City College boys to whom I was drawn. Or was I still looking for the crippled little brother I had hated and loved and controlled? Steve was markedly deaf, not adept at lipreading, and, as I had done with a deaf friend earlier, I stopped being an echo of *The New Yorker*—mouthing Parker and Benchley witticisms—and limited myself, except in bed, to simple, important sentences. Not that there weren't wit and play. He could be funny, sardonic, inventive, and poetic and say strange things, like the fact that he was enamored of my white fingernails—I didn't paint them and he thought it naively charming. I could play, too, but it had to be in short, clear sentences. He told me, almost immediately after we met, that he had had for a long time fierce headaches and periods of projectile vomiting as he became increasingly deaf. His physician father took him to his most prestigious peers. They could make no diagnosis. It was a young doctor friend, just out of residency as a neurologist, who diagnosed Steve's condition as brain tumors. He was taken to Boston where the leading brain surgeon of his day, Harvey Cushing, operated on him, and Steve was sure that—although the deafness was irreversible—he would become stronger, almost well. In the meantime, he was writing poetry, which he would show me someday when it was polished and perfected, and was enormously enjoying his fellowship at a large hospital as part of an experimental team working in the early quests of endocrinology. His work with hundreds of white mice created some stimulating scenes at the dinner table. Having to inject hundreds of them in the course of some days, he would put a few in a vest pocket or in a jacket pocket. Forgetting to take them out, he brought them home to leap out on the dinner table following the smell of food. His mother, a heavy woman, shrieked at the sight of the speedy, red-eyed little beasts, and, with extraordinary dexterity for her age and size, swiftly climbed a nearby bookcase. The maid dashed back to the kitchen and the women guests (there were always guests—old friends, habitual droppers-in) would run to hide in the nearby bathroom while the men and I howled in glee watching the delicate white creatures put their nervous little pulsating noses into mounds of rice, twittering around the steaming bowl of beef Stroganoff.

Among the visitors who came as honored guests, not as hungry, lonely schleppers, was a family of high life, of very *goyische* grown children, beautifully dressed and given to airs and often to broad, frank statements, laughing at themselves and each other. They were to me, Bronx and Hunter College bred, like people in the movies, or the guests of the artistic Bergsons for whom I had once been a mother's helper. Their father, a silent man (he wanted to hide his Yiddish accent, I suspected), had a reputation for enjoying high-colonic enemas with a particular blond *shikse* nurse. The mother, a scatty, pretty woman with a charming pan-Continental accent, constantly strived to show how unspoiled and practical she was. No Billie Burke she. Every once in a while she would ask her driver to take her to a wholesale market, where, she gleamingly boasted, she bought crates of spinach and lettuce at wonderfully cheap rates. That the vegetables were hardly ever consumed and had to be thrown out while they rotted waiting to be eaten didn't concern her. She had been efficient, practical, and a knowing duenna of her large household.

One laughing daughter spoke of her honeymoon: "For a week I didn't see anything in Italy but the ceiling above my bed in the hotel." A young princeling son, ashamed of a plebeian taste, refused to remember *liverwurst*, a vulgar, working-class food, but insisted in calling it "you know what I mean; I can't remember its name," when we ordered picnic sandwiches. It was a fecund family, several of the older daughters already mothers, some growing bellies, all speaking of babies, babies.

I envied them, not their clothing and glamour but their babies and wanted one so urgently it was as painful and insistent a hunger as sex. I had to have a baby (maybe a return to home, for which I was often homesick among these elegant strangers, and to life with my baby sister—rocking her, feeding her, holding her on my lap). I must have, I had to have, I could not be denied a baby. At first Steve was reluctant, he didn't like babies, we couldn't afford one, and what would happen to my college career, particularly now that I was enjoying being a full English major, a difficult achievement in Hunter College? I suspect he had other reasons but did not express them: Was he truly optimistic about his health, did he know something about his brain tumors that he wouldn't tell me? I never knew. So frightening was the idea to him that when I did become pregnant he arranged an abortion for me, this time done by a friendly, redheaded doctor who told me to lie down to see if the anesthesia mask would fit. Fully believing that he meant this as a preliminary for an appointment, I obeyed and woke up to find that he had already performed the abortion, generously allowing me no time for fear or pain.

Soon after, I was pregnant again and this time I begged Steve to let me go through with the pregnancy. I would keep the baby out of his way if he wanted me to; I could go back to college at night; his father and mother would be very happy to have a grandchild. Please. Please. He finally consented. I don't think he was greatly interested in my pregnancy, which was remarkably uneventful; I was obviously a well-equipped baby-making machine, the body sharing the intense eagerness, seconding it, encouraging it, putting nothing in its way, not even the common morning sickness. Steve was politely solicitous now and then, as his delicately keyed nature asked of him. Amazing things were going on in the endocrinology laboratory that were much more singular and brought him home with an incandescence of triumph on his face. One evening he announced that they had changed the sex of some mice. Another jubilant evening he announced that they had turned a hen into a rooster and were confident of achieving the reverse a few days hence. He described the women who could not conceive—because of endocrine problems, it was conjectured—and how they carried condoms of semen between their breasts to keep them body-warm and usable for testing when they reached the endocrinology clinic. His greatest triumph was a slow one and for those pioneer years, magical.

There was a young, well-informed lab assistant whose voice was as high as a woman's, who, Steve told me, had small breasts and undescended testes, very little body hair, and—another typical aberration—the full thighs of a woman, not the slightly concave structure that was masculine. The young man, Dan, asked Steve if he could help him. Steve hesitated. There might be temporary failures or, after months of treatment, total failure; Dan was to be fully aware of the fact that there were absolutely no guarantees. Dan, undiscouraged, entered an experimental course of hormone injections in a balance of inhibitors and stimulants designed by Steve. I got to know shy, self-conscious Dan on his occasional visits to our house to receive instructions from Steve and the reiterated reminders not to expect too much. There was no danger, really, but the risk of wasted time and hope. Did Dan understand that? Yes, of course.

I very often answered the phone when Dan called for information or a meeting, and the calls were in the same bashful, high voice for months and months until once, I heard the name and dropped the phone. It was Dan, his voice now seeming to thunder on the phone—the manner still shyly polite, the voice that of a man. In time Dan lost his breasts, grew face hair, talked volubly—almost uncontrollably for a while—in his new deep voice and began to court a young neighbor he had always admired and who had been a friend. The end of the story, as in all white-magic stories, was that he married the girl, became the father of two children, and lived masculinely happily forever after. This achievement, and the fact that he worked endocrine miracles for sterile women who now conceived and carried babies to full term, brought Steve world renown—a fact I didn't know until we received letters of condolence from scientific societies and endocrinologists in Sweden, France, Germany, and even Russia when he died, still in his early thirties.

Occasionally, during the long waiting times for the baby and developments with Dan, and with his hopeful childless women, he turned fully to me, his attentions expressed in oblique ways more meaningful than the usual cliches of admiration and lovemaking. One night, staring at me, he said, "What is it, I wonder, that keeps you from being altogether beautiful? You're very near, but not quite, and I like that; I love whatever that little imperfection, that not-quite thing, might be." Another time, he asked me whether I had ever heard Wagner's *Die Walküre*. I said I hadn't and he hummed a bit of "Du bist der Lenz." I understood the German but not the context. He explained that Siegmund was singing to Sieglinde as his springtime, his revival, of new freshets of love and hope. "Du bist der Lenz," Steve said, sang itself every time he was near me. (And Steve often returns to me as my fecund, fearless youth, garlanded with the pale greens and tiny buds of spring, their roots rising from a pregnant belly.)

Shortly before I was due to deliver, Steve prepared an ingenious chart that could record intervals and intensity of labor pains and thus kept me interested and distracted through many of the early hours of pain. Finally they took me to the hospital: Steve, his father, and an old family friend whose life was incomplete without a nightly visit to the house. Steve's father came into the delivery room with me and kept talking to me, telling me when to push, when to breathe easily. At the very end of labor, when he told me the baby was about to come out, I asked for something to make me go away, become unconscious; it was too sad to lose this close, constant companion that had lived in me; I didn't want to be there for the separation. An hour later, I came to and was shown a perfect little girl with enchanting tiny fingers and wisps of blond-red hair. Lifted and whipped around by breezes of ecstasy, I did not sleep for two days and nights, calling everyone I knew—my mother, my college friends, to tell them about the wonderful thing I had done. A few days later, sitting at home among a luxury of presents, the likes of which I had never before received, the ecstasy ebbed and I gathered around myself a vulnerability I had never before experienced. I had taught myself during my adolescence that I was responsible to and for no one but myself. Now I had entered a universal fate—I had given a hostage to fortune, as Bacon had put it, I was a participant in the sorrows that came with a great flood of the Yangtze River in China, of earthquakes in Guatemala, of malaria in Africa, of wars and famine. I was a presence in every terrifying headline in the newspapers. A child was my passport to all of humanity. It wasn't a depression but a sad sobriety, made sadder by the fact that my nipples became ulcerated and I couldn't nurse my baby, as I had eagerly looked forward to doing.

She thrived as her father began to fail. His hearing grew worse, and I realized—a knife stuck in my chest—that in counting change to pay a taxi driver, he did not look at the coins but sorted them out by feeling their size and weight. He was losing his sight as well. His failing senses and the realization that his brain tumors were back or, as he suspected and I found out later, had never been altogether removed, made him withdraw from us. He still worked and continued to for a year or two until his gait became uncertain and he began to suffer convulsions. He then left his work, stayed at home, and ultimately became bedridden. When Lexie found him in a convulsion and ran to me asking, "What's the matter with Daddy?" I explained that he had the flu and a bad chill made him shake. She said nothing but obviously didn't believe me. The second time she saw him convulsed and distorted, she asked no questions. I made no explanation but became altogether determined to take her with me to another place, out of the sight of his suffering. And I wondered how Grandpa, a wise physician, who knew what must ultimately happen to his son, had not warned me or even prevented me from having a child who might inherit her father's frailties. The old man respected me, loved me, toasted me and my patience, my valor and good looks, when he lifted his glass at family parties and yet was willing—eager—to pull me into potential doom—and maybe his dazzling little granddaughter with me—for a few years of happiness for his son. I had noticed before, of course, that love had the head of Janus—an opener and a closer, a friend and a foe, a giver and a taker, an enhancer and a destroyer. Poor Grandpa Janus was not free to choose; he had to give his good face to Steve and, despite his love for me and my child, turn the destroyer face to me.

8

Lexie: Farewell

ILL left Europe earlier than I did. I stayed on for a week or two with my sister, a valiant walker, in Paris, through which I urged her—she mustn't miss the view of the back of Notre-Dame and its buttresses, she must see my favorite little church, we must wander through the Marché aux Puces, she must examine with me—in spite of angry concierges—a few authentically medieval buildings I had found, etc., etc.—until I noticed that her espadrilles were bloodstained by the abrasions on her unaccustomed, tortured (by me, I guiltily felt) feet. I returned home soon after, leaving her to her own pace and the care of less-exigent friends.

I was met at the airport by Bill and Lexie. She looked strange, not plump as I was accustomed to seeing her, but bloated, her face doughy and tautly expressionless as if she were hiding pain. When we got home I asked Bill what he thought might be the matter with her. He said he didn't know, but she had become very silent, still working at school studies and music, but without vigor and enthusiasm. In spite of her bloated look she wasn't eating much and occasionally complained of strange shooting pains in her back and head, not easily defined, not easily placed. I questioned her. She answered evasively, "I don't know; I just feel odd and bad sometimes. Maybe I have mononucleosis like my friend Bessie had." We started a round of medical visits—

she, I discovered, with a surer knowledge of what we were looking for than I. She had read in medical books all about her father's condition, which had ultimately been disclosed to her after his death, and checked her still-vague symptoms with his. They did not, of course, match at the onset of her illness, but she suspected that she carried a form of his disease as I was trying to avoid such a recognition. We went from doctor to doctor recommended by anxious physician friends. No diagnosis, no help. As she grew more and more listless, and obviously in great pain, she sought out other healers. We found our way to a far end of Brooklyn to a healer she had heard about and in whose ministrations she put desperate faith, and I willing to follow whatever lead made her optimistic. We paid him a substantial fee, and she followed the curious diet and exercises according to his instructions and then, quietly, without a word, conceded that she was no better and sank back into a fatalistic, tired somnolence.

It was generally agreed upon, finally, that there was one man to see, an elderly neurologist, loved and held in awe as the head for many years of neurology at Bellevue. His office was a set of old-fashioned worn settees, a few magazines of elderly vintage on a bamboo table, and on the walls a photo of Harvey Cushing and one of Einstein (I think). He came out to us shortly after we arrived and greeted us with old-fashioned courtesy. Then he conducted Lexie gently into an examining room of which I got only a glimpse of metal, leather tables, white sheets, and blank walls, the usual chillingly clinical room. They were together for some time, he talking softly to her in a tone I could hear, but no distinct words. When they emerged, he asked her to go to the bathroom, where she would find a jar for a urine specimen, a subterfuge, I realized, for being alone with me for a minute or two. As soon as she closed the bathroom door, he looked at me for a silent moment or two and then sadly, reluctantly, asked, "Is this your only child?" He didn't have to say more. I recognized doom and died with it. On the way home I kept chattering at her brightly like a manic puppet: how nice the doctor was and how optimistic and would she like to go to the movies and to a Chinese restaurant for supper? Would she like to invite her friend

Bessie to come with us? and on and senselessly, ceaselessly on.

That same afternoon, I went to a corner drugstore on Third Avenue (we then lived near Park Avenue in Murray Hill) and called the surgeon who had assisted Harvey Cushing at Steve's operation. He had been in touch with the neurologist at Bellevue. He told me, his voice low and unhappy, "I'm afraid that your daughter has what her father did. I'm sorry, very sorry for you both." It was arranged by the family and physician friends that she be operated on for multiple spinal cord tumors—*benign*, to me an ironic word when it refers to growths that can be as deadly as cancer in their destruction—by a reputable surgeon who had trained with Cushing's disciple. Bill arranged for a private room in Beth Israel Hospital, where Lexie was tested for a few more days and then, finally, taken to the operating room. I kissed her as she lay on the table and told her that in a few hours she would come back and be well. For some reason, the only thing I said to the young assistant surgeon who was accompanying her was, "Don't let her be afraid." I didn't know, I still don't, why I said that, except to express in some oblique way, my own terror. Unable to sit in her empty room I wandered about the halls and finally into a waiting room to find a woman sobbing loudly; her own little girl was undergoing a brain operation. I told her I was in similar trouble, my daughter was undergoing an operation on her spinal cord and we talked—she weeping, I dry eyed—in praise of our children, how wonderful and good they were, how smart in school, how helpful at home. She, a religious Jewish woman, asked why God was hurting her in this way? I, nonreligious, began to think of God, or Nature, or Life, as one of the most powerful of the criminally insane, a judgment I returned to several later times.

After much of the day had gone in the giving and taking of consolations, I was called back to Lexie's room where she lay, still anesthetized. I waited for her to wake up and at last that night she did. She recognized me and smiled and then said with studied calm, "I think I can't move my legs." It's only the anaesthetic, I said, incapable of accepting this second death. The next day a resident came in to prick her legs with needles. It was true. She had no sensation from the waist down. Within the next twenty-four hours they returned her to the operating room to find out what had gone wrong and, if possible, to correct it, but she remained, day after day, paralyzed from the waist down. Always greatly courageous, strengthened by the hopefulness of youth— she was then fourteen—she kept assuring me she would surely recover the use of her legs. "Don't worry, Mom." I went to the hospital early every morning, each awakening out of nightmare sleep a stone of despair around my neck. We didn't always talk, through those endless hot summer days. Sometimes we read, she improving her French and Latin since she knew she was in line for the top medals in both studies at Hunter High School. She wrote engagingly illustrated notes to her friends and teachers and invented origami forms of colored papers. She was polite and patient with visitors except when a large group gathered and occasionally argued, voice rising over voice, which made her tense and irritable, unlike her controlled, aristocratic self. I limited visitors, particularly careful to weed out all but the most considerate after an incident that sent her into a black depression. Late one evening after I had gone, a doctor had come in, introduced himself as a psychiatrist, and without preliminaries asked her bluntly, "What would you do if you couldn't walk again?" She didn't know what to say but was thrust into a frightened bewilderment she had never allowed herself before, especially since her surgeons had told her she would recover the use of her legs in time. When I heard about the encounter and saw her speechless face the next morning, I asked to speak with him. He was out, not due for another day or two. I left notes but he never came to see me. The only way I could expend my fury was not to pay his considerable bill for a "consultation" to which he had not been invited and in my rejection of the bill spilled out my hatred for him, his incompetence, and his cruelty.

When the hospital thought she was ready to be discharged after weeks on weeks, on crutches and dangling legs, a young intern offered to teach her to walk. Her long stay, her courage and maturity had impressed a number of the young doctors who came in to visit as frequently as they could, and this particular intern had been especially attentive. Of course, we offered to pay him, knowing how little—if anything—interns earned at the time. He was pleased with the offer and did show up twice in one week, making the first tentative efforts at teaching her to flex her knees and bend her ankles, which she began to do, feebly at first but jubilantly, full of hope and plans to return to school in the coming semester. The young man however never showed again, and it was my turn to help her walk again, as I had when she was an infant, in a quite different mood then.

Without trained skill, frightened that I might do her injury, and not capable of supporting her body steadily, I inquired about physiotherapists who would make house visits. We found no one but were guided to the Rusk Institute where we were interviewed by a tall Scandinavian doctor with a comforting manner illuminated by a large, full-faced smile. She was admitted the next day and stayed about two weeks, clearly enjoying the progress she was making and, especially, the company of youngsters whom she could help. Sometimes on crutches, sometimes in a wheelchair, she moved among them, becoming herself an amateur assistant therapist. She wrote notes for the girl with twisted hands and read stories to a little boy who was a spastic and found it difficult to hold a book. She talked to and soothed others and by her very presence, the doctors told me, served as a source of hope for the others as well as herself.

When she came home, still wobbly but walking, there was the problem of negotiating the one long flight of stairs from the street to our apartment. Hanging on to the banister and to me she climbed the stairs, up and down for hours at a time, day after day, in the same persistent, unconquerable way she had once learned, in one endless day of skids and falls, to roller-skate and later, also in one fierce day, to ride a bicycle. When she had mastered the house stairs, insisting that I let her do them alone, I only to watch from the top step, she began to speak of returning to school, now, very soon, with the opening of the fall term. Fine, I would take her to and from school every day until she was easy on the subway stairs. She wouldn't have it; she would go and return alone. I could not insist, although I tried. I had to allow room for her valor and try, again, my own. For at least a month my days were filled with hideous imaginings: falls on the subway stairs should someone dash by, pushing her, or worse still, crowd her on the platform and upset her shaky equilibrium. I must have gone about my ordinary household duties quite automatically, my whole gutted body and frantic imagination fixed on subway stairs and platforms and tracks and Lexie's uncertain walk.

In her final semester, in spite of the loss of much school time, she won both the French and Latin medals and submitted a paper that was offered to a learned journal by one of her Latin teachers. It was published; her subject was "Tacitus as a Novelist," the essay praised for its scholarship and originality. She applied for admission to the two-year accelerated program at the University of Chicago and was admitted among a group of gifted, advanced students but could not enter—she was too young—until the next year when she would be seventeen. In the course of that year she worked as an assistant to an editor of children's books and wrote her own book of her time in Hunter High School, a school whose intellectual atmosphere she liked to describe as of a mind-set whose favorite joke was "Euripedes? Well, then Eumenides." Her book (mentioned before) was accepted for publication with the understanding she was to make a few changes in it. She was not interested: An advance of money meant nothing to her, and furthermore this was a practice piece.

I was proud and frightened when I put her and her friend Bessie, who was in the same program, on the train to Chicago. After the first note, which told me she had arrived safely and liked the dormitory room she shared with Bessie, came a second describing days of testing in every conceivable subject to its scholastic limits and a happy report of her odd and wonderful program. Because she didn't like mathematics, she scored very low and was assigned a freshman class. Her French was good enough to place her in a graduate school French philosophy course, while her Latin score also put her into the graduate school. She had wanted to take some music courses but, having completed the examination, was told that the university lacked courses advanced enough for her. It was suggested she consult with the music department for permission to attend student rehearsals and concerts and she was offered the use of a piano when she wanted to practice or compose. The rest, she said, was pleasant grazing here and there—maybe comparative religions, maybe Middle English.

When she came home for the Christmas vacation of her second year I noticed that she said "What? What did you say? Are you losing that mellifluous voice with age?" I couldn't admit, I wouldn't, that she might be growing deaf like her father, but the little poisonous thing I now carried in my stomach proclaimed itself clearly, sharply, again. Whether I would admit it or not, she *was* hard of hearing. I took her to a performance of *Madame Butterfly*, which she knew and loved, and found all my muscles and organs taut and straining to make her hear, hoping crazily that the great effort of my body would bring forth full sound for her, the effort more painfully intense during the humming chorus, which she especially loved. (Not a cryer, I find myself tearful when I hear the humming chorus now, weeping not for poor Butterfly but for my daughter and my impassioned, fruitless willing that she hear it.)

During her time at the university she had made a new close friend, Laura, and through Laura met Greg, whom, Lexie announced shortly after graduation, she was going to marry. Since they were of different backgrounds and she underaged, the marriage was performed by someone with no religious affiliations. I thought about whether she could, with a weakened bladder, manage a sex life; I wondered if she could cope physically with the responsibilities of marriage, if she could ever bear children. I voiced none of these doubts; what she wanted she must have, her time might be short, as her father's had been. I bought us both splendid dresses and decorated the house gaily, invited guests to a sumptuous feast—acted out, in short, a happy, promising event. Greg shortly left to study in a special army training school and she, entering a new, shocking course of alternately hating and loving me that lasted until her death, went to live with one of her father's relatives. She resented it, but I made ways of keeping in touch with her and could see her sicken again—deafer, her vision growing misty, her face again doughy and motionlessly controlled. After a few weeks, the relative phoned to tell me she was quite sick. I took her home and had her examined again. The judgments were brief and sure: She had a regrowth of the spinal tumors and a newer growth of brain tumors, to follow her father's fate. She would need, immediately, a brain operation. I had the Red Cross locate Greg and bring him back to New York. As a soldier in the army he had the right to have her admitted to Walter Reed Hospital in Washington, where I stayed through the days of surgery and intensive care. When I was finally permitted to see her, she was sitting up in bed brightly, her head bound in a white turban of bandage. She greeted me affectionately and said, "Sit down, be calm, I want to tell you something." The hollow thing I was sat down and waited. She said matter-of-factly, "I have about five years to live." I began to cry. She said, "Please don't cry, but listen to the things I have planned for us to do together. I'll dictate essays and stories and a book to you. You can read research for me and I can tell you how we'll use it. It'll be a busy, productive time, you'll see."

Greg, Bill, and I brought her home. She was bedridden, at times incontinent. Laura and Greg—I had intimations that they were living together—and other friends came frequently. I asked Lexie from time to time whether she had any project in mind, any research for me to do. No, she said angrily, just get her a large pad and big crayons. On the pad she wrote that she was not afraid of dying, that her death would be a step toward a higher evolutionary form, that was all. Her incontinence increased and one night, when she had repeated attacks of diarrhea, a great humiliation to her and a source of renewed anger toward me, I changed her bedclothes several times and washed sheets after she fell into exhausted sleep (to know I was washing soiled sheets would make her angrier with both of us). Because she didn't want attention from me, I asked her if it wouldn't be better to hire a nurse to care for her. No, no, and no. She didn't want a nurse, and I was to leave her alone as much as possible, and please close the door.

When I asked her one day what she might want for lunch, she said that she wanted me to bring her a bottle of crème de menthe. She drank a bottle a day thereafter. I wondered why it was only and always crème de menthe but I would have given her anything she wanted, including drugs if she asked for them and if I knew where to find them. At least, I hoped, the crème de menthe would dull the persistent pains in her head and make her less furiously angry with her incontinence. And night after night, for many months, I thought of ways to kill her before she went into seizures or became incapable of breathing, and to kill myself as well. What kind of poisons would do it painlessly and where would I get them? How did one buy a gun? From whom? I circled and circled and circled, night after night, searching for our quick deaths until she succeeded, possibly with her friends, in devising her own solution.

One afternoon, while I was sitting holding a newspaper before me to look busy, Laura came out of Lexie's room, closed the door tightly, and handed me a piece of paper on which Lexie had written her will in large, crayoned words. All the records and books I had given her were to be now the property of Laura, Greg, and Bessie. The only music I was to keep, because I was fond of it, was the recording of "Die Schöne Mullerin," sung by Aksel Schiøtz (who was also to die some years later, of brain tumors). It seems now to me that the liquor she drank was practice for taking it with a lethal drug a friend was to supply from a hospital or university lab, for her readiness to die when she chose to. She died two or three days after she presented me with the will, an act of great fury mitigated by a tiny touch of love. The next few days were a surrealist film spaced through with white blanks: a newspaper cameraman—*Daily News*—tried to push his way in to take pictures of the girl who had committed suicide. How had he found out? Greg? Laura? The many-eared superintendent? Something or other went on about an autopsy, the results kept discreetly private by officials who were friends of our physician friends. We were told—where, how, by whom, what the words were, I can't see or hear—that Lexie had died of a dose of cyanide taken with alcohol. By the time of her funeral,

I hated her for all the suffering she had gone through, which I could not prevent, and because she had left me. I expressed my isolation from her publicly by not throwing, as others did, a rose into her grave (an idiotic, sentimental gesture) and never had inscribed the headstone she asked for in her will, a stone that would quote Emily Dickinson: "The Soul selects her own Society" (clearly not mine). I visited her grave only once—a mound of grass divided by narrow, strict cement paths from other mounds of grass and meaningless to me. I chose to know her as a little girl who was a bird for one full day.

9

Greg and Laura

WHEN Lexie was married she changed her name to that of her husband, Jordan. She decided as well that her first name, Alexandra, was no longer to be Lexie. She was to be Sally Jordan and was adamant about changing her identity to that of a new person: perhaps Sally with a future supplanting the doomed Lexie. I of course had difficulty calling her by her new name but I tried, as I would try anything to please her. But when her friend came into the room in which I was sitting and announced that she thought Sally was dead, I couldn't understand for a moment who she was talking about, rejecting the fact under the unaccustomed name.

Her husband, Greg, and the friend, Laura, did not allow her to fade into death or me to sit absorbing death. They were shortly married and too often telephoned me. First it was Greg who said he had written a poem about a dead girl, a good poem, he thought; would I like to see it? I said no thank you and wished him luck in publishing it, maybe in *The New Yorker*. This was followed by chummy, "Mommy, we need your advice" sorts of calls. Would Orchard Street be a good place to buy inexpensive sheets, and what about pots and pans? I answered as briefly and curtly as I could but didn't altogether discourage them from calling; I had been, after all, the groom's mother-in-law and his authority on domestic matters. The day I stopped such queries altogether began with a call asking about sites along the East River for sunning and picnicking. It was such a lovely Saturday, and they wanted to make the most of it. I mentioned a few areas and hung up. Hours later, in high, merry voices, they asked for a recipe for chicken they planned to serve friends that evening. He: How small do you make the pieces? She: Do you marinate them? He: How much garlic do you put in? She: How long do they have to cook? And so on. I answered all their questions and, overwhelmed, finally, by that contented, coarse cruelty, told them not to call again on such matters and all others. They didn't. I don't know what happened to them and am replete with not caring. Not true. I loathe them as carefree carriers of killing tidings, proud of their roles in high drama, young and picnicking in the sun, entertaining friends, while I was full of a dead girl over whom they had triumphed.

10

Flight: To Mexico

FTER Lexie's death and burial and the unbearable drip of
consolations and condolences to which I could make no
response except the meaningless "thank you," I could no
longer stay in New York, no longer answer the telephone calls
or well-meant notes, each a blow. I asked Bill to go with me to
Mexico, maybe to be soothed by the generous sun, distracted by
the ebullient markets, by living in a tongue other than English.
Maybe, maybe, I could soften some of the Dickinson "lead," the
metallic coldness that was my cloak and climate. After a few
blank days in Mexico City, we took off for Oaxaca, one of the
most amiable and distracting of Mexican cities. Bill and I spent
our evenings sitting at the side of the town square, sipping beer,
watching the departures and arrivals of country people, of the
respectably dressed city natives come to eat in the restaurants
around this *zócalo* and to wait for the concert in the ornate
bandstand. We watched the long, matted-haired hippies in their
split denims, their girls wearing unwashed Mayan *huipiles*, saun-
tering around the square like conquering heroes. (Why? Perhaps
because thus they thought they had trampled their parents' re-
spectabilities.) The rug salesmen were lifting the last Mexican-
eagle-crushing-the-foreign-serpent rugs to their shoulders. The
women were bundling their rebozos and gathering up their sleeping babies sprawled on the sidewalks, readying to make the home-

ward trek to Teotitlán del Valle, Mitla, Tula, and far-distant villages in the hills. The marimba band began to trickle onto the bandstand, a few practicing the swirls and twirls of their parts in the ensembles.

As usual, Bill spoke very little, but I was accustomed to that and set my attention on the sights and sounds about me, even staring at the lean, yellow dogs, the color and shape of starvation and rabies, dogs I feared and loathed. As we sipped our beer, watching and listening in some sort of tired peace, a woman moved out of the passing crowd and came directly toward us.

She was dressed in a wide, brilliantly colored skirt and a rose-embroidered Tejuana blouse. She might actually, costume and stride, have *been* a Tejuana except for pink cheeks and a crown of blond hair held with silver dangling pins. "I like what you look like," she said. "Can I sit with you for a moment?" I knew loneliness when I saw it, but this was a novel approach that appealed to me, and Bill might find her more interesting than he found me. She began to speak, almost instantly after she was seated and ordered a glass of beer, about her life in Oaxaca. She taught midwifery and a class in ethnology at the local university. Her ethnology came from the wildernesses, hardly explored, where she ventured to live with primitive peoples isolated in hot jungle lands. They taught her their modes of living and thought, their styles of cooking and childbearing and child raising. She taught the women how to deliver babies more safely and how to feed them nutritiously. She became their general doctor when the local herbs, barks, and grasses they preferred didn't help; she became their social worker, arbiter of quarrels, and, inevitably, an authoritative anthropologist.

Bill went home, having stayed only a few days, while I still needed his presence, or someone's, raw and empty as I was. I could not return to the apartment in which Lexie had died, but what would I do alone in Mexico? On her suggestion I moved into Lini's—that was the woman's name—apartment, part of it a shop of crafts and objects she received for sale from her jungle friends. Between the shop, the classes, and an occasional boarder like myself, she earned just about enough to support herself and a young, beautiful, and exigent daughter who yearned loudly and incessantly for the pretty things her classmates had—the embossed school boxes, the polish on their nails, the ribbons in their hair, the foamy party skirts—and she got them, often from me. (I needed a daughter, anyone's daughter, to spoil.) Sleeping in Lini's apartment, eating with her, and talking with her into long nights, I learned a good deal about her life, later recorded in an autobiography. She had managed to crawl out of a harsh, vindictive childhood to find the education she desperately wanted, amassing enough learning to make her a qualified nurse with capacities that earned her broad-ranging jobs. Like most of the young of the thirties and forties, she felt with the left but, unlike many of us, acted vigorously in its defense. She went to Spain to treat Abraham Lincoln Brigade soldiers at the front. There she fell in love with, and was loved by, a brigade soldier, an event I often suspected, as did others, somewhat enriched by reading Hemingway. On their return to the States he moved out of her orbit and married someone else. She was subsequently married twice and had a daughter by each husband, the first child kept by the husband, the second—the girl I knew and spoiled—left as Lini's charge.

Her fame as the red Florence Nightingale spread quickly, and in the glowering McCarthy days she was barred from institutions that had eagerly used her services before. Nor could she get a job as a private nurse with no respectable credentials to show; she had been stripped of them. She was reduced to housework, but that too was difficult; no one wanted a housekeeper who brought a baby, a possible longtime cryer, a carrier of measles and chicken pox, a thing that had to be looked to frequently, into her house. With her last money Lini bought a ticket for Mexico, which, she knew, was hospitable to Spanish refugees who escaped Franco, and wasn't she, in a way, one of them? In Mexico she searched out displaced Spaniards through whom she found work, among her jobs exploration and instruction in jungle wilderness. When we met she must have been about forty, the round body carried with a proud air, the crown of yellow hair kept determinedly yellow and tinkling with little bells on hairpins, the Tejuana skirts swinging jauntily, almost defiantly.

I sought her out at other times to stay with her in Jalapa, where she also taught and sold crafts and tropical native dresses, and found her later in Cuernavaca, in a large house on an immense lawn that held a pool—her very own house, the house she had earned in the course of her long struggle for comfort and security. Although she held several official positions now, was a power in the town, she still took in lodgers, limiting them to bed and breakfast. Some remained constant, winter-after-winter visitors, some were repelled by her "if you don't like it, don't eat it" response to a legitimate complaint (for instance, the quality of the butter, not one of Mexico's stellar products). I found her "take it or leave it" a sign of increasing confidence and pride in her achievements and position. I watched without comment and applauded silently.

To go back to my first stay with Lini, in Oaxaca: She was expecting a visit from her American daughter and needed my room. I wouldn't mind finding another for a couple of weeks? Of course I didn't mind and went out on a search for shelter, not nearly ready for a return to New York even if it did mean being alone in Mexico. There was an antiquely Spanish cheap hotel not too far from the center, and I moved into one of its rooms—a large, bare room unadorned except for the worn lace cover on the bed and a chrome of faded, weeping madonna high on one wall. The rest was broad, sunny space with a few niches set into one wall to serve as closets. Next door was the bathroom, also immense and unadorned except for a toilet, quite close to the shower, which lacked a curtain. When in use the shower enthusiastically sprayed the door, the toilet, and the floor tiles and then slowly, slowly, its waters gurgled down a languid drain. There were few clients in the Santa Rosa Hotel—as I remember its name—and I felt perfectly comfortable in the bathroom, as if it were part of my suite. Of course it had to happen: A man entered the unlocked door and urinated while I was in the shower. My face was turned to the wall when he began, but then I turned to see him shaking his penis, the most private and ludicrous act I can think of. This hidalgo lifted his hand to his broad straw hat, took it off to make a low drunken bow, hiding his penis on the downward sweep of his hat. With the other hand, he groped for the towel hanging on the door behind him and handed it to me. His penis under his hat, my breasts and pubic hair just about covered by the small towel, we introduced ourselves politely to each other, with repetitions of *"Mucho gusto, mucho gusto."* He asked me if I would have lunch with him the next day. I replied *"con placer,"* having no such intention.

I did meet him, though, my guide into several weird weeks. He was lithe, blond, with crystalline blue eyes. He didn't like his Dutch name and introduced himself as Lundgren, a Scandinavian seaman, hunter, archaeologist, adventurer, and writer. This was his third visit to Mexico, the first in Oaxaca. Would I take him around, show him what I thought was important? With pleasure; I had nothing else to do. A unique friendship took root, a chaste friendship. He had a wife whom he truly loved; she was coming to join him soon. In spite of his pleas of ignorance I found Lundgren well informed about the local Zapotecs and Miztecs; he knew their gods and what the dry old grins on their faces might mean. He pointed out distortions of anatomy, abnormalities that were conspicuous in all Mexican cultures; they apparently prized the grotesque. We admired together and pondered the *"danzantes,"* a frieze of men of different races (how did the ancients know them?) and estimated the present worth of the gold found at Monte Alban. We explored the wonderfully ebullient Saturday market at the edge of town and rode buses that took us to neighboring markets and villages. We watched the villagers of Teotitlán weave copies of Miró canvases, visited with expert potters in Coyotepecá and resisted the earnest salesmanship in Tecolutla's rebozo stalls.

Every local fiesta found us singing and dancing with the rest. The fiesta at Tula of the imponderably old, huge, *ahuehuete* tree commemorated the martyrdom of one of the saints sheltered in the endearing miniature church behind the tree. Having finished

a bottle of tequila with my help, Lundgren took a harmonica out
of his pocket and soon had everyone dancing around the ancient
of trees. To fill the thin harmonica sound, someone brought a
loudspeaker and old records, their scratchy tunes booming over
the village roofs. Lundgren held me more tightly than he had
before as we danced and seemed more heated than in other
friendly touchings, like walking arm in arm: to him habitual; to
me, having wanted and missed touching too long, it felt like an
elixir, melting my frozen blood. We danced like zanies, inventing
steps, singing and laughing and drunk. We were the last couple
under the tree, stopping only when we were dragged by the night's
new *compadres* to the last truck returning to Oaxaca. In the truck
I nestled close to Lundgren, pulled his arm around my shoulder,
his other arm around my waist, re-creating the tight embrace of
the dancing as it had grown wilder, Dionysian. Wrapped around
each other we fell asleep, hardly aware of getting out of the truck
and climbing into our separate beds.

The next morning, still disheveled and flushed, not quite
solidly on his feet, he came into my room to tell me that he was
going to the airport, to meet his wife, arriving from San Francisco.
He had spoken of her before, telling me that he had followed
her through many streets of Shanghai when he was on shore
leave there as a young sailor and finally, by his persistent pursuit
and courtship, had persuaded her to leave China when his ship
was ready to sail off. He had told me that she was the daughter
of a powerful man who had taken a concubine for a second wife
who produced a second, favored family, leaving the first in difficult straits although they continued to live in the same spacious
compound. Her mother further separated the children from their
father by converting to Catholicism, the children along with her,
changing their Chinese names to Irish Catholic. Margaret, Lundgren's wife, hated the strict nuns in her new school and their
pictures and stories of tortured saints. She hated her father, who
made his first children use a humiliating back gate, the gate of
the servants, to enter their house. Lundgren also told me several
heroic stories of getting her out of China; he had a full repertoire.
One had her hiding in his cabin until the ship was well out to

sea and then presenting her to the captain who, seduced by her beauty and charm, let her stay on as the ship's seamstress. Another tale told of cutting her hair and presenting her as a capable cabin boy; she was hired. Another described carrying her on board as a large bundle of purchases he was taking home to his mother. At other times, he told of having her delivered to the ship's cook in a huge sack of potatoes. The cook was, of course, his friend. Margaret later told a simpler story of paying her way.

While Lundgren was at the airport I sat in the *zócalo* talking with a few of the rebozo vendors from Mitla, exchanging quips with the older ones, those of the sharp-eyed falcon faces. Lundgren returned after an hour or two, greeted me and our Mitla friends, and then walked away a few paces to bring a Chinese girl, drinking a Coke at a nearby table, to meet us. The poised older women welcomed her with the customary courtly Mexican greetings. The rest of us stared at the girl, disbelieving her uncanny perfection, the unreal Chinese doll we had all seen in gift shops and accepted as a foreign fantasy. Here she was, that doll, enfolded in silks, her delicate face held in two curves of black satin hair. She came forward and shook everyone's hand with a little bow, a soft smile playing about a lightly rouged blossom mouth. When I greeted her she said, in accented but meticulous English that her husband had written much about me and that she was grateful that I had been such a good companion to him. I looked as long as I politely could into the long, shining eyes and the flower smile to read unspoken meanings, or at least one double entendre. I detected none. As we three walked away from the Indian group with the usual wishes that things go well, that we sleep soundly and the final adios—go with God—Margaret said merrily that she must try to look more Oaxacan, less Chinese. I would help her, wouldn't I? Again, she thanked me for my friendship with her husband; it had changed his mood and the tenor of his letters to her, recently free of cries of aloneness.

Life with Margaret (her name seemed strange to me for quite a while, so bound up with blond saints and ladies of chivalry) quickly became intimate, burgeoning with surprises and change, change I needed and maybe helped make. I told her many details of my life, the travails and the pleasures, confidences I could not give a man; they required a woman. She told me of her childhood, her brothers and sisters who were now scattered—California, France, Thailand—leaving her mother, a neglected aristocrat, living alone in China, sustained only by her religion. From time to time I found Margaret examining me as I had at first examined her. Pulling me in front of a cracked mirror in the hotel hallway, she showed me once how well we looked together, her black smooth hair in contrast to my yellow-brown thatch, a wilderness thing; my round blue eyes contrasted to her black shining arrows; my broad European mouth as against her small, perfectly outlined lips. She pulled me to her, put one arm strongly around my waist and drew my arm over her shoulder. I moved away; this was too much like an adolescent crush I had once lived. I had walked with my adolescent friend in just this entwined way, an act of defiance, a hoped-for suggestion of illicit sex and a lively appreciation of the contrasts we offered: the light and the dark, the slender and the plump.

Margaret, in spite of my mild protests, was eager to re-create the small scenes of my youth, more avid than I had ever been, insisting and insisting that we walk on the main streets, around the zócalo and through the market in this lover's knot, quite strange to Mexicans, except among cantina pals supporting each other's lurching bodies. No women conducted themselves in such a manner. Each morning she called down the hall (I had moved to another room with its own curtainless shower and defenseless toilet) to ask what I was wearing that day. I hadn't much of a tropical wardrobe, but she found something in her valise to harmonize with my choice so that we made a pleasing composition of shapes and colors. She never spoke of sex or made an overt sexual gesture; the compositions we shaped were seemingly enough for her. (If there were more to come, I would certainly have had the husband, for the familiarity of a male body if for no other reason. I tried to imagine, as I had several times before, what women did together sexually and what my mind saw—the clash of breasts, the fingerings, the tonguings—didn't appeal to me.)

We lived on a cooperative ebb and flow of money. Mine was a fairly steady but by no means generous allowance from Bill. Lundgren's money came from his mother when she could spare it; Margaret depended on small amounts from her sister in San Francisco. When our fortunes were high we ate in the most expensive restaurants and bought the objects we had coveted during lean times—the fine knives with defiant mottoes carved into the handles for Lundgren, Oaxacan figurines and ceramics for me, old posters and photographs for Margaret. When we were close to the last pesos Margaret would set herself on a stool in the market and without permission or a stall fee, set up in business as a dealer in pictures: some of the posters and old photographs she had gathered locally, a few small Chinese landscape paintings she had brought with her, and a series of prints of willowy, sinuous geishas. Her wares did not sell too well; the Mexicans could not afford them or were shocked by some of the geisha portraits. Tourists bought an old sentimental postcard, a portrait of Zapata or Pancho Villa, and let the rest go, not Mexican enough to take home.

On the third day of a week of rice and beans eaten at the cheapest stall in the market, Margaret decided to sell herself as a Chinese cook, I to be her assistant, to serve the small American colony and the boardinghouses that kept Americans. Carrying a long striped Oaxacan bag swollen with vegetables, *zapotes,* and *mamey,* she knocked at what she thought might be appropriate doors, sometimes gestured out by a servant already in residence, sometimes welcomed as the Oriental princess she appeared to be. I washed and chopped the vegetables, the prime chore of Chinese cooking, and helped serve, enjoying it all as a short-lived adventure. After we had served twenty or so dinners, the taste for Chinese variations on Mexican themes slackened off, partially the fault of jealous local cooks who spread it about— look at how peculiar we were, separately and together—that we were *brujas* (witches), a ready Mexican accusation. Counting up our accumulated moneys one evening we found that we had enough money for a long bus ride to Mexico City where we might do better. Lundgren might, for one, dig out his camera and sell Mexican pictures to Scandinavian magazines which would welcome a bit of exotica from a distant world. She would make delicate Oriental-style sketches of the people, the parks, the villas and sell them locally.

In his wanderings Lundgren had picked up a good repertoire of cheap hotels in Mexico City. Shortly after we left the bus station we settled into a modest, almost-clean inn that asked about two dollars a night (1950s prices); no private toilets or showers; there were a few off the hallways. They photographed and sketched while I made notes for a book I might someday write about Mexico. When someone's money came in we went dancing in one of the inexpensive tough places on San Juan de Letrán, then a harsh, low-life street. The three of us danced together until an American boy joined us and we became a foursome of two couples, each woman safe from menace by being attached to a man clearly in possession. (The rule seemed to be that a woman who danced with the same man all the time could not be approached by other men. Those who danced with different partners were open territory—whores, which they probably were.) Lundgren liked the threesome dancing best and held us both through the long slow wails of sad songs and the quick, merry steps of borrowed Haitian merengues and Puerto Rican salsas, the music and dancing lifted by tequila and mescal, its raw partner.

After returning from a dancing night, dazzled and dizzied with music and liquor, our man would not let me go to my room but insisted that I stay with them, that I share their bed. I did. He was asleep within two minutes of hitting the pillow. Margaret stayed awake, stroking my arm and neck lazily. She leaned her head forward to kiss me, missed my mouth, turned away and slid into sleep. I went back to my room with difficulty, turning mistaken doorknobs, earning shouts of indignation. I never quite understood what happened that night or the attitudes and events that foreshadowed it. Did they feel that they were in some way married to me as well as to each other? Was I some grotesque phantom child for whom they saved the tenderest part of the *carne asada*, for whom they left the largest portion of guacamole?

Was I a third of a triplet or a twin to each, a dream lover to each? What was my contribution—becoming docile child, twin, wife, husband, anything they wanted me to be and, I couldn't deny it, I eagerly wanted to be? Or did I serve none of these roles, rather a figure in some occult machinations I couldn't fathom? Hung over, unmagicked, I decided to get out of Mexico and out of these lives: to plot a reasonable course for myself although I wasn't quite sure what that meant; maybe resume life with Bill or find work in New York and live on my own. At breakfast I told Margaret and Lundgren that I was ready to return to New York. As if I had snapped a chain they recoiled from me. We were separate now, no longer three in one. Later that week they announced they too were leaving, returning to Europe. Margaret's sister had offered them a loan of the passage money to be paid back at some future time.

Our farewells were a return to the same intimate, ritualistic qualities that had made me happy and uneasy before. We stood close together in the center of their room, he the tall one, the priest, the shaman, in the middle. He said a few words to a crude clay bird he wore around his neck, took it off and put it on mine, assuring me that this was the happy bird that would touch my days with rainbows and gold. Margaret removed her dress and asked me to take mine off. (I remember well that it was a green corduroy skirt and a green cotton sweater.) She put on my skirt and sweater, stroking them at her waist and under her breasts as if there were sacred ointments in the cloth. After a few moments of stroking and smoothing, she reached for a cardboard box on her bed. "This is for you, your marriage dress, as this," touching the green corduroy skirt, "is mine." Out of the box she lifted a length of peach-colored lace worked in a pattern of chrysanthemums, exquisitely gossamer, awesomely delicate. "My sister was married in this dress and gave it to me to hand on to someone I truly loved. It's yours. We're married to each other, all three of us. Don't forget. Never."

They did not accompany me to the airport, and I was relieved that they hadn't; enough of ceremonious partings. We never saw each other again although I always carried a strand of attachment to them, a suggestion that we were indissolubly attached to one another. I was close to finding Margaret once when I was traveling in northern Europe but decided not to see her. Still afraid of the power she might exert? Afraid of my response to her? Afraid that she might have become an ordinary Chinese matron? I wore the marriage dress once, not too comfortably, obsessed with the fear of soiling it or ripping a strand of the lace, marring the petals of a chrysanthemum. Although I could not consciously accept the dress as a symbol of my "marriage," as anything but an expression of Margaret's mysteries, I carried the dress from place to foreign place with a care I lavished on no other possession. But the gossamer loveliness is now gone, probably stolen by a hotel maid who may have cut it up to make a blouse, to twist as a scarf around her hat, to use as a veil to be worn at mass. I rather hope it has become a veil to wear in church, yet another place of puzzlement and mysteries.

11

Marriage, and Out

M Y marriage to Bill is misted with uncomfortable questions, the uncertain answers often embarrassing, sometimes hoarse with anger. I first met him when I was
envoy from the firm in which I worked as female Figaro, a job
described elsewhere. One day my adroit speech and decent manners were sent off to discuss a problem that troubled my boss and
Bill's people. I remember little of that first encounter; our next
meeting comes sharp. Attending one of Bill's office parties I met
his senior partner, a confidently aggressive man who put his mark
on me and then, in order to pace his way through the niceties
of greeting other guests, turned me over to Bill with a quick,
"Keep an eye on her." Bill did and continued to when a few
members of the party, gaudy with laughter and drink, moved
down to the old Lafayette Hotel on University Place for late
supper. In the course of our conversation I told Bill that I would
soon leave my job and return to Mexico, possibly to try some
articles. I must have described (I imagine seductively) prowling
the huge markets, sitting for Mexican artists who drew me in the
angular Orozco manner, and incidents that fostered an intimacy
with an American girl who had come to Mexico for the delivery
of her illegitimate child, at whose baptism and registration as an
American citizen I was a witness. Besides, I told him, I was in
love with the easygoing, peacocks-on-the-lawns Mexico City (I

speak of forty years ago), its brilliant skies punctuated with the snowcaps of Popocatepetl and Ixtacihuatl, its white-clothed wandering peasants and the girls with red and purple strands of wool woven through lustrous black braids. Ergo, Bill's letter shortly after I left New York, announcing that he would arrive in a couple of weeks. It did not especially excite or even particularly please me; my life was a sufficiently generous cornucopia constantly spilling splendors for my eyes, my ears, and my omnivorous interest.

When I chose to think of it—like my tongue searching out the pain of a sore tooth—I rather wished that the letter had come from Jerry, my umbilical cord for five years, my partner in the twinings of love and lust, but my tongue soon lost its way to the tooth, which then lost its pain. Here was a consequential move by a man who was married and the father of young children, a man I hardly knew. How would it be to travel with him? Would he match my tastes for passions and languors, for extravagant declarations and gestures? Would he be a joyful man as Jerry had been? Could he dance the heated rhythms of Latin America Jerry had taught me, or the slow snakiness of Harlem ballrooms? To hell with all that, why not try, why not find out what was being offered? Although my self-portrait of independence and integrity in love tried to hide it, there was somewhere in my mind a hope that I might marry a man who would rescue me from the dour life of a single parent when my pesos ran out, as well as the money that was keeping Lexie in her country school. Maybe I would no longer have to endure the long sad twilights when I called for her at a friend's house after my working day ended and walked home with her trying to be entertaining while my mind worriedly wandered among a cheap, nutritious supper to prepare, the washing and ironing to do, scrubbing the bathroom and the kitchen. Lexie's life would certainly be lighter, gayer, if I were at home when she returned from school and had a father to greet when he came home in the evening. Bill's reason for coming to me, I assumed, was to help him sever himself from a soured marriage, to fall into the pleasures of a new attachment, the ideal, of course, this time around.

He came, eager, disheveled, and oddly winsome; there was youthful appeal in his smile, a mist of shyness. After two or three days of showing him my favorite places in Mexico City, we took a train—a long day's ride—to Oaxaca. I was somewhat puzzled, surprised that he had not asked me to join him in his Mexico City hotel nor had he made any attempt to come to me at night. Jerry would not have wasted such time, but there was no reason to be impatient; we would undoubtedly share a room in Oaxaca and in other towns of the itinerary I had planned for us. My patient optimism was, however, stretched to discomfort at his continued lack of sexual interest, always explained: The altitude tired him; Mexican food didn't agree with him; maybe he shouldn't have drunk that last bottle of Carta Blanca beer. These complaints came only at night, I noticed, and I couldn't help equating them with the female, "I have a headache, dear," the base of many-tongued, feeble jokes.

During the day he was amiable, willing to follow whatever paths I ran. His courtship technique was good humor floating on a stream of jokes and that appealing winsomeness. But at night—in enchanting Oaxaca, in Tehuantepec, the home of the most colorful and mighty women of Mexico, among the Greek warriorlike machos of Las Casas—still exhaustion, too-spicy tacos, a general malaise. So, I made the overtures, committing the immortal error, imagining that I could lead him into plea-sures, expertise, enthusiasm; that he would soon, under my tu-telage, become a lively, imaginative bed partner. And I had high hopes for tropical, fleshly Acapulco. There we lived in a cabin brushed by palms, awash in bougainvillea and passion flowers. Who could turn with the sun on a white beach along with other ripe, oiled, golden bodies; who could drink rum out of a coconut shell under the susurrus of banana leaves; who could be caressed by dulcet evening breezes and listen to burning love songs without yielding to their seduction? Bill could, and I began to find him distasteful to look at, concentrating on a few fat blackheads, staring at his deeply tobacco-stained teeth. Frustrated, insulted and angry, I announced one morning that I was returning to Mexico City; we weren't doing well together, and I saw no reason for going on. He pleaded with me to stay; he was not himself, upset by his wife's threats that she would not allow him to visit his children after their divorce. Please give him a little time. I consented. He became more affectionate and tried with clearly feigned passion to prove greater interest and prowess, but the hoped-for joyousness and spontaneity weren't there. Still, I thought I could inspire him beyond the pattern he soon returned to: the swift mount, the quick release, and off into sleep. I would, I must, keep trying to create a happy husband and a happy father for my daughter.

On whipped-up waves of hope, willing myself to love him (as I did, because I needed to love), I consented to marry him when we returned to New York. He left for Reno first, to establish the required weeks of residency. I followed at the proper time for the dusty romance (for which I had a strong distaste) of a Reno wedding. With the shrug and the *ni modo* (no matter) I had learned in Mexico, I went to Nevada—to find Bill in some difficulties. He had a night or two before dashed a hired car into a cow, demolishing both car and cow. It had happened on an unlit back road he had taken on his return from the house of a woman with whom he had spent the evening. I was startled by both his honesty and the fact that he felt free to make dates so near the time of our marriage. I said nothing, quite certain that he had not initiated the date, that it had been proposed by the woman; I had begun to know his passive, "take-me" style.

After a few days of assaulting and cajoling the slot machines of Reno, a few forays into blackjack and roulette, and hours of spirited horseplay with young new divorcées at Bill's ranch, we were married in a small, unadorned office, the short ceremony performed by an anonymous man who droned in an anonymous voice. Documents and money quickly exchanged, we left for a bibulous lunch, courtesy of the ranch and Bill's new friends. Back in New York we settled into a capacious Village apartment. Lexie and Bill, her new father, pleased each other, he admiring her accomplishments, she warmed by his good nature and jokes.

Accustomed to flies in my ointments, I accepted with stoicism Bill's mother's refusal to meet me for a considerable time after our marriage, although she herself had been divorced and re-married at a time when those were scandalous acts. More trying was Bill's dominating partner, George. On the few occasions when we danced together he held me so tightly that I was sure he was trying to break my back; there was no libido in an embrace harsh enough to suggest violence. (That destructive hold was to be repeated several times later in my life. Was there something in me that evoked it?) George also enjoyed, in the course of a few private conversations with me, recalling devilish, mouth-watering schemes to keep Bill away from his former wife, at least for a few infuriating hours. There were stories of going to out-of-town racetracks and devising one clever ruse or another that made Bill miss the last evening train back. And there were the golf games he and some friends kept slowly going and going until it was time for Bill's late return to yet another domestic quarrel. With some ingenuity I managed to avoid more of these stories and the triumphant finale, "Boy, was she mad when he got to his house!" It required no brilliance to recognize these stories as threats to myself, George to dominate my life when and how he could.

It wasn't George, though, who made me feel, after a year or two of marriage, that I was sinking into quicksand. I had lost my footing, my confidence, my enthusiasm for creating a solid mar-riage. I tried coquettishness, playfulness, sentimental gestures like sending Bill, away on a business trip, the words and notes of old love songs. He thought it was a charming idea but quite unrelated to my personal charms. Or were there none? What did he find wrong with me? Was it the smell of my perfume or lack of a distinctive, exciting body odor? Was it the smell of tobacco on my breath? He reeked of it and I didn't mind. Was it my eagerness that repelled him?

Although we were impeccable in our dealings with each oth-er's children, there were few other grounds on which we didn't quarrel: his indifference, his carelessness, his insensitivity, my quickness to take offense. He accused me of not wanting to bear his children. I shrilled back that one made children with sex, in small supply in our house. To avoid quarreling, to some degree for Lexie's sake, we often spent endless hours at concerts and listening to records (one of those frequently played was Beethoven's C Minor piano sonata, opus 111, performed by Artur Schnabel, which I acknowledge as a gift from Bill, since I had not known it before.

Visits to the homes of friends in the suburbs were icy little torments. There should have been talk during the rides and maybe joking, maybe touching, but instead there were long silences like heavy clouds that didn't dampen the fire in my flesh, on my skin, begging to be touched, to be embraced. When we reached our destination he would display himself with the winsomeness I had grown to loathe. Dimpling prettily, playing wittily, he responded always to the most vigorously flirtatious of the women, the bold takers. It was also sourly interesting and painful to watch him, at other times, with men, in whose society he was easy and strong; to hear the jauntiness in his voice; to observe the light step with which he went off to a field day of golf, drinking, and poker in the company of men only. These were usually spring outings and my bitchy mind thought of him in this exultant mood as "Queen of the May," hinting to myself a thought that became a conviction later: He was quite possibly a neuter, one of a vast number in a world that, with a few venturesome scientific exceptions, refuses to recognize them.

After my return from the Scandinavian-Chinese-American triplets adventures in Mexico following Lexie's death, I became again the wife and hostess of our handsome apartment off Park Avenue, seeing to it that the bold Italian lamps were well dusted and the cushions on the gray velvet settees, which I still remember with distinct affection, were properly plumped. We invited guests for whom I cooked decent meals; I conducted Bill's out-of-town customers to the South Street Seaport (then free of affectations), to the Frick Collection, and to Chinatown. I sympathized with lovesick friends and young relatives; bought beer and thick sandwiches for Bill's poker nights. Moving through the required paces with distant cordiality, I felt nothing, still walled in ice and lead.

One Sunday afternoon while Bill was playing golf, I went

with a friend to a performance of Honegger's *King David* at one of the Lower Fifth Avenue churches. As we walked uptown afterward, I felt a throttling pressure in my chest. I could not talk with my friend; there was no breath, nor breath for walking. My friend hailed a taxi and stayed with me (by this time I was heaving and gasping) until Bill came home. The next morning we went to the office of a physician Bill liked and respected. He was a dashing man, immaculately assembled and of swift, confident judgments and speech; actorish. Of course, he said after a quick examination, anyone like myself who had lived through my six years of agony, suppressing complaint and mourning, was, naturally, subject to a heart attack. Such extraordinary control insisted on payment—a heart attack, for instance. I must enter his hospital immediately.

I knew that women of my age rarely had heart attacks. I called an old physician friend, told him of the judgment of Bill's friend, and asked whether it was possible for a woman who was still menstruating to suffer a heart attack. He hesitated, said it was rare but, hesitating again, possible. Having had earlier experiences of the protection of one physician by another (part of the Hippocratic oath?), a sort of Round Table loyalty that shielded the hasty and incompetent, leaving a patient in the hands of Lady Luck, I kept my doubts, too indifferent to voice them, or maybe I was welcoming the finality of a heart attack. Nor did Bill suggest exploring a second opinion.

In the hospital, during the process of gasping out my uneventful medical history, I revealed that I thought I was pregnant; I had missed two periods. The details of the abortion procedure escape me. Surely this, my first legal abortion, was as neat, unhurried, and solicitous as the adolescent illegal ones had been harried and grim. After the abortion and three weeks in the hospital, which remain a blank except for a recall of my accustomed chanting: "discouraged, *découragée, scoraggiato; descorazonada*, disheartened," I returned home carrying a small vial of nitroglycerin and the histrionic doctor's warnings that I was to live carefully: a set of stairs might kill me, or a sudden shock. I was to live delicately, like a Victorian lady given to the vapors.

In a short, skeptical time I became careless, began to smoke again and to conduct my pathless life without a thought to my pulse or heartbeats.

With the disappearance of this last baby, both conversation and sex disappeared almost entirely from the marriage, leaving us further isolated from each other, I in a deepening tunnel of isolation while Bill had his business, his friends, his outings. During an opera performance at the Metropolitan, a performance to which I went alone because Bill was away, I looked around and a thought took me—coolly, no wonder, no agitation—"It's funny; everyone has a face but me." Some days later, making my way through a midtown lunchtime crowd, I found myself repeating, "Interesting, everyone has a face, not I." As I brushed my hair before my dressing table mirror, the face I looked at seemed remotely familiar, the face of a teacher I had known at P.S. 59, the face of a saleswoman in a shop I had frequented years before, the face of the mother of a childhood friend, a face only remotely resembling the one I expected in the mirror. That, too, was a mildly interesting phenomenon, nothing to get excited about. It was a suitable accompaniment to my denial of food and sleep, this denying my face, my calling card for a world I no longer cared to impress with my singularity or even existence. The knowledge of having no face of my own did ultimately become disturbing; the stubbornness of wanting to live, of finding my face, took over. The search for that face led to psychoanalysis, a few years of wandering in the jungles and swamps, the light and the dark, of my memories, my dreams, and my emotions.

My first analytic sessions were conversations, a mode of exploring my styles of thinking, my interests. It was decided that my facelessness needed five analytic hours a week and might take some years to disappear. Since it would come off the top of Bill's income (which, by the way, I never knew), he had no objection to the expense that would take responsibility for my life off his hands. He went to another analyst, a man he liked very much, who startled him, the classic "nice guy," by asking, early in their work, "Why are you such a son of a bitch?" Bill seemed rather pleased to have been appointed a thoroughly macho aggressor and hoped for further extraordinary revelations. Unfortunately his doctor died after a few sessions, and Bill would go to no one else. In the meantime I underwent an exhaustive set of medical tests to find out whether I had had heart disease or not. The physician recommended by my analyst said that I had been attacked by pericarditis that time and had no essential heart weakness.

Because I had heard that dreams were important I willed myself to dream and amassed Alice in Wonderland and Grimm's fairy tales and Pearl White scenes of which, to my regret, I kept no notes. Sometimes they came in clusters, like TV miniseries, I the gypsy heroine of chases in deep ravines and flashing my raggle-taggle skirts as I leaped among perilous crags. Other dreams were gentler and often difficult to probe. A dream of appearing among the plump-bellied, sweetly draped maidens who surrounded Botticelli's Primavera led into long, wondrous explorations of what the women meant to me. They were introduced with my description of a linen tablecloth embroidered with bits of Botticelli background, blossom-strewn cloth I had seen in Florence and longed to have, desperately longed, although I have never had a piercing greed for possessions. Why did I have to have that cloth with its never-to-fade, immortal flowers? Perhaps I needed it to assure myself that my marriage, already ripped by frailties, would become a new springtime; I as one of the round-bellied beauties would give birth again, maybe to my dead mother, my daughter. The Renaissance girls who had lived dancingly for centuries might infuse me with their immortality, with their forever-fertility, with resurrections.

Still quite vivid are the dreams that opened and closed my analysis. The very first week on the couch produced a scene in a cabin of a ship, not actually a cabin, rather an office that held a big, shining wheel, now untouched because the captain was busy discussing my voyage. My mother was there, the expression on her face both pleased and anxious. The captain told us that I would be traveling a long journey, touching both Bothnia and Bithynia. My mother's response was to warn me that I would need clothing for both cold and warm climates and medicine for seasickness. Bill, in a metal suit and wearing a robot's expressionless face, said nothing but handed the captain sheaves of money with stiff, angular gestures, like the automaton he appeared to be. He walked out after a final payment, my mother kissed me good-bye, and I was left with the captain, who admonished me never to touch the wheel until he had taught me to direct the ship, some time soon, maybe.

The dreams that marked my readiness to leave the couch (and the drawing I had stared at for years, growing quite attached to it as I studied every stroke on cheek and skirt) came as two separate scenes. The first marked the end of a long train journey, I leaping off the train liltingly, swinging sacks and large bags that were extraordinarily light despite their number and size. No one met me, but it was a happy destination, the station an enchantment of Tiffany lamps bound in the sinuous art nouveau rhythms of an old Paris Métro station. The second and final dream was a not-very-clever but telling pun. I was in my kitchen, cooking. I noticed that instead of the usual four burners the stove now had six, and the small, ordinary flames I had been accustomed to had burst into tall, blue flame-flowers held in sun yellow pods, the blue and yellow throbbing and singing. I awoke from the dream laughing. "I'm there! I'm cooking with gas! More burners, all flaming brilliantly; the world shining and singing, decorated as I like it. Bill can stay, Bill can go. I can cope with him, I can cope without him." As in adolescence I was again invincible, indestructible, inviolable.

After thirteen years of a marriage that should never have existed—Bill's role as Lexie's father fading out of our grotesque play during the years of her illness and death (he avoided unpleasantness, much less tragedy—not uncommon)—I felt there was no point in staying tied to him. But, carrying the loss of my mother, my sister, my daughter, I found it difficult to accept another, even in this lackluster life. There came the point, late in my analysis, when I knew that I could live without him or, if he consented, with him, and I told him so. He mentioned, in a by-the-way manner, that he was seeing a woman, a recently divorced old flame. He made sure I understood the situation by scattering scraps of half-torn notes of phone numbers and addresses for me to examine and discard. (Why didn't he call from his office? It would have been less cruel but less conclusive in its effect on me.) I finally suggested he leave and he did, neglecting to take his golf clubs, which stayed on for months—maybe an indication that he wasn't quite sure he wanted to be rid of me, more likely a symptom of his extraordinary, self-protecting forgetfulness.

Shortly before we separated I was offered a small advance by a publisher friend to write a guidebook of New York City. To my amazement and delight it was highly praised and sold well, launching me on a travel-writing career, the next stop a long, book-length stay in Mexico. While I was working and living there, Bill phoned me to ask if I would consent to a Mexican divorce; not, of course, that he was planning to remarry, not at all, but it might make matters between us clear and final. Flying on the wings of a promising career and basking in the glow of a fervent new affair, I readily consented. I knew that he would not have called me unless he were interested in marrying again; he didn't know how to live alone. I was high on a variety of pleasures; why shouldn't he enjoy himself too? I sent him the papers he needed immediately.

Three years or so after he was remarried he died suddenly, of a heart attack, I think. I had never known him to be seriously ill and saw his death as the result of nonmedical causes, the result of an act that was tantamount to self-strangulation. I had known him through our years together as the perfect salesman personality, who made no harsh or even definite judgments; amiability was the essential air he breathed except at home with me. He would enter no controversy of any kind other than a dispute that might, for example, involve the dating of a musical event, for which he had an astonishing memory. And who could quarrel with him about the dates of De Reszke's triumphs? He was very well liked in his business world, agreeable, yielding, his talk laced with harmless quips and mild gossip. As I watched and listened I began to imagine I saw him with his arms crossed protectively over his chest, shielding himself from challenge of any kind. On the news of his death I saw vividly the arms creep up to his neck and, still crossed, tighten around his throat until he fell, without breath, without life, strangled. The image is still sharp and deep, as deep and strong as the conviction that he would have divorced that wife and married another, divorced and married again and then again, never acknowledging his neuter proclivities but finding unforgivable faults in the wives who, through one lack or another failed him while he denied us intimate conversation, denied us sex, reduced us to nonbeings (to a variety of neuters too?).

Those appalled by this rather harsh portrait and skeptical of my "neuter" theory might find more acceptable explanations of Bill in a short biography of his youth. His mother, an ambitious girl, married an ineffectual young man, generally referred to as a nonentity. Bill may have loved his gentle, inept father, but his forceful mother took him over completely, fostering in him, as he grew older, the contempt she felt for his father. As she taught and directed him, she awed him in her rise from good job to more prestigious job.

When he was seventeen or eighteen, his mother remarried and took Bill to live with her and her husband. The new father (a man I learned to respect and love, incidentally) had come through a tortured youth to be educated into an esteemed profession. A man who had struggled through life on the strength of extreme controls and disciplines found the boy infuriating: his sloppiness, his loose handling of time and objects, his casual school attendance, his slouching through life an immoral contrast to the strict exigencies of his own life. Embittering this contrast there must have been the usual possessiveness, the husband for wife, the son for mother.

The fury of the strict man, the humiliation of the loose, undirected youth forced tempestuous quarrels. Unprepared, Bill was pushed out, homeless. Quite possibly he never forgave his mother for not standing with him, later expressed by denying his wives their roles as anchors, emotional and sexual, in his life. Escaping them as his mother had escaped him, choosing to ally himself with his blood father, he became the careless, floating man of his mother's critical legends.

A not-entirely-surprising consequence of Bill's death was the discovery that he had not changed his will after our divorce— certainly not out of affection for me but his general distractedness. The will still read as before: I was to control all his worldly goods with the added compliment that I could be trusted to be fair to his children, his mother, and his sisters, to make judicious distributions of moneys to them. The house furnishings, books, and pictures were to remain mine. Without ever having met her, I was now doubly insulted for his third wife. He had let it be known among mutual friends that though she was much more fun than I, they were not to expect that she be as clever or intellectually keen, and now he hadn't acknowledged his party girl's property rights. Other than my executor's fee and arranging to keep my modest alimony stipend, I signed a waiver that took all other properties and moneys away from me, I pleased to be rid of that which wasn't justly mine, inherited from a man I hadn't liked for some time.

Foolish little comedies, some tainted with sadness, colored my life after I was divorced and living alone in New York during intervals between work trips abroad. One of a group of friends I had inherited from Bill was an aspiring woman writer whose proposals for articles and books fell like airless balloons. Thinking that the quiet, dedicated atmosphere of a literary colony would infuse her with inspiration and skill, she applied for an invitation to one of them and was accepted. In the course of conversation with a young writer there, she discovered that his assignment from a prestigious periodical was to write a long article, already contracted for, on the same subject she was working on. Hilda had begun her attempts at writing much earlier than I, struggling painfully for a footing in the world of ringing words and here was I, infinitely less ambitious and almost by accident propelled into a position that gave me significant space. I knew she was hurt and angry, but for a time she contained herself; I expected she would find the proper time and place for settling scores. A few weeks after her return from the sterile Olympus she phoned to gossip and burble on pleasantly. I wondered at the long-winded affability. Then: She was sure I wouldn't mind, I would understand; she would like to use my apartment one evening to meet a man friend. I said of course she might. She arrived about an hour before her rendezvous, twittering thanks and, using strips and lengths she carried in a straw basket, draped bits of silk over my candid lamps, designed my gray velvet couch cushions into seductive arrangements on my bed, filled a coffee mug with sticks wafting incense; long Russian cigarettes appeared in a Japanese tray. (My nasty mind went back to the movie decors of my childhood; this was a houri's den into which Rudolph Valentino must soon stride.) I left her, saying I would not be back until midnight and be assured that I would make no mention of this incident to anyone. Although my life had been enriched in recent years by multicolored travel and the satisfaction of writing books that were not wildly remunerative but well received, I still fell into occasional pits of loneliness, especially in New York, the deepest pit of remembered sorrows. I walked out of my apartment at about eight o'clock into weather that murmured with me, *"Il pleure dans mon coeur comme il pleut sur la ville,"* the cold rain icier with my aloneness and anger with Hilda. She might have avoided the contrast: my solitary life with hers, the husband, the children, the lover between my sheets, but this was her revenge for my professional triumph.

I found a movie I hardly saw, wrapped in my dank dark, and found when I emerged that it was only eleven o'clock: an hour to kill and no window-shopping on caged and bolted Madison Avenue. I dawdled over a hot chocolate in a coffee shop on Lexington and then walked around in the rain pacing away the minutes until midnight. As arranged, the key was under my doormat. When I walked into my apartment I was enveloped in the theatrical odors of incense and warm perfumed damp oozing out of the bathroom. The bed had been hastily covered, lumpily tracing body shapes. Two wet towels hung in the bathroom, and in the living room, centered on a table, a vase holding one perfect rose—telling clichés, almost verbal descriptions of a night of love. Hilda called me the next day to thank me again and to tell me how lovely the evening had been. I cut her short; excuse me, my doorbell was ringing.

Solitary possession of a conveniently situated apartment was also a lure to a number of men I knew, including two who had been my friends, the husbands of friends. One sack of rectitude and purportedly unshakable fidelity enfolded me in awkward embraces and kisses in a taxi, breathlessly urging that we go to my house, please. Another, on the excuse of discussing with me a lucrative literary job, had hardly hung up his coat when he turned to the attack. I tore away from him to position myself at the far end of my big round dining table. The chase around and around the table might have been staged by Harpo Marx. I laughed as I eluded him from table to bedroom, to hallway, to kitchen. Exhausted, infuriated, he gave up, flinging at me as he reached for his coat a common accusation: "I always suspected you were a lesbian; now I'm sure." The male ego among my gentlemen friends, married, mainly, took these rebuffs hard.

12

Who and Where Am I?

ARRIAGE gone; my analysis a halo of bright lights; a book contract and airline tickets in my purse; the big round Eames table, the old Steinway piano, the small gray velvet couches I was fond of, the trunkful of dishes, and excess clothing stored, to come to life at some future time. Favorite books, pictures, sculpture, and records distributed among friends; they must not be imprisoned and muted; they must live, must be seen and heard. As I stood surrounded by the valises I would take for a long stay in Mexico, keys in hand to surrender to the caretaker of the brownstone I was leaving, Joe, the friend who was to drive me to the airport, arrived. His first question after we started off was, "What's your Mexican address; where will I forward your mail or phone you?" "Oh, I'll find someplace after a few days in a hotel." After a pause, "How can you go off this way into a shapeless distance?" His question suddenly made me feel cold and naked, afraid and unreal. Who was I if I didn't have streets and numbers dangling from my name? I was going to be lost, going to disappear, bereft of significant symbols that shaped *me*. It was while we were tunneling under the river toward Queens and the airport that I had a lightning revelation, Saint Paul on the road to Damascus, that served me the rest of my life, making it possible to leave one country and language for another with undisturbed ease. No matter that I did or didn't have the streets, the numbers, I was I and remained I; gathered together, very rarely dissolved or lost, firm in my anticipation of wonderful things to see and learn, to nestle comfortably in almost any civilization.

And if I ever wavered slightly, there was my magic box that contained recordings of *Otello*, of *Der Rosenkavalier*, of *Don Giovanni*, lieder sung by Lotte Lehmann, and chamber music by Schubert, Brahms, Beethoven—my lodestones. As Senora, as Miss, as Mrs., as Madame, as Mademoiselle, as Signora, as la Americana, as Ka-a-a-te, as Catalina, I subsequently lived in about forty houses and flats, from a one-room, bathtub-in-the-kitchen, toilet-in-the-hall flat on the rue du Dragon in Paris, to a large green-shuttered double studio—still missed and mourned—on the lovely, half-hidden via Margutta in Rome, and on to a duplex apartment bearing a plaque commemorating its use by Artur Rubinstein, later inhabited by Leonard Bernstein in my temporary absence. That was in Jerusalem's Mishkenot Shananim, the aristocratic guest house that was Israel's obeisance to the arts. (My landlady on the via Margutta introduced herself, as many Roman landladies did, as a Contessa. She was both a Visconti and a Gonzaga, she said—and who was I to deny her the mask of nobility that would awe American tenants, dazzle us into paying high rentals?)

One or two other shelters stay firmly in my memory: a huge flat on the rue du Faubourg-St.-Honoré in Paris, its eighteenth-century furnishings, tapestries, and paintings torn away by the Nazis from the Jewish family that owned it. The apartment was so large and forlorn that I lived only in the bedroom and the kitchen, walking through the bitter emptiness as rapidly as I could. Another flat, on the via delle Vite near the Piazza di Spagna in Rome, offered a series of colorful enlightenments. It had peculiarities: a tiny living room; a minimal dinette; a small balcony from which I listened to the local women quarreling over laundry space on the lines that crisscrossed the yard; an immense bedroom, mirrored at sides and ceiling, a pink satin throw on the bed; unusually broad and deep closets; and a sybarite's bathroom. Clearly the bedroom, closets, and bathroom were the focal spaces. The purposes of the layout of the apartment—and I assumed it echoed others in the house—became more obvious when, coming home late several nights, I saw women I had earlier passed on the stairs in wrappers or ordinary street clothing now parading in low-slung blouses and tasseled skirts, swinging large black pocketbooks as they paraded and leaned near doorways, paraded again and leaned again between our house and the piazza. Living with these ladies made it quite easy to elicit phone service, no mean achievement. On the advice of a Roman friend, I applied to the phone bureau announcing that I was in a "private business" and urgently needed a phone for my livelihood, *per piacere*. Three days later a leering, efficient young man installed my phone. As a tip he wanted a kiss; I forced a bundle of lire into his hand, no kiss. The flat produced two minor problems, less easily resolved: Did I greet my neighbors when I saw them sashaying at midnight in front of our house or ignore them while they were in their line of duty? It took time to settle that dilemma, trying one approach or another until it became clear that the women preferred to ignore me. So, we remained blind to one another except in daylight hours when we exchanged the minimal *buongiorno*. Then there were the numbers and kinds of telephone calls I had to answer. At two in the morning (many mornings), "Is Rosa there?" At three on another morning, *"Come stai, bella? Si posso venire adesso, fra qualche minuti?"* Having denied that I was the *bella* the caller was yearning for, I had next to cope with his willingness to make do with me, the unknown *bella* with the voice of a diva and the charming accent. "How about it? I'm really dying to meet you." I often went on my Roman rounds foggy with lack of sleep, but I can't say it wasn't stimulating, all of it: the flat, the neighbors, the phone calls, and imagining myself as some of my night callers might have imagined me.

13

My Sister, Sylvia

It has been said before in several idioms and styles that whoever planned the wondrous universe had aberrational periods that belonged to the criminally insane—monster newborns, diseases of doom among children, and the humiliations, the painful depletions of old age.

Two years after Lexie's death and at a time when psychoanalysis was beginning to return my face to me and my so-called heart disease had been correctly diagnosed as an attack of pericarditis that had left no permanent injuries, my sister, eight years younger than myself, began to die. She had been my second child—my brother, crippled by malnutrition in his earliest years, my first. As the eldest in a European household, it was my duty to take her carriage down four flights of stairs, return for her and carefully place her in her carriage, then rock her to sleep in the fresh air—I in permanent elderly shade while my brother played stickball, howling and dancing in the bright sun. I had resented her birth, the source of screams from my mother's bedroom, a guilty reminder of the hideous pain I must have caused my mother at my birth. I would not look at the baby for at least a week but slinked from house to school, from room to room, to avoid her. I could not, however, long resist her golden eyes and toes like pink petals and, as she grew older, her gentleness, a peaceable contrast to the noisy battering at life and each other that was the rough climate of my brother and myself. One of our rare agreements, tacit but steady, was that we would teach her our particular skills. His contribution was dancing and she became a superb dancer, better than her mentor. Our joint contribution was the dozens of songs we knew, which she sang more musically than we did in a surprisingly full, unerring voice. I taught her to read before her school did and, when she was older, and I living elsewhere, took her to Klein's to pick out clothing. (As if it lay here on the desk before me, I see a white dress with bright flowers that we bought for her elementary school graduation party.) Although she didn't ask for it, she was always one of our responsibilities, a light burden we carried willingly. After my mother's death, Sylvia's graduation from college, my brother's induction into the army, I found her an apartment near mine, shopped and cooked with her, and asked too many maternal questions about her work, demanding jobs she performed with skill and confidence. One of our joint pleasures was to meet friends at the Village Vanguard, not far from our apartments, and especially fun for Sylvia who had been picked out by Leadbelly, then the lead performer at the club, as his preferred dance partner. Leaving his twelve-string guitar backstage after singing— as no one has since—"Midnight Special," "Take This Hammer," and, his closing signature, Woody Guthrie's "Good Night, Irene," he came out front looking for the "little round gal" (a rough but accurate description of Sylvia) and would lead her, neither faltering, through a diabolic series of steps they invented as the music urged them. He never danced with me and rarely with anyone else but the "little round gal."

Unlike many sisters, we were genuinely fond of each other (the fact that mine was a maternal rather than a sibling's role colored our responses toward each other). We understood each other uncannily well. When, for instance, she would receive a large jar of mirabelles packed in France, she would call to ask me if I felt better, knowing that my sending her something she delighted in and couldn't afford would partially melt away the ice that still encrusted me on glacial days.

Her cuddly roundness matched itself in marriage to a slim,

elegant young man, a product, as we were, of the city colleges. It was not a marriage I understood, but then I didn't understand my own or those of several friends—or maybe marriage as a usable institution in the twentieth century. Possibly to seal the stretches drifting between them, and certainly because she loved babies and wanted to sing to them her many songs, she had three babies within five or six years, all by cesarean section, the first a cruel trial of days on days of labor before the obstetricians would agree that surgical intervention was called for. As cesarean children they didn't have to struggle their way through dark, crushing channels and emerged looking like freshly enameled baby dolls in Christmas displays.

She was an enthusiastic if exhausted young mother and, like our mother, playful and laughing with her children, not too concerned about the smears on clothing and dirt in the hair that the older two collected in their narrow backyard. It was a pretty little yard and was attached to a long, narrow path that touched on every backyard of the block. It was a good, easy place to let a four-year-old wander; some backyard or other would welcome him or direct him home. Their father was not quite approving of this freedom from neatness and boundaries, but tasting on weekends the puny quarrels, the quick wails, the birdcalls of "Daddy, I want," the spilled milk, the upset applesauce that made the floors perilous skating rinks, he stifled criticism and took on a few household chores—washing dishes, and changing the baby's diapers. Unlike the combative toddlers the baby, a girl, was a contented cooer, a decorative thing, responsive and pleasing.

When the little boy was six, in the first grade, the first little girl three, and the baby about six months old, Sylvia began to have intense and constant aches in and around her abdomen. She couldn't locate the pain exactly but it grew increasingly unbearable. Finally she had to take to her bed, suffering hideously and at times only semiconscious. Her mother-in-law and I cared for the children while her husband took her from doctor to doctor for various abdominal tests, which showed no sign of illness in that region. She began to slip out of consciousness frequently and her few periods of seeming lucidity became irrational spates of words. She was taken to a brain surgeon. Very reluctantly, because of my recent loss of Lexie, her husband revealed what I was already guessing: She seemed to have a brain disturbance, the pain in her abdomen an erratic substitute for the unlocated pain in her head. The diagnosis was confirmed and again confirmed: She had the dread brain tumor, not benign this time but cancerous. Taking the children with us, her husband and I drove to Mount Sinai Hospital where she was to be operated on, although the doctors held out no hope for ultimate normalcy; she was so damaged that at best she might probably live on as a brainless vegetable. In the course of the long ride from Forest Hills to Mount Sinai, Sylvia spoke gaily and incessantly about the streets we passed, about the corruption in the city government, inventing criminal roles for the borough presidents, the head of the police department, talking about them in a high, affected voice. I stayed in the car with the children while their father took her into the hospital. As if they knew that something terrible was about to happen, the baby began to sob; the older two wailed "Momma, Momma." I was not permitted to cry; I had youngsters to placate and reassure, not very successfully. They wept all the way home, I driving with the baby in my lap and the other two clustered as close to me as brakes and steering would allow.

The next day I was with her in the hospital; the old, accustomed vigil. She knew who I was, she didn't know who I was; a recognition of realities, a return to her secret, diseased world. She was fed very lightly because she was to have surgery the next day, and she cried because she was hungry and the bad people wouldn't give her anything to eat. When her husband came in the late afternoon she cried again, pleading, "Poppa, poppa, get me out of this bad place; they're ugly, they're mean, they took away my ice cream." That night Mount Sinai could find no special nurse, and I stayed on with instructions from her young surgeon not to let her sleep. I had to slap her hands, to make conversation with her, as to a child, as to a demented adult, pushing her head gently back and forth to wake her out of the unconsciousness she seemed to long for. This went on, the slapping, the pushing, the talking, those nightmare hours until morning when they took my sister for surgery. I sat in the waiting room for I don't know how long, until her husband arrived and, shoftly after, the young surgeon. He told us, his voice low and burdened, that she had died in the course of the operation. And, he added gently, it might be a good thing. Had she lived, she would have had to be institutionalized, far from the children to whom she would be a dreadful presence if they tried to see her. I have always suspected that the young doctor had made no attempt to correct whatever it was he might have found but simply helped her die, and I have always been grateful to him.

I didn't settle into mourning; it was the accustomed color and climate of my life at that time. Besides, the children needed constant attention. If I hadn't read it somewhere, I would not have believed that young children react to the loss of their mother with such distinct voyages into melancholia. The little boy refused to go to school in the fear, it seemed, that his house, his sisters, his grandmother, his aunt would disapppear while he was away. When we finally persuaded him to return, I taking him to school and calling for him, he spent much of his free time on the telephone with his father to reassure himself that he was in his office and would be at home for supper. In order to be able to go to sleep he kept the end of his dog's leash between his teeth and although it was chewed up and dirty, we were grateful for—and to—it. The three-year-old, not yet in nursery school, spent the day on her bed, her face turned to the wall as if she were trying to see through it, to penetrate it. I offered all sorts of blandishments—we would go to Woolworth's to buy papers and crayons and ribbons of which she could make the chain loops she liked so much. "No, thank you, Kate." Would she like to go to the ice-cream parlor and have a big chocolate cone? "No, thank you, Kate." Should we go next door and see the new kittens that Susie, the big cat, had just given birth to? "No, thank you, Kate." She would not budge until her father came home; she had her supper and went back to staring at the wall at the side of her bed. It wasn't until months later, after she had been treated at a school for sorrowing children like herself, that she stopped staring at the wall, waiting for her mother to walk through it.

The seven-month-old ate and slept normally but had stopped chortling and gurgling and made no attempt to turn over or to progress to any of the developmental stages expected of her. She was inert, and her muscle tone had turned to silken flab. We had to exercise her legs and arms and massage them for a long time before she ventured movements of her own.

Shortly after, their father hired a superbly understanding Jamaican lady who cared for them affectionately and devotedly. She stayed with them for two to three years, until their father remarried—so assiduously careful about making a new life for himself and his children that he never told them anything about their blood mother—a lack I think I see manifested in their curious, ambivalent attitudes toward reminders of her in conversation (tactfully rare) or in photos.

Sylvia's death had on me not only the effect of forever-loss, still as strongly present as that of Lexie, but—with brain tumors in my direct family and carried by my daughter not only from her father but possibly by something in my genes as well—it made of me a self-appointed Typhoid Mary of brain tumors. I would not hold or handle any child, no matter how appealing, no matter how a parent might thrust it at me for approval. I was afraid of the contamination I carried. I'm not sure I'm free of that fear yet. (Particularly since the Great Joker has recently decreed that I have one too—nothing to worry about at my age, and unlikely to trouble me before I am skull and bones.)

14

The Dross

IT was a Sunday evening after one of the habitual repetitions of Mexico City Sundays several friends and I had shaped and happily clung to. First, a breakfast of chocolate and *pan dulces* in a cafe near the Bellas Artes Museum where, breakfast over, we attended the weekly morning concerts. Then home for a large *comida*, a siesta, and either the bullfight at four o'clock sharp (the only "sharp" in all of Mexican life) or a movie at one of the grand, bedizened, befountained movie palaces on the Avenida de la Reforma.

We had gathered that particular Sunday evening for a birthday party of one of our circle. As I placed a bowl of guacamole on a side table, a wave of nausea rocked me. I knew the sensation and looked up at the chandelier. It was swinging gently from side to side, as were the drapes at the front window. "Earthquake!" several voices shouted as the guests began to dash about blindly, frantically, searching for exits from this sixth-floor apartment. Head for the elevator? Clearly unsafe. Run down the stairs? They might collapse and bury us in concrete and the steel of banisters. Our host shouted, "Stay put! Don't try to get out. Maybe this will be one of the ordinary little ones." It was: The drapes swung back to stillness; the chandelier settled into its one space. A few newly arrived American friends remained uneasy but were soon lost in admiration of the "cool hands" of whom I had become a

member through my longer stay in Mexico, my fair command
of Spanish, and the friendship of several Mexicans. By this time
a seasoned acquaintance of minor earthquakes, I talked casually
about my experiences. None of them was particularly memorable
except for the time I tried to mount a flight of stairs that ground
on each other like giant teeth, and the one big tremor that picked
up my sleeping body and threw it to the floor several feet from
my bed. Other earthquake stories were told, diminishing the
hoped-for gaiety of the party, and most of the guests left early
except for one friend with whom I had been discussing my search
for new housing.

I had had quite enough of sharing a tight house with a tall,
professorial neuter who appointed himself my guru and allowed
me few moments free of his instructions, unrequested, unwanted,
toward the better life as he had learned it in a spiritual voyage,
wandering among ashrams from Poona to Madras, from Bombay
to Calcutta. The friend with whom I had been speaking at the
earthquake party had been at one time attached to a place nearer
the center of the city, a boardinghouse at number seven on the
street called Paris—a house that had earned local fame for its
owners and its guests. He suggested I inquire there. When I asked
for a room I was told that the only one available was a tiny house
of one room plus bathroom in the yard adjoining the big house.
I had no objection to that cabin furnished in devoutly Mexican
style: crude leather seats, a bedcover of bright, striped *manta*, an
assortment of green dishes from Oaxaca, and a Totonaco goddess
grinning down at me from the bathroom door. True, the street
floor did invite an occasional scorpion, one hideous little creature
nesting in a shoe I was about to put on. True, the yard attracted
rats who wandered away from the hordes that danced the night
away in an adjoining street pit lined with garbage and feces. But
I could observe the comings and goings of the house and was
often invited to meet a refulgent variety of people, a number of
them especially attractive as representatives of the arts and contemporary history.

The duenna of the house, a sweet-tempered gentlewoman,
was Señora Arenal, the mother of two distinguished daughters,

one of them in medicine—I don't remember precisely what division. The other, Angelica, of the taut, alert face, a face constantly poised for intellectual combat, was the wife of David Siqueiros, then held by many to be Mexico's leading painter. The wife rejected my crude, inimical, American existence; the husband was absently, vaguely cordial when we met. Other than a greeting from the painter, we never spoke. I didn't particularly mind since there were other guests with whom to converse, particularly people who had fled Franco's Spain to shelter in Mexico, which offered them—as it offered refugee Jews—safekeeping, even the dignity of a Loyalist government in exile. One man whose face resembled a noble, classical bust of an ancient philosopher had been head of the library network of Madrid; another was a renowned writer; another, a close assistant to the heroic firebrand La Pasionária. One appealing, poorly dressed, and shy group always huddled together, its members tied together by their lack of Spanish, their suspicion of Mexican foods, and, I suspect, homesickness. They were all young with a number of little children whom they would take for walks on the Reforma and quickly back again, afraid of the traffic and the dark people in this big, strange city far from Moscow and Kiev and Yalta. I was told that they were on their way to Nicaragua, to Guatemala, to other Central American countries, to fill jobs in Soviet consulates. Several of us wondered and kept on wondering how their bewildered naïveté managed in a language and a set of mores so distant from their own.

Among the Spanish, Mexican, Slavic faces, the most compelling—at least to me—was that of Siqueiros. There was little of the Indian in his face as there was in the faces of his rivals, Diego Rivera and Rivera's wife, Frida Kahlo, both of whom had Jewish blood and yet looked like the indigenes of their paintings. What I found so absorbing in his face was its softness, a womanliness—an aging woman—toward which it was sloping. As some elderly women develop craggy eyebrows and wiry facial hair, some of their masculine counterparts turn to an almost hairless creaminess; a silky droop of cheek; soft, plump eyelids. Siqueiros's voice, though, was sharp and vehement, particularly in its assaults on the government that had imprisoned him (not without recognizing that he deserved special privileges, like the freedom and space to paint, like streams of visitors and the small luxuries that were the right of a famous painter, a national monument).

It was in this multilingual, multicolored Paris seven, a changing show directed by the esteemed painter and his sharp, beautiful, dedicated wife, that I met Miguel, with whom I began to travel and explore Mexico after we became close friends. Following one roaring tequila-floated party that lasted into dawn, Miguel and I, carrying minimal bundles of clothing, started on the long journey to a distant hacienda he had known as a child. During a breakfast of coffee and sweet rolls at Sanborn's lovely old, tiled house we were joined by a friend of Miguel. He gave us instructions on which train to take, which bus from the train, and when we got to the end of the bus line we were to go to the big market and ask for Sweet Pea; everyone knew Sweet Pea for his extraordinary flowerlike face. I slept fitfully on the train and on the bus, a little worried about spending the night with Miguel, obviously an essence of this long trip. Would I enjoy it? Would he? I didn't want any change; I enjoyed him just as he was, a witty Mexican who had been educated in the States but had vivid memories of Mexico, had studied photographs of the places of his beginnings and insisted that elderly relatives tell him stories of the old days. Now he wanted to return to their reality, and I was delighted to be taken to his obscure villages, as he had taken me to other evocative places—the mineral baths of Mexican kings; the enclaves of magic makers; small, abandoned sites of ruins; thieves' markets; much. They had always been day trips. Was I ready for tonight? OK, OK, I was not a young virgin and friendships with men often pointed this ultimate way. Invitations to bed had come from a number of Mexicans, fairly numerous and no longer flattering, particularly when I realized that my prime attraction was an exoticism of sun-bleached hair and sun-darkened skin, which made an effective frame for blue eyes that blazed out of a tanned face. I was not so much desirable as I was a rarity, an aesthetic pleasure. Miguel had not been one of the

exigent suitors; there was one half-hearted suggestion, hardly a
pressing request, and dropped with my refusal, as light as his bid.
Since we had both made our first shots in the game and dropped
it, we hadn't gone on. Now?

After hours of bus and train we found Sweet Pea, easily
recognizable by the folds and sad innocence of his face. He helped
us into the back of his truck, which was full of bales, our seats
for the next hour, each bump on the rough road a blow. Traveling
through miles of cactus, the sword-bladed expanse cut in one
place by an abandoned, toylike railroad train and in another by
a sloping chapel with an eroded doorway, we came to a gutted
hacienda, a victim of the 1910–12 revolution, our base for the
day. It must once have been magnificent, with a kitchen immense
enough to prepare courtly dinners for fifty guests or more. Here
and there now a few cracked benches, dust-covered platters, and
a huge urn with one smashed ear. The large *sala* held a red-
velvet couch sliced by furious swords, which left it vomiting gray
stuffing. A few pieces of ornate, wobbly furniture, a shred of
satin, a dangle of faded tassel, were witness to despoiled splendor.
At the back of the house we found a bedroom with usable pillows,
two limp quilts, and a couple of old but clean sheets. We assumed
that an ancient caretaker still slept here and had disappeared when
the local grapevine told him that Miguel, whose family he had
once fought, was returning. We never saw him.

Company we did have, however. It was Claudia, Sweet Pea's
now-and-then girlfriend. She was splendid, opulently curved and
brightly colored and as tempting as a bowl of tropical fruit. We
had picked her up for the last lap of the truck ride and found her
well-informed on many subjects and as lovely squatting on a sack
of corn as she was standing upright, waving vigorously at passersby, flashing her marvelously white teeth at them, each smile
a gift. She inspected with us the defunct stables, the storage
houses, and a second family chapel, still gleaming with the old
gilt that once blazed the altar. Claudia had some wonderful things
to say about these *chingado* landowners who made slaves of their
peasants, of their women workers who kept their babies drugged
and quiet, as Russian women serfs had, here by drugging them

with nipples soaked in *pulque*, a sort of beer. While we later walked through the fields of cactus from which the hacienda had made *pulque*, mescal, and tequila and the fortune that came with their sale, we heard the distant sounds of a fair and market being set up. We followed the excited voices, the hoarse groans of a calliope, and soon came on the wild-eyed wooden horses of the carousel, clay pipes to shoot down for prizes (elderly Kewpie dolls), a huge scale and hammer that proved whether a man was a "mama's boy" or a "Cadillac macho," depending on how mightily he swung the hammer.

While Miguel and Sweet Pea, whom we found at the fair, shot down pipes and little ducks, Claudia and I inspected the vegetables and fruits of the adjoining market and some of the small objects for sale. We stopped at a row of pretty, handknit purses suspended on a line above one fruit stall. Claudia examined a few inside and out and suddenly, quickly, paid for one I thought thoroughly unattractive. She pulled me hurriedly from the stall to the area behind the shooting gallery, then, looking carefully around, opened the purse. It was full of money—small moneys, but full. "Claudia, that's where he keeps his earnings, that poor man. Give it back, give it back now or I'll tell the police." "What police?" she laughed. "If there were any around they would take it for themselves; that dumb *campesino* would never see it in any case." I knew she was right and could only look at her disapprovingly, repeating, "That poor man, what will he take back to his family?" "What do I care about his family? He probably stole the purses from someone else and maybe the change too." Difficult as it was to be indignant with wild, ravishing Claudia, I tried to make her regret her theft, restore the money, but gave up when she bought a bottle of tequila for it, to drink with the tacos and empanadas I bought for our strolling picnic.

It was now full night, the stars thick, a light breeze swinging through the fair, carrying thin strips of music. The food and the tequila went down smoothly, making us even more talkative than before, Claudia roaring with laughter at each quip she uttered. After some vague time Miguel and I realized that Claudia and

Sweet Pea were gone. As I tried to rise from the bench on which we had been sitting, I found my legs unwilling to hold me. With Miguel's arms supporting and directing me, we reached the bedroom of the decayed hacienda. I heaved a great breath when we got to the door, and with it a flood of vomit filled my mouth. I reached the garden door of the bedroom and vomited, blaming the disgusting act on Claudia's theft, on Sweet Pea's weird face, on my own stupidity in allowing myself to be bedded down with Miguel when I didn't know whether I wanted him, on my disgusting old trait of, "I don't really want it but don't want to let it go." After I stopped heaving, Miguel helped me to the bed.

I remember nothing else until the next morning, when I found myself undressed except for a half slip that had been pulled up to cover my breasts and smoothed down to cover my thighs. My mouth burned with vomit and self-hatred; I couldn't lift my eyes to look at Miguel lying next to me. When I summoned the courage to open them there was no Miguel. Only a magnificent passionflower, boldly shaped and colored, lying on the pillow next to mine. I washed at an outdoor tap, then returned to the bedroom to dress, trembling with unhappiness and shame. As I was putting on my lipstick and combing my hair, sure that Miguel had left me and I couldn't blame him—but how would I get back to Mexico City?—he appeared with a full smile and a second passionflower, which he placed beside the first. I tried to apologize: I'm sorry I made a fool and pig of myself last night. I'm sorry I spoiled your night. Lend me your revolver; I'm going to shoot myself. He flicked my cheek and said, "Let's forget it. I'll get us some breakfast." As I sat wishing I were dead, he brought in coffee and rolls and ate heartily while I nibbled and sipped, muttering a repetition of apologies. He would not let me go on: "These things happen; forget it."

Miguel and I remained friends, he as adviser and guide to obscure places, I as provider of occasional good restaurant meals and supplier of a new warm sweater or freshly starched shirt. It was he who taught me to ride (no great achievement because my mounts were tired old nags with no protest in them), taught me to recognize the salient features of Huastec idols, introduced me to the masterworks of the Olmecs, and told me stories of the revolution as he heard them from his elders. I met a few personages, quite, quite old, of some of the stories during a long horseback ride in the bare, dry, inhospitable land that was Miguel's *tierra*. He was astonished by a new *supermercado*—"and it even has Coca-Cola"—half in admiration, half in contempt. Several *pulquerías* now looked like modern city bars, but were not for the elderly who stumbled their way to back alleys, to swinging doors parting from their hinges, machetes, knives, and guns still the companions of their drunken angers. Miguel wouldn't let me enter one of these, the most picturesquely, dustily worn, but Sweet Pea and Claudia, whom we would bump into now and then, did go in. Standing outside, wary of the lurching entrances and exits, I once heard Claudia's high, strong, ranchera voice, accompanied by an uncertain trumpet, fill the mescal-heavy air.

I never saw Sweet Pea again but did meet with Claudia in Mexico City. As always, she talked volubly, choosing at one time to give me an informative lecture on how the maguey cactus leaves were pounded into cloth by the Aztecs, who used the needle at the end of each leaf to sew the pieces of cloth together. She was encyclopedic about the exact treatment of the maguey plant to produce *pulque*, which many of the local children drank freely, producing a swaying populace that did not go to school but brawled lazily on their village paths. And on and on she went, through the making of mescal and tequila, taking long sips from bottles of each type as she talked.

On one visit to my apartment, already well fortified with tequila, she asked for a few drops more, *"por favorcita."* After gulping them down she burst into tears. She had been remembering the agonies of childbirth twelve years before (not, I noted, the agony of separation from the child who lived with her father in another country) and shrieked and wailed about her torn flesh, every muscle and vein being ripped out of her body. I knew that very few women remember the pains of childbirth, but I listened.

Always vivid and explicit, with a surprising command of anatomical terms, she described floods of blood, engorgements, rippings, and tearings, the matter that I knew in Frida Kahlo's paintings and that Claudia probably knew as well, making the paintings her own life, as she made any poignant piece of autobiographical material her very own.

Miguel knew her moods and stories and never accused her of lying to her face but warned me against her. "Why?" I asked. "What's the harm of a few colorful lies?" "You'll see, she'll use the lies and you in some unpleasant way." I stayed in touch with her. One night during the rainy season she phoned to ask if she could sleep on my couch; she didn't feel like waiting for the bus in the wet night, and she was so near my house. I said of course, gave her some coffee when she arrived, helped her put sheets on the couch, and went to my bed. I was aroused from a deep sleep by the sound of sobbing close to my ear. I woke to find Claudia in my bed, big tears pouring out of those incomparable cat green eyes. She was mourning her mother's death, she said, a mother who was a saint, who fed all the poor in the neighborhood. (I had heard it differently: an ordinary woman with ordinary impulses, kindly enough, but no Virgin of Guadalupe.) "And," Claudia went on, "she held me like this," putting her arms tightly around me. "When I sobbed and hiccupped after the crying, she would stroke me like this," and Claudia's long-fingered hand ran eagerly down my thigh and around my buttocks. I began to pull away but she held me firmly with one arm and hand while with her other hand she pulled at my hair to bring my mouth to hers. Fierce and strong as she was, I managed to tear out of her grasp and, leaping out of bed, shouted, "Get the hell out of here! I don't want you and never will, as a sex partner. Get out. Now!" She made a courtly gesture, as if in regret and apology, but I pointed to the bathroom, told her she could use it for five minutes and then out, home, wherever that was; maybe with the whores in the Zona Rosa, maybe with the lesbians who haunted Frida's house.

She tried several times to see me. I always refused, not only because of the sexual overtures but because I was tired of the wild tales and tempestuous emotions that were essentially acting, acting as she might have seen it in paintings, in the movies, acting out anyone's dramatic stories to weave into the pastiche that was Claudia. Though she was the most beautiful woman I had ever seen, and I am always grateful to beautiful women, I had had enough, more than enough.

At thirty-five I had made it: a Hollywood party and pursuit by a star. Who could ask for anything more, particularly a woman whose father had convinced her that her generous mouth was modeled on the grotesque smile that once advertised Luna Park in Coney Island, a woman whose father had spewed forth constant nastiness on her Charlie Chaplin walk (the walk of ballerinas, later discovered—but too late to use as contradiction or consolation).

The Caliban side of memory has left no tuneful, pleasant murmur, no splendid images of this Hollywood celebration of my powerful allure. There remains only the vague knowledge of a crowded, extravagantly dressed party in a vast house fitted with furniture that had nothing to do with people; it was a bizarre movie set. Adorning this indoor scenery were the expected big-party appurtenances: pots of caviar, notable champagne, white-gloved waiters, sentimental songs oozing out of some concealed sound box, and, of course, euphoria in high decibels. In the course of circulating among almost-recognized faces, sorting out one darling starlet from another, straining to identify the man who looked like Charles Boyer, or was it Cary Grant (the champagne assembled attractive collages), I was stopped by a middle-aged actor, still quite attractive, with an international playboy accent; the sophisticated, cynically pseudoromantic blue blood. I knew him and his work, and it was a heady surprise to have him bring me champagne and make conversation with me, mainly about himself and his work, pleased that I remembered much of it. The courtier in him then turned to me: I was intelligent, a novelty in this stinkpot of ignorance and stupidity, quite charming, and so unusual looking with those Slavic cheekbones he had always adored. Drawing me behind a heavy damask drape, he said it would be a great pleasure, an honor, if I went home with him.

My usual promising and dangerous "Why not?" laced with flattery and wine, consented. We left by a side door and through a formal garden manned by white marble demigods staring balefully into the moonlit shrubbery. He conducted me to a dashing leather-lined car, and in his now-exaggerated international accent, assured me of extraordinary pleasures to come. Negotiating the legendary hills and green coves that sheltered stars' houses, we finally arrived at something of a *Schloss* complete with spreads of carved wood, a run of broad turrets, ornate, heavy locks: the Germanic baronial look. The room into which my hero led me after my cape was taken by a manservant was all *Schloss* again, this area the hunting hall, an imitation of the halls in which birds and minnesingers sang the baron's loves and might. The rugs were, suitably, bearskins, the walls hung with the fierce horns and insulted snouts of hunt animals. Ranged around an enormous wooden table were seats made of broad leather slings held by thick brass studs. I could almost hear, as I looked around, the clank of beakers and platters and the howling of mighty trenchermen. However, here were no minnesingers, no trenchermen, no maces, no clubs, only animal skins and heads and a man who spoke affectedly, and myself. He kissed me gently, sat me in a cushioned chair at the end of the long room and then seated himself on a thronelike, richly carved seat at the opposite side of the hall. Well settled on his throne, he shouted across the room, "Look at me, keep looking at me!"

I smiled and looked. Slowly, as if following the passages of an ancient ritual, he took off his dinner jacket, his patent leather pumps, his black silk socks and black garters, revealing milk white shanks. Still dressed in his shirt and bow tie, still wearing his trousers, he slowly pulled down the zipper on his trousers and tenderly released his penis. "Too limp, *n'est-ce pas?*" he called. I said nothing. "We'll fix that soon." "I'm sure," I called back to him. He began to stroke his penis, first with one thin white hand and the other, soon both hands in a steady rhythm. I watched, waiting for my part in this odd play. As his penis slowly reached full size and rigidity, he stopped looking at me, not acknowledging my presence at all but concentrating, accelerating his rhythm. I sat there with growing distaste, like the taste of vomit, in my mouth. At most this was a novelty I had never before observed, and I didn't think much of the whole performance. As his lordship's head fell lower and lower, centered on his privates (the wrong word in this context), I examined the hall for an exit. There was only one, the metal-bound door behind his throne. I hugged the wall as I approached him and the door on tiptoe, feeling like the heroine of an early, idiotic spy film. Not a look, not a word from him, cocooned in his solitary ecstasy. I had served as a catalyst; that task accomplished, I was completely erasable.

On the other side of the door, I found the manservant, almost as if he had known I would be out of the hall by this time. He helped me with my coat and telephoned for a taxi, and I was out and away, carrying a combination of disgust and entertainment, storing in my mental sack yet another of life's infinity of ridiculous patterns. In the course of my bemused return there came to my mind a scene from Malory's *Morte d'Artur*, neither a parallel to my recent experience, nor altogether removed from it. In Malory's book, the great lover Tristan turns his ladylove Isolde with the flat of his sword to show off excitedly her fine hips and full breasts to the other knights of his circle. She remains silent, unprotesting, as I had been in my knight's use of me. Thus ended the tale of the Lady Caterina as unenthusiastic voyeur and assistant to the knight of the blue-white shanks.

Difficult to define the urge in some people to destroy a smooth surface, to lacerate without hesitation the glistening, purple swell of an eggplant, to roil the surface of a silken lake. Alone and appearing not to be lonely; my smooth surface seemingly unmarred; durable, steady, after careful nurturing over the years; I was both challenge and temptation at times to several uncertain, groping people I encountered in my travels, staying with their needs until they became burdensome, then wandering away to free myself, to repair my near violated protections. Sometimes the dabbler in my calm waters was a girl looking for a stance to imitate, mine for a change, a stop in the whirling pace of changing adolescent roles, from Hedda Gabler to Electra. Sometimes it was the cling of a soft-lipped boy lost in a flurry of signposts he would not decipher. There was the woman to calm through one-night love-stands—overtures she hoped would blossom into magnificent "Tristans and Isoldes." In short I was called on variously to be mother, sister, wife, daughter to a fair number of people, careful to appear sympathetic—which I usually was—and usually ready to twist out of their meshes as tactfully as I could.

Ruth was my most difficult assignment, not recognized until I was well mired in it; I should have been more clever and resisted the awkward costume in which she was preparing to dress me. I knew her as the wife of a lively entrepreneur, a jester who coasted prosperously on good-natured shrewdness and a boundless supply of jokes. About a year after his death Ruth began to plan her life without him. Left well off, well housed, and well dressed, she was lost in the lack of directions he had designed for her. She entered my life importantly when I agreed to spend two or three winter months with her in a Mexican town. Since she planned to buy the flat she had acquired for us and I was not interested in, or financially capable of, ownership, it seemed reasonable for me to pay less than half the rental for a small bedroom and the use of a hall bathroom rather than the suite of large bedroom and bright, attached bathroom that became hers. Shortly after we settled in she hired a handyman to restore our decayed garden and a full-time maid to serve our household needs. At first I was contented to have someone else take charge of matters at which I was no longer adept, or eager to be. An uneasy curiosity set in, however, when I realized that she never consulted me about menus, about variations of the well-balanced *comidas*, wholesome and dull. I didn't complain or suggest changes; I couldn't, without appearing critical, and she was, by way of her efficiency and larger investment, the boss. So I said nothing, perking up my tastebuds with hot-sauced tacos stuffed and fried by Maria, my favorite street vendor.

I was then working on the second or third draft of my book

on Mexico, finding the work increasingly difficult, not because of my accustomed finicky habits of careful selecting and polishing (as if I were practicing a lapidary craft), but because of the noise outside my windows, which swelled with the calls of children going to and from a neighboring school, among them wailing baby sisters and brothers and chattering maids who broke off their twittering with loud calls and dashes to three- and four-year-olds threatening to entangle themselves in adult legs and bicycle wheels. Fortunately, I was invited to use the typewriter and studio of other friends in a capacious house a street or two distant from the school. It was an amiable arrangement that often included an invitation to breakfast, prepared by a more imaginative maid than ours. In all innocence—or was it?—I described to Ruth the novel pancakes and rolls I had eaten at the Walkers', suggesting casually that our maid might be spurred on to similar small wonders. Ruth's voice and face blazed: "Why don't you get yourself adopted by those Walkers, those failed artists, who can certainly afford to share their house and food with you. I'm sure you will have a better time with them than you have with me." She was probably referring to the too-many Scrabble games we played too many evenings, games I invariably lost because she had long ago memorized a Scrabble dictionary while I had no equipment but my ordinary vocabulary and was not, by nature, an avid competitor.

Her fantasy of the companionship that I had failed to sustain began to take on verbal shape, tainted with nostalgia and some venom. When her husband was alive, she told me, they had taken a winter house in Morelia. He would go out early Sunday mornings to bring back the small, crisp *bolillos* put aside for him by the best baker in town. He then fixed a pretty tray and served her a fresh *bolillo* and coffee in bed while the maid rolled in a cart laden with papaya, pineapple, oranges, *zapotes*, and sweet little red bananas. Returning to the kitchen, the maid chopped up the lively ingredients that made the pungent sauce for *huevos rancheros* and heated the tortillas the couple later shared in the dining room. Breakfast over, they would take long walks or search the local flea markets for an oddity, an antique, a curio that caught her fancy. Then, after a good Sunday dinner and a couple of siesta hours, they would have friends in to listen to records or maybe go to the movies. She had hoped that we would spend such pleasant Sundays together, she and I. (Did she really mean, I wondered as she spoke, that I was to be a sort of Susanna to her Countess, or worse still, the young Octavian to her Marschallin? Ridiculous.) But I had for some time been uneasy over Ruth's jealousy of the Walkers, the fact that I preferred to work in their house rather than the room she had arranged for me. (I was of course exaggerating, dramatizing, the noise of the children under my window, she insisted.) The guilt valve that now and then ruled my life fell open, and I rebuked myself for spending too much time away from her, for not attempting to buy Sunday rolls, being indifferent to Scrabble. Then it hit, the recoil: I couldn't, wouldn't, be her husband or play the devoted marriage game she wanted to revive. The guilt valve snapped shut.

I began to gather my papers, to pick up Mexican toys for children in the States, to arrange my luggage, taking great care to avoid Ruth's visitor, a cousin from New Jersey who croaked, whenever she could corner me, that for Ruth's great favors, her indulgences, the cheap room and board, I was to thank God every day. And as well—the serf making the most primitive obeisances to her lady—I was to kiss her ass every day. On hearing this new story, too mad to be altogether humiliating, the Walkers insisted that I spend my remaining Mexican days with them. I never saw Ruth or her cousin again.

I gathered together once more the wariness that examined the uses I might be put to and by whom. There were slips that I didn't really mind. Being a sucker occasionally, in spite of the facade I held on to, was basically native to me and not the most uncomfortable role, I decided, to play in a world of ceaseless duets of egos and hubris, struggles for minuscule powers I found stupid and rarely fruitful.

15

The Gold

ALDO was—beyond the Borromini churches, the Carravaggios, the war-torn cats of the Piazza Argentina, the superb dignity of the Basilica of Santa Sabina on the Aventine and the city glowing gold in the late afternoon sun—my favorite Roman presence. He was a *fusto*, a strong tree trunk, thick and tall, a crisp-haired centurion who might have been painted by Mantegna; of rough, coarse bark that covered troubling sensibilities and keen, delicate insights he seemed to save for me, his *"professoressa,"* in private conversations while his wife, as much my friend, was out shopping. Uneducated, just barely literate (he once asked whether his name, which appeared in my book on Rome, with thanks, was printed in all other copies or in his copy alone; he never knew how a book came into being), he was practiced in the street smarts that were the ground-base of his life. However, he was not quite smart enough for the wealthier manipulators whose company he always yearned for, got, and deeply regretted. The regret had always to be expressed in a contemptuous shrug, as an aristocrat shrugs off losses of fame and fortune, as American officers he had known in his boyhood shrugged off petty thefts and lost bets years before.

Aldo had been born in a basement room on one of the mean, sluttish streets of Trastevere, the get of a soldier and a careless girl. They both disappeared while he was still an infant; he was taken in by a relative, a young widow with several small children whom she supported by sewing, knitting, and selling greens in a local market while the little girls took care of each other and the household: a crowding of beds, a table, a crude stove; an outdoor toilet was shared by the rest of their tenement neighbors. The boys were among those immortalized in the Italian film *Shoeshine*, earning a few lire and food, chocolate, and cigarettes to resell; running errands and pimping for the American soldiers. Aldo, with his intelligence and amiability, must have been one of the most successful of these entrepreneurs and procurers, a major provider for the family (whom he helped, incidentally, all his years, the dim muddy as well as the glistening silvery).

Though he shared kisses and curses with the rest of the family, he learned from the older children that his mother and father were different from theirs. The widow, now "aunt," told him his father was a soldier and possibly had been killed or resettled in the north where there were jobs, and was probably not, in any case, likely to return to Rome. His mother? The aunt knew nothing about her except that her name was Anna Ferretti, a distant relative of her dead husband. The aunt said she couldn't remember any more and discouraged further conversation about the mother of whom the boy began to dream, to picture in scenes of affectionate meetings. When he was sixteen and working at odd jobs that required strength and ingenuity, he began to put aside bits of money to use in a search for his mother. He questioned an old ex-policeman of the area, the priest in the corner church, a neighborhood cobbler. Only the daughter of the tobacconist, now a matron with a light mustache and four children, had a few misty recollections of Anna when they were girls together. She had heard some time ago that Anna had gotten into trouble on the other side of the river and had then gone south to Naples or some place around there, where she had relatives. The woman seemed to know more, Aldo suspected, but refused to speak it. When he had put together a sum on which to start his journey, Aldo said good-bye to his family and set out southward for Naples. The accumulated money, not much to begin with, didn't last very long. Stopping in villages, cleaning out the bones and entrails of a butcher shop one day, plucking chickens another, carrying water to masons working in the sweltering sun, he earned enough to buy his daily food. He slept in tool sheds, under trees, under the portico of a ruin, anywhere. He rarely had enough money for a bus or train but walked and hitched his way toward Naples.

Following taciturn suggestions from a few Trasteverini he had questioned, he made his way to the fish stalls on the Naples waterfront. One of the vendors to whom he mentioned the Ferrettis directed him to a crone who, the man said, knew everyone in Naples back to the Spanish kings and even before, to Saint Peter the fisherman. As Aldo approached her (this little scene in his odyssey remained especially vivid in his mind), she quickly drew her basket of fish closer and whipped her skirt, shining with scales, over it to protect her wares from a big, broad boy who was undoubtedly a thief. He greeted her with all the polite deference his untutored youth could muster, hoping she might be impressed with the fact that he had walked most of the way from Rome to find relatives named Ferretti. Maybe she knew them? Yes, she knew an old couple, very old, and their children and grandchildren, gone now, all gone, to work in Torino, San Paolo, and Brooklyn across the ocean. As she bumbled on in her narratives of wandering Neapolitans, he broke in—again most politely—to ask where he might find these relatives. She pointed him to a house at the edge of the market where, probably, the old, old Ferretti and his old woman lived in a basement room. The old man's wandering memory, she added, couldn't recall what he had done an hour ago but was as sharp and clear as a newspaper page when it came to the history of his tribe.

The ancient couple were apparently afraid to let anyone in, or were deaf; it required considerable banging and shouting of the name Ferretti to see the door cracked open a bit and then wider. Aldo introduced himself as a great-nephew, the son of Anna Ferretti. The old man looked at him suspiciously for a while, his tired eyes and bulbous nose pulled down to the toothless mouth in a wary grimace. The woman continued to cut a thick slice off the bread she held against her chest and, after a lightning appraisal of the boy, gave him a chunk, growling, "*Mangia.*" The man turned his eyes away from Aldo, seeming to trace on a wall the brambles and patches of memory. Finally, "Yes, I remember her. She stopped here a few years ago or was it last year, on her way to, I think, Torre del Greco, where she had been offered a job." Aldo took his leave as soon as he could, vigorously shaking the old man's hand and kissing the wrinkled cheek of the old woman, who thrust at him another chunk of bread and a tomato wrapped in brown paper to serve as his next meal.

Torre del Greco was not the town, but his mother was known by some of its shop people, one of whom, a specialist in ribbons and combs and lipsticks, directed the boy to a village close by, describing the house Aldo was to look for. It turned out to be a large house with a deeply eaved porch on which lolled several women, some of them young, several near middle age, all of them in bright kimonos, ribbons in their hair, globes of rouge on their cheeks, their eyes gleaming out of dark pastes. Aldo approached the women and asked if they knew, or if one of them might be, Anna Ferretti. A woman in a pink kimono, no longer young yet still pretty, with large blue eyes like his own and crisp hair like his own flying out of her glittering comb, rose quickly to approach him. He rushed toward her yelling, "Mama, it's me, your son! You are my mother, I know it. You even look like me." As he reached to embrace her she stopped him with a raw, rasping whisper, "Don't say those words here. Or anywhere. Never." And turning to her friends she explained, "This is a crazy kid who belongs to some distant relatives in Rome. He's an orphan, I've heard, but not mine." Turning back to the boy she hissed, "Get the hell out of here and don't ever come back."

He never did and told the full story only twice: first to his wife and then to me. *Ebrea* that I was—and he laughed to see my face tighten when he repeated the anti-Semitic quips directed at Jewish dealers on the via del Babuino—I understood him, he said, maybe because I was of an old tribe that traveled stubbornly to find its kin, somewhat as he had. Although I couldn't always understand his Romanesco (except for the smutty words I had

learned in my Bronx childhood from Italian neighbors) and my
Italian was weak kneed during the first days of our friendship, I
did have a sense of understanding him, of being an affectionate
witness, never a judge, of all he was and probably felt. It was a
steady, serene sort of love entirely unfettered by sexual webs. I
loved his wife without quite understanding her, nearer my own
non-Mediterranean culture yet opaque to me in several ways.
(One gossip of our acquaintance could not resist the Roman
cliché, here the cliché of a bored, jealous woman, that Aldo was
in love with me or that I was in love with him, or both; a hot
romance was burning right under his poor wife's undiscerning
eyes. She turned her Anglo-Saxon ear away from the Roman
muttering and we three spent much of our lives, when I lived
in Rome, together in easy pleasure and affection.)

Aldo's adult life remained dedicated to proving that he was a
nobleman, the benevolent, egalitarian lord of Trastevere, never
the discard of a whore. Immortally marked by the profligacy and
open-handedness of the American soldiers for whom he had been
a clever, swift Figaro, an aristocrat he became—with help from
his generous wife. He drove an Alfa Romeo later exchanged for
a sleek Ferrari. His summer shirts were of fine handkerchief linen,
matched by heavier linen trousers, blue, green, pristine white,
the most fashionable confections of Yves St. Laurent. It was
watching a great power, a galaxy of glittering stars, to see him,
informal, affable, Lorenzo de Medici, Il Magnifico, enter the
choicest of restaurants or, if the mood suited him, mom and pop
places in the lost, winding alleys of the medieval city. He was
welcomed into the kitchens to taste, to choose his menu, to joke,
to praise. He graced the waiters, too, with his affability and
immense tips.

At the same time he courted those he considered really big
spenders and was readily accepted into their lairs because of his
earthy appeal, his dashing wardrobe, and because a few shrewd
eyes guessed him an easy sucker, ready to be taken. At first it
was steep card games with experts ready to fleece the refulgent
innocent lamb. And fleeced he was, for sums that had to be

borrowed at high interest rates. Almost wiped out and frightened by the keen card sharps, he left their circle after settling his debts and looked around for another big-shot arena. It was, early on, dinner and light bets at the racetrack, where friends introduced him to several of their friends who bet more heavily. They, in turn, introduced him to *their* friends who didn't bother with the refinements of dinner, light talk, and light bets. These men spent their time with jockeys and trainers and dark-capped whisperers. No longer was it dining and tossing around a few thousand lire with his wife, his friends, and their wives, but a pacing about to join a deeply concentrated cluster of men, extraordinarily monosyllabic and restrained for Italians. Even Aldo's innate exuberance and ease were veiled, muffled in the presence of these taciturn experts, their crisp short phrases and tight gestures. Aldo thought of these men, he told me later, as members of a secret society, a society he didn't understand yet found exciting, controlling arcane mysteries he thought he might share. On hints from the cabal he made bets on his own; he lost. He combined bets with his cohorts and lost again, or so he was told. Undiscouraged—after all, large losses were the privilege of rich, untroubled men—he spent many evenings with this gang who had assured him he needn't be bothered by a temporary bad streak; the money would soon be regained and with it much more. Bothered by his losses? Not on their lives. He wasn't worried, he knew they would bring in a fortune on the inside dope they had from the stables; the horses' mouths, so to speak.

To maintain his racetrack career Aldo was forced to borrow from his friends, but the debts didn't worry him. (His obsessive, ambitious, eager optimism was, to me, Neronian, a characteristic of Rienzi too and of half-mad D'Annunzio; a particularly Italian quality.) His pot of gold flew apart one night with an explosion of gunshot close to his ear; the swift roar dashed by the side of his face to settle in a bloody hole in the temple of his companion, who slid from his seat, dead. Without a moment's hesitation Aldo ran to his Ferrari in the car park and drove directly home. There he found a policeman waiting for him. He was accused of being one of a mob of mafiosi by the officials at the station to which he was taken. His mob was contesting territories, racetrack chicanery one area, with a powerful group from Sicily intent on wiping out Aldo's friends. Aldo swore he knew nothing of mobs nor their clandestine activities; he just might have suspected something dangerous was going on but found it safer to remain the rich, unsuspecting fool interested only in betting on the horses.

Italian law decides that one is guilty until proved innocent. Aldo was never proved to have been a member of any gang, never a mafioso, but shadows hung over him; he was not a clearly free man. He was kept in Rome's Regina Coeli prison for three months, always splendidly dressed in the fresh clothing his wife brought him daily, eating well on the meals she provided as well as the king-size Havana cigars he didn't puff much but loved to use for significant gesturing. After his release and for some years thereafter, the police would make impromptu visits, asking him questions he truly could not answer, much as he might have enjoyed seeing himself as one privy to big gang secrets. The visits ultimately stopped altogether. Aldo now contented himself with less-hazardous pursuits, mainly in varieties of wheeling and dealing: putting one antiquarian in touch with another, indicating valuable properties to potential purchasers for a fee (he seemed to know everyone in Rome), glorying in his Prince of Rome role, sporting his Savile Row and Paris wardrobe, his friendly address still laced with choice Trasteverino obscenities. He became again the dinner companion who commandeered every restaurant we entered with his full-sun, larger-than-lifeness—my favorite sidekick of halcyon months in Rome, my favorite illiterate street-smart, but not quite enough, shoeshine boy, my latter-day impetuous, unwise, generous, grand Renaissance duke.

In the course of a Caribbean island vacation—Martinique, St. Lucia, Grenada—Bill and I decided to explore the little-visited island of Domenica. We found a mail plane that serviced the St. Lucia-Domenica run daily. In the small room-size cabin crammed with mailbags and assorted bundles, we met the one other passenger, a handsome light brown man, rather portly, with a mildly authoritative air and courtly speech. After we took off in the plane that had the substance of a kite, he asked us why we were going to Domenica, which had so few tourists. That was primarily our reason, we told him, and because we had heard it was lyrical, spoke an attractive tongue, and had not succumbed to modernity. In the exchange of names he informed us that he was an inspector of island schools; his mission was to meet with the principals of various high schools to find students deserving of scholarships in English universities, then offered by the British government.

It was a wild flight. The bundles of freight and mail rolled against our legs and bumped from one side to another of our frail capsule. A sudden windstorm drove it, time and time again, fearsomely toward high hills. The insouciant pilot, singing out to the wind, "No, you don't, damn you," twisted the plane away as it dived toward each hill. We made it, to be met by a ferry manned by black boys in English sailor suits—broad white collars, white round hats, and all—like Gilbert and Sullivan tars. They helped us with our luggage, found us seats, and, with the bundles and mail, disappeared to the far end of the ferry. Mr. Bradley, the school supervisor, sat with us, his first words after we were settled: "We, both of you and I, share an immortal attachment. One lives with many people but meets the threat of imminent death with very few. I shall never forget you; we are tied together." He then greeted two Englishmen, introduced as exporters of cocoa and vanilla. They had Empire manners, ironically overpolite to the tars who arranged their packages and to the boy who served tea. During a conversation that gave us local information and lauded the beauty of the island (we did not discover Jean Rhys's descriptions of the island until much later), they also extolled the finely balanced race relationships of Domenica. I wondered about this balance, knowing that there were comparatively few white people in an almost totally black population. Having moved on from the speech on "balance," when I asked about the numbers of whites and blacks on the island, one of the Empire builders brought forth the word *tolerance*. My egalitarian hackles began to rise, and I sputtered with no tact or

grace at all, "Who tolerates whom? And why the word that sug-
gests mature patience with immature peoples, a word that might
have been used by an eighteenth-century Russian landowner
about his favorite serfs. What right have you to tolerate people
who were here long before you invaded, your right to tolerate
founded on the greed of British enterprise and your Oxbridge,
Empire-builder accent?" As I went on stuttering, scolding, repetitious with anger, the men left their seats with the excuse of
greeting people at the other end of the ferry. Mr. Bradley, who
had not said a word while he listened, bade us a friendly "enjoy
yourselves" as we left the ferry and invited us to a party at the
home of Roseau's school principal. It was to take place the following night; we accepted, "with pleasure."

After spending much of the next morning on a long veranda
of our hotel on the main street of Roseau, watching people passing, trying to catch their soft, lilting speech mingled with reminders of old French, we hired a car to take us to a leafy watering
hole. Its underground rivulets propelled us around and around
in a hypnotic, smooth rhythm on which we floated effortlessly,
our upturned eyes filled with the yellows, reds, greens of the
leaves and pods of the cocoa plants above. Waking from the
afternoon siesta into which the whole town sank, we dressed and
waited for Mr. Bradley to drive us to the principal's house. Like
most of Roseau in those years the principal lived in a simple
wooden house. Its interior, however, strikingly contradicted the
plain shell: on the shelves of the living room pieces of rare Wedg-
wood, the sparkle of Lalique glasses, a group of Ming figurines.
The principal greeted us cordially and introduced us to his wife
who wore a subtly draped cloth of gold dress whose design I
studied enviously and admiringly as she led us to an array of
champagne flutes bubbling with French wine. An adjoining table
offered a huge bright-green cabbage scooped out to hold a tall
mound of gray black caviar. Chomping on caviar-laden biscuits,
on several types of French pâté and cheeses, we studied the
compelling drawings and etchings on the walls. I can't remember
the substance of our several conversations with other guests, but
I hear spritely voices and see faces of animated welcome. Mr.

Bradley had, we suspected, spoken of my outburst on the ferry and had thus helped open the island to us: several lively parties, picnics, and teas laid out in appealing places. We met our Oxbridge friends once or twice, greeted each other perfunctorily and moved on. We didn't mind—we had the cordial island Mr. Bradley and his friends had made for us.

Our island odyssey also took us to Trinidad where we arranged for a trip on a bauxite freighter bound for Dutch Guiana to pick up large quantities of the light powder that would become aluminum. With some fear of an imagined crew of near pirates and other roughs of unknown origins stamped on my mind by early movies, I gallantly agreed to board this certainly filthy ship subject to all the dangers my fertile imagination could conjure up. She turned out to be spanking white, free of roughs and dirt. She was oddly shaped, as bauxite freighters were (are still?), and captained by a Norwegian whose employers owned several vessels that made the journey by way of the Surinam River, which narrowed to the Cottica and then narrowed further to streams whose tricky snakelike turns required guidance by local pilots in small boats. Our first port of call was Paramaribo, reached on a Sunday. In front of a stolid official building and all about its square lay dozens of inert male bodies. This was revolution, insurrection, massacre. I turned to our Norwegian captain, aghast, and asked him what he thought had happened and were we in danger among these dreadful events? He laughed and said that all these men were resting, either too drunk to stumble home or just plain sleepy this siestatime; they found the ground convenient and amply comfortable.

Our quarters of blond Swedish woods and handsome textiles consisted of a full bedroom, bathroom, and living room centered on a large table. The quarters next to ours—quite similar—were used by the captain and his immediate assistants. The rest of the ship was an immensely long row of wide bauxite bins on which we took walks under the tropical sun or paced our way through lashing tropical rains, and over whose rails we photographed exotic tropical plants each time the awkward ship was deliberately

crashed into the jungle to be backed out for a new direction on
another coiling river. (The white railing, strict and straight when
we left Trinidad, looked like spaghetti at the end of the trip.)
About where the Surinam became the Cottica we were accosted
by swift canoes that carried Djukas, handsome blacks still living
rather as they might have lived in Africa centuries before, the
men wearing loincloths, the women in minimal cotton sarongs,
the babies shining naked. The canoes were filled with merry boys
who waved and gestured for us to throw them the gifts they knew
we had brought from Trinidad—hard candies in small sacks and
minute cakes of soap. They were not recently replanted Africans,
we were told, but escaped slaves who had run from the Dutch
settlers with whom, at some long-gone time, they had done battle
and won. For a number of years the Dutch government had sent
them an annual gift of money; one group of Djukas still owned
a ceremonial sword ceded as a symbol of Holland's defeat. The
Djukas were never molested again and live their lives of fish,
plantains, and cheap sweets in peace and the cleanliness of small
cakes of American soap.

Bill and I ate frequent meals with the captain except for
breakfasts, which we always had alone in our suite. The table
was laden with at least six hard-boiled eggs, two or three varieties
of cheese, a mound of rolls and breads, two kinds of herring,
and several bowls of jelly. While we were making solid inroads
on the extravagant meal, the cook would come in to ask us what
kind of eggs—scrambled, once-over, sunny-side up—we might
want, his face pleading for an order. He was bleakly crestfallen
when we said that we had enough, more than enough, thank
you. So we ordered fried eggs each morning and threw them
down the toilet, hearing our parents' voices shouting at us that
to waste food was criminal. But the remembered voices were
easier to bear than the cook's despairing face. He was a soft, fat,
elderly Scandinavian and, like a number of such men I had
observed, was beginning to look like an old woman, with pen-
dulous breasts and a tender white skin wrinkled as silk wrinkles.
For a reason I could never fathom he appointed me his particular
charge, standing over me chanting, "Eat, eat. You shkinny

[which I was not]. You get shick, you go to hoshpital, you die. Eat, eat." He didn't limit himself to standing over me at the table; he would follow me under tropical rains and piercing sun across the bauxite bins, offering me dainty, freshly made sandwiches and newly baked cookies, moaning, "Eat, eat. You terrible shkinny, you go to hoshpital, you die." His crazy, impassioned concern for my health made it difficult to refuse him and I stuffed myself uncomfortably to arrive in the bauxite village of Mungo five pounds over my shkinny weight. He was a nuisance, old Sven, a disturbance that sometimes marred my enchantment with the jungle, the willful rivers, the Djukas, but I liked the solicitude, the pesky pursuits, the burden of being too-much cared for as my grandparents might have burdened me, had I ever known them.

There were other friends in London, but Esther was my London hearth, refuge from weeks of iced bones in damp flats whose windows sneered an unremitting gray. She was refuge from the rains that washed words from my notebook as I stood before Saint Helen's Church in Bishopsgate, from the wet streets of John Stow's Elizabethan town that I slogged through slowly, meticulously, for the book on London I had been commissioned to write.

She was extraordinarily pretty, with a generous, white-toothed smile, a crop of lively dark hair, and, in spite of the birth of four children, a lissome figure undisturbed by an awesome appetite. Dazzlingly energetic and not bound by society's ordinary practices, she might suddenly decide to invite a large miscellany of people at five in the afternoon for dinner at eight that same evening. Pirouetting gaily from bowl to stove to platters, she stuffed dozens of calabasas to fry in Mexican style, roasted several chickens in Moroccan style, prepared vats of salad and Italian risottos and baked several rich cakes. By the time her guests arrived—and few in dully-fed London would refuse her invitations—she would be wearing a torero suit held over from the time she aspired to be a Spanish dancer—the once-zippered front now held by two frank safety pins to accommodate the slightly matured belly—or a rainbow flow of exotica she had picked up on the Portobello Road. Her guests were a collection of anyone she liked (with rare exceptions, she liked everyone): a clerk in a local store, someone she had conversed with on a bus, a disheveled genius and his minor-guru lover, as well as a number of the more "bourgeois" (at least on the surface). I found a number of lasting friendships and stimulating acquaintances during those high-colored soirees in the once-conventional English house whose spaces became bizarre under Esther's drive for the exotic. The salon was stepped like a theater arena, the dining room hung with Indian cloths to shape a large tent. A tall African drum stood at the head of the stairs that led to her bedroom, which was draped in lustrous purple satin. Huge Moroccan cushions became seats in the living room, not easy to sit on securely but satisfactorily distant from the cliché of chintz couches and armchairs in the time-worn English style she abhorred.

One couple I met over a glass of Yugoslav wine (they are still close friends) offered me their son of sixteen, waiting to enter Oxford, as my London guide. He had curiosity and wit, endless buoyant energy, and, most useful and impressive of all, a deep rich voice and the educated speech of Westminster College. Voice and vocabulary were the tools that gave him the confidence to phone the authorities of the Guild Hall as secretary to an important American writer, asking for special appointments and the viewing of rooms and objects not open to the general public. Voice and accent worked for admission to hidden almshouses, to unknown corners of Chiswick, and to Sion House. And he had a rich repertoire of Victorian songs: "Come into the Garden, Maud," et cetera, which enlivened the worn streets of Spitalfields and the abandoned magnificence of Hawksmoor churches. He was the most entertaining and efficient guide I ever had and is still a cherished friend although time and distance have thinned our encounters.

Another couple I met at one of Esther's parties were émigrés from Eastern Europe, she a plump, smiling woman with the warm, salubrious look of a tub of fresh butter. He was short, thin, swarthy, and introduced himself, whenever he was addressed, as a writer dedicated to freeing the world from inhibited sex. After several desultory, halting conversations, his message tuneless and repetitious, he suggested, in a formal voice and manner—not a breath of eroticism or even urgency in it—that we, he and I, go to Paris together for an "amorous weekend." As lagniappe, or if we failed to mesh, he offered me an introduction to a famous lesbian (Natalie something, I think), rich, powerful, and the ruler of a large and devoted Amazon court. I declined both offers as formally as he had made them. He never spoke to me again, even when we rubbed elbows reaching for the same heaped platter of pasta carbonara.

The wine ran luxuriantly, the abundance of high-scented dishes filled the crowded salon, threatening the strength of the bamboo tables from China, while the noises of intellectual combat and laughter poured into the quiet Hampstead street. In wandering among these replete, chattering groups I learned a number of facts of various lives put by Esther in an envelope she blithely labeled "English eccentricity." I didn't agree with her limiting category but began to gather more and more life-style patterns into the collection I had amassed, and eagerly kept amassing, all my life. There was the plain, flat-shoed, tweed-skirted matron who lived with her husband and three children in the staid suburban town of Guildford. She was tiddly enough, one bibulous evening, to tell me that she and her husband took a monthly weekend in Paris to join a *"partouze"* group, all strangers to them, and went from man to woman to man, as they fancied or were fancied, in quick, energetic coupling—the more the better—or, once in a while, to shape a group of "who was doing what to whom" in imitation of the Indian sculptures at Khajuraho. When I asked her to describe the room in which all this fun and games took place, she said, "Nothing much, an old ballet studio with one mirrored wall, mats on the floor, and douche bags hanging here and there for sort of cleaning up." Once or twice she had gone with her husband on a business trip to Japan and found a masseuse who not only oiled and stroked her muscles but treated her to extra pleasures; delicious. She was planning to return soon to that masseuse in Tokyo.

Another design for living was revealed to me by two homosexuals. They shared the same house Monday through Friday,
and each weekend, the younger went to stay with a former lover
whom he sort of missed and for whom he felt a bit sorry. His
weekday partner had no objections to the arrangement; it all
worked smoothly.

It was at Esther's, too, that I met the dashing Eric von something, a former actor. (Half the male population of London, it
sometimes seemed to me, were unemployed actors, past or present.) Eric dressed in dessicated splendor—a worn, belaced, satin
shirt, a leftover of a cavalier role, and stained red velvet knee
breeches, also a stage souvenir. I found him appealing because
he was so painfully careful to hold together what he liked to refer
to as his "persona." Not only was his wardrobe of the theater,
but his voice wandered from the dulcet tones of Romeo's wooing
to Lear's howling furies. And in his worn carriage and face there
was still some fading beauty, carefully maintained by tight un-
dergarments, I suspect, and discreet makeup.

Some years later, while I was living in Italy, I was joined by
a friend who traveled with me from Rome to London. Since I
no longer had an apartment there, Mary and I had to find a place
for a week or two, not a hotel, too expensive; possibly a "bed and
breakfast." I remembered that Eric, who lived off Hampstead
Heath, rented out a couple of rooms in his house when he could
find the proper tenants. Although he could hardly afford to be,
he was very choosy; Mary and I became two of the chosen.

It was a small but comfortable house and, in the main, neatly
and conventionally furnished. It was the objects of decor that
mesmerized us both. Near the front door there was a small,
discreet plaque that pictured a nude, classic Apollo, a garland
on his lovely curls. Inside the door, standing on a bookcase was
the figure of a little peasant boy in a wide, long shirt. If one
touched the bottom of the shirt, as Eric demonstrated, it tilted
high in front to release a large erect penis. Our gleaming bathroom, airy and large, featured almost-full-length photographs of
Greta Garbo, Bette Davis, and Joan Crawford and over the sink
in which we brushed our teeth and washed our faces was a big

photograph of a brutish young man dressed in leather and hung with heavy chains. His trousers were wide open to reveal a bushy crop of pubic hair and a powerful penis that seemed to threaten us as we washed. The hand soap was penis-shaped, as was the larger bath soap. There was no place, except the balcony kitchen, that did not remind us of the preferences of the house. Eric was a solicitous host; we were offered extra blankets against the damp London night air and were very well and tastefully fed at breakfast. He also took us for long, interesting walks that almost always seemed to end up at one particular pub, clearly the preferred meeting place of local homosexuals. Mary was an innocent and slow to recognize that Eric took us to his and his friends' favored pub because he thought it would please us to be among other lesbians. I found Eric's supposition funny, but she was appalled, insulted. So we left to settle into a dour, dim room in a slovenly house in Marylebone. No more lavish breakfasts, no curious soaps, no sadomasochism, no idolized movie stars; boring, boring.

But back to Esther, whose love of the theatrical gesture, which lived well with the Orientalish fantasy decor of her house, urged her to buy a tall secondhand London taxi she had painted a sort of gold. It was actually a practical choice: It used cheap diesel fuel and its roomy interior held her four children comfortably. Occasionally she was hailed by a passenger whom she would pick up and whose fare she turned down for the pleasure of observing the startled look on her passenger's face and the satisfaction of offering a service for no reward except "Thank you, I do thank you." In order to ride with her and her children, something I did frequently, I had to sit on a cushion-covered wooden box next to her seat, not the most comfortable perch for longish journeys, though I enjoyed them greatly.

One memorable holiday weekend, when her husband was away, Esther and I bundled the children and bags of sweaters and woolen socks into the golden chariot. On the way out of town I searched for an open sweets shop among the many tightly shut and finally found one that armed me with sacks of chocolates, toffees, and biscuits, tranquilizers for the restless gaggle in the back. My technique was to throw over my shoulder an assorted handful of sweets when I heard the rustlings of an incipient quarrel or the wail of "Mummy, she's ———." Not surprisingly, it rained and rained, a common accompaniment to English outings. Our first stop, after a look at Hastings, and a short lecture from me on its significance, was the village of Battle where the three little girls sheltered under a set of eaves, digging into a bagful of sweets, while Esther and I and the youngest, a valiant little boy of four, scrambled along the bastions—the remains of abbey and ancient tower. Placated by the promise of chips, lots of chips, with their lunch in Rye, the children allowed me a short time to become enamored of Winchelsea's glorious ghost of a church and the splendid tombs, their marble carved in the fashions of seven or eight centuries ago.

After lunch, heavy with the promised chips, the children permitted me to walk them through cobbled streets and houses like flower-painted toys for a glimpse of the house in which Henry James had lived and worked. Then they were ready to move on. Where? Esther, who had a strong leaning toward the occult (I accompanied her to several sessions with seers and soothsayers who impressed her more profoundly, more convincingly, than they did me), had developed a friendship during one of those sessions with a fortune-teller and astrologer who lived with a friend about twenty kilometers from Rye. Always as sure of a welcome as she was welcoming, she telephoned and suggested we might visit. Tired, wet, and chilled, the children fell asleep on the couches near the fireplace after a tea of cocoa and sandwiches while Esther and our hosts spoke of the importance of attending the Midsummer Eve rituals on Glastonbury Tor and discussed whether the plinths at Stonehenge were really a satanic work. They thought it was quite possible; no other explanations suited them. Then, as a polite host, one gentleman turned to me, examined my hands, felt the bumps of my head, and traced the lines on my forehead. His prophecy for me was that I would someday write a very successful play. (Decades later, I'm still waiting.)

When it was time to rouse the sleeping children and pour

them back into the taxi, we asked our host about local inns. Was there one in which we might spend the night? We dashed from one suggested inn to another and, since it was a holiday weekend, found no room anywhere. The night grew wetter and colder, the children slept sprawled out on the seat and floor of the cab covered with coats and scarves, while I grew more and more uneasy, tired and despairing, as the unsuccessful quest dragged on. Esther, as always cheery and optimistic, had one of her swift inspirations: Try the local police. We found the station of a small village and she twinklingly presented her dilemma to the sleepy constable, who yielded to her charm and her problem. He lifted the phone, conducted a short conversation, and turned to us, smiling. "My friend, Mrs. Ashton, doesn't usually take in people but she will put you and your children up for tonight." He drew us a map of local roads to lead us to the Ashton farm, where we were greeted by a sturdy, apple-cheeked woman who helped us carry the sleeping children into the house and up the stairs to a large room that held several cots, once the beds of her children, now grown and gone, she said. She covered the children tenderly, tucked them in warmly, and pointed out two beds in an adjoining room that Esther and I could use. Noticing that I was less bouncy, feeling the wet cold more painfully than Esther and older than she, Mrs. Ashton covered me with a pile of comforters and, as I was burrowing contentedly into my warm, dry cocoon, insisted I drink the cup of hot cocoa she had brought up from the kitchen along with a hot water bottle for my feet.

The next morning was clear, sharp—a bright, rare gift. Breakfast was large enough for a family of ten adults because, Mrs. Ashton explained—beaming down on the piles of buttered scones, the platters of eggs and sausages, and bowls of porridge— she had not yet learned, and didn't want to, that her big children were not going to dash down the stairs and noisily surround the broad, wooden kitchen table. Our troops ate enough under Mrs. Ashton's urging to make impressive dents in the platters and bowls and, with egg, butter, and crumbs still tinting their faces, ran out to find tire swings on trees and cats, rabbits, and ducks to fondle and chase. Mr. Ashton, whom we had not yet met, a man with a craggy face, dark and Celtic, emerged from the barn leading a pony for the children to ride. From his pockets he took large green apples, one for each child, and with a shy nod to us ladies returned to the barn.

With the generosity of children, they forgave us the long, cold, sleepy rides, the crazy explorations of bastions and authors' houses, and settled their memories, for a long time, on Mrs. Ashton, on her tire swings and her pony, her affectionate farewell embraces and "Come back soon, all of you," accompanied by a large bundle of sandwiches and sweet biscuits. I have been considerately treated in houses in Chester Square, warmed in cottages edging the forbidding Yorkshire moors, cordially served tea in a shop in Wales, but none of these acts of hospitality was as pleasing as the generosity and solicitude of the lonely Ashtons revived for a morning by the wholesome greed of children and the tunes of their play.

Faultless Esther had one monumental fault; she could not, constitutionally, genetically perhaps, be on time or anywhere near appointed time. I have an album of remembered pictures of myself standing on obscure, unsheltered corners in London under a vulnerable umbrella, my feet and hands turning into fins, waiting for as long as two hours until she finally drove up in her chariot burbling explanations and apologies. Worse than the long street waits, though, were our drives to the airport to get me onto a plane back to New York for my annual visit. I always announced firmly that I intended to take a taxi, thinking mainly of my own peace of mind, of avoiding the nausea of anxiety the riding with her would surely induce. "Nonsense," she said, "it's much too expensive and I have my taxi here and the time, plenty of time." I kept insisting on taking a taxi, afraid of her strange measure of time, quite contrary to mine, which forced me to be at stations and airports well ahead of schedule. She was adamant and I tried to appease her with a compromise: I would take a taxi to Victoria Station and board a reliable airport bus, not expensive at all. "Don't be silly; why struggle with luggage in and out of taxis and buses; it will all be easier and more comfortable if I drive you."

I argued and pleaded, afraid to hurt her feelings, to appear un-responsive to her concern, but I often thought of disappearing during the night to sit out untroubled waiting hours in Heathrow. However, she usually arranged one of her splendid dinners as a farewell party for me that lasted late into the night before my morning departure. So I stayed the night at her house, and my luggage with me.

I was entirely at her mercy, tortured by her generosity. My stomach was pierced with knives, my intestines twisted into knots of agony when, in the one hour she had allowed between her house in Hampstead and Heathrow Airport, she stopped to buy a string for one of the children's guitars, stopped to examine a rug she might buy, stopped to make an appointment with a piano teacher, stopped to look at a pair of boots for her eldest daughter, stopped and stopped while I continued to die. We usually made it by two minutes, hobbling breathlessly under my baggage and sacks. Once we pushed our way to barriers that were already closing. She helped me leap over them and threw the baggage after me. When my breath returned to normal during the flight, I swore that I would absolutely never, never allow her to take me to a plane again, not to announce a departure, to phone my good-byes from the airport. But I let her cajole me into trying her again and again. She wouldn't make any stops, she swore. And there I was once more, watching the speeding clock as she selected vegetables to make a stew for a sick friend, as she tele-phoned one of her children who was home sick with a cold, and, and. It stopped altogether when I dashed past immigration offi-cials who chased me to the plane, which was about to raise its ramp and close its doors. Why they let me go I'll never know, but even Esther was impressed with our close call, which she thought was exciting and I torture.

Living on the crest of ebullience and impulse, dashing with dizzying energy in several directions simultaneously, called, I frequently suspected, for a crash. It came: as listlessness, inde-cision, indifference, and a lost, expressionless face. At first she resisted psychotherapy but finally arranged for treatment, amaz-ingly on time for each session. After a few months she was soaring again, tearing around in her golden taxi, now in a job as driver and guide to foreign tourists, making them welcome in her good Spanish and French and her nervy, entertaining improvisations on Italian. Her amiability and charm earned her exquisite quarters and meals as well as weighty tips. And with a sense of her own growing responsibility and competence as a professional, she learned to obey the clock—with a few lapses, always forgiven her.

She died young; gallant, dashing, impulsive, generous until her last breath.

16

Game of Metaphors

IS name, of course, was not Zorba but some called him that because of his "Greekness": the free gestures, the seductive smile, the brazen nerve, the superhuman energy and radiance. He didn't look like the stage and screen versions of the big Zorba but was rather a Mercury, the swift young messenger of the gods, the mercurial catalyst of the alchemists. He never appeared at breakfast, not even to share a small glass of champagne that our table had decided was a graceful "good morning" ritual, nor the good-bye salute to our princess of ships, the *France*, on her last voyage. As we got to know him, Albert, a tablemate, and I became his friends and admirers, Albert actually an adorer, and for ancient, understandable reasons. A minor functionary in a remote embassy, Albert was tall and leathery, a British country gentleman steadily dressed in tweed jackets patched with suede elbows, a Britisher with hair carefully parted at the side and slicked down, not one hair out of place. He did not, of course, wear a topee but one could see him in it, its brim cutting straight across his sun-dried, wrinkled forehead. I could also see him circling a statue of Apollo, entranced with the music of its callipygous curves and the beflowered curls on its forehead. Albert loved our Zorba with the love the Englishmen have lavished on Greeks (and other Mediterraneans) for centuries; in the flesh when they dared. Albert's was not a face that lit up, but a faint glow washed over it when he spoke with our Greek who always appeared at lunchtime, fresh white-linen suited and glowing. He never told of it, but others did, that during our first-class sedate dinner dances led on by elderly musicians, he explored the second- and third-class areas. Dispensing gifts of laughter and wine and bounding peasant dance steps with as many boys and girls as he could touch, he played the night away. Then, we were told, he had himself vigorously pummeled in the massage room, dashed between hot and cold showers after a punishing sauna, and emerged a god, the quintessence of antique, alluring perfection, my Mercury, Albert's Apollo.

Because Albert loathed a pouter-pigeon American woman heavy with gems who sat at our table, he never asked her to dance. He was equally contemptuous of the two daughters of a French financier, curly, pretty, wound about each other, burbling incessantly. So, for most evenings we had each other, he and I, as dance partners. As I expected, the first dances were calm, staid fox-trots with a small flurry of dip for a closing fillip. Albert soon found them boring and preferred to stride along the deck, a rigidly paced swift machine, I hardly able to keep up. He talked. He talked about his wife, a "worthy" woman, he said (I hated him for the condescending word), a woman of integrity who spent many hours at charity teas, who visited the failing with flowers and scones. "Why do you hate her so?" I asked after a while. "I don't hate her at all, my dear, you're quite mistaken. She leads her life fruitfully and efficiently, takes solid and sensible care of our four children, and manages the house, the money, the horses, as well as if I weren't there at all, which I frequently am not. I would call it a good marriage, a neat symbiosis of decencies earned and well used, plus amiability when we are with each other and measure the children against their peers in school and against each other." A long pause. "Sex is, when I return, somewhat lusty for a short time, designed, I rather suspect, as proof of celibate hunger on both our parts during separations." "You're not sure she's faithful?" "Faithful to whom? To me? I don't reject an easy opportunity when I'm abroad, why should she? And in any case, a minor fling might be quite pleasurable for her. Both her mother and grandmother were Yorkshire women, and she still slips into addressing everyone, except on formal, cautious occasions, as 'Luv.' You noticed the profligate use of it, I'm sure, when you were in the north of England, found it an endearing greeting, which often, at least to me—I may be wrong—promises intimacy." "She must be a strong woman," I said, "to conduct her life in your aura of polite coolness and still manage a reasonably pleasurable life." "Yes," he answered, "she is strong, very strong, and that's why I married her and would like, at some time, to leave her, forever. She doesn't really need me, and my salary checks would keep coming in to support her and the children. Love in your sense and maybe hers I may lack, but centuries of British rectitude and responsibilities stiffened by army mores still act effectively." "Would you include me along with the strong ones?" I asked after a pause. "Oh, absolutely. What are you doing here alone on a luxury liner, on your way to England to do what and with whom? You mention writing, but no men, and you obviously haven't any close attachments or plans for nesting with anyone; off on your own to prove how self-sufficient you are." He stared at my disconcerted face for a moment, then, "Let's dance."

In the ballroom he swung me into a waltz, which grew faster and faster, not so much bound in sensuality as in a tight wrestle hold, his arm bending my back sharply, painfully. Could this rigid man be trying to break my back, the staff of the will and independence be scorned? (A sharp memory of a similar assault as dancing returned to me from Ciudad Trujillo, and a dimmer recollection from an encounter in New York.) Was he trying to destroy my short legs, which he would not permit to stop in that waltz, and another and yet another, allowing for no pause until he was dragging me around, grinning as he looked down at my sweaty, twisted face? He frightened me; he hated me. I pulled out of his iron arm as soon as the interminable music stopped and turned on him, gasping, "Are we back to strengths, to breaking my body and spirits? What are you trying to prove now? That men are stronger than women? Of course they are, physically at least. Were you proving that I was altogether weak, that your arm might snap my back, your feet break my ankles, that you could reduce me to awkward pulp while others looked on? What real strength does that give you? Does making a rag doll of me turn you into Achilles?" He left me trembling at the corner of the ballroom, trying to smooth my shambled hair and cover my cracked lipstick, and soon came back with a biscuit mounded with caviar and a glass of wine. "Sit down, rest, and maybe later we'll talk." I drank the wine. My hand still shook as I tried to powder my damp face.

As we walked, contemplatively and slowly now, his satanic dancer's grin replaced by the expressionless leather mask, he talked: "As you know, I was born in India, not far from Bombay, where I was, in my twenties, attached to a small government office seeing to a variety of matters—a little police work, a little soldiering, conclaves with the older natives concerning local disputes, nothing distinguished. To go back, though: During one period of leave, my father, a middle-aged British schoolmaster teaching in Bombay, met my mother, already reaching spinsterhood, in London. He married her mainly out of loneliness, I think, and took her back to India. She loathed India and Indians, their disorder, their noise and dirt, their red spit of betel juice, their speech, and found my father a plodding, dull man. I? One of the mistakes that followed her departure from England. Leaving me with my father, she returned to neat, sweet Devon to share a house with an old friend and remembered me twice a year: once with a Christmas card, once with a birthday toy that was, year after year, too young and useless for me. I was looked after in a casual way by my father when he wasn't busy working or drinking and chatting at the club; cricket as the afternoon cooled. The woman who took care of me when I was very young was our scrawny cleaner-cook, affectionate and playful with me until I was about seven. Then it stopped, possibly because my father thought I was becoming too attached to her; he was extremely wary of Anglo-Indian relationships, although it was persistently whispered that he kept an Indian woman in a nearby village. My companions were the gardener, a boy of all work, and several schoolmates. The rest of my adolescent landscape seemed peopled with tinkling, black-braided girls one must not pay attention to. But I couldn't help comparing the brisk movements of the British mothers of my school friends and their strong, calling-to-hounds voices with the quiet, graceful Indian girls who walked along the roads, their ankles shining with bangles, bangles clicking prettily on their arms, their nubile bodies now revealed, now hidden, in the moving folds and swells of blue, lavender, pink saris. I couldn't very well stand on the road and stare at the girls, imagining the full, ripe breasts and roundness of hips I had seen only in sculptures, so I started walking regularly the short distance to town where there was a building under construction. This gave me—and others—an excuse to stare at Rajasthani women wearing swinging gypsy skirts climbing with bricks balanced on flat baskets they wore as hats from one level of building to another; agile, full-bodied, smelling, I imagined, of flowers and spices and sweat; so seductive, so terribly wantable. But I couldn't have them or even get near them, so I had to give up these voyeur's visits, too painfully exciting.

"At twenty—still a virgin—I was shipped off to England and marriage to a second cousin. She had much more tact and patience than my mother; she bided her time through the birth of four children in India and then, when I was moved to an inconvenient, remote location, suggested that it was time for her and the children to return to England. I would, of course, be expected to write and visit as often as I had leave. And here I am, going back for one of those visits, back to the woman who didn't have the frailty to hesitate when questioned about the welfare and education of our children, about a fuller life for herself. Nor was she overconcerned about my new bachelorhood, its ephemeral pleasures, its dun loneliness.

"My mother is a faded picture, my wife a sturdy cottage with durable chintz furniture, but I do have a love, a true love. She is Indian, with that Indian-goddess curve of belly, trilling fringes of earring in her lobes. She is a deaf-mute, sometimes blind, altogether and always dependent on me. I am her whole world and carefully explain with touch and gestures what I want of her. She always understands. She cooks for me and massages my feet; I stroke her breasts and lie in her, moving, as slowly and heatedly as her face asks. Where is she? Where do I keep her? Constantly with me, wherever I am, wherever I travel. You think I'm mad, that she's a figment of my imagination, but she fills and enfolds my life. She is my eternal, immutable love, in no way touched by a few meaningless stray encounters."

I avoided Albert for a few days, unwilling to connect with him and his fantasy. He stayed out of my way, probably to distance himself from the unusual intimacy of our conversation. The necessary, polite table talk gradually eased into ordinary conversation again, but the deaf-mute, sometimes blind Indian girl never reappeared except in my mind, where she took her place with tragic young heroines like doomed Ophelia, consumptive Mimi, abandoned Butterfly.

Finally expelled from our golden-egg, the *France*, Mercury, Albert, and I sat looking at the rainswept windows of the train station at Southampton. The Greek was, as always, happy. His small Hermès address book was full of promise—a girl in London's Mayfair, a girl in Shepherd's Bush, a girl in Islington and all, naturally, waiting for him and the valuable presents he would bring. Albert was less happy as his eyes followed the streaks of rain on the windows. He was ready to go home to Sussex but, he said unexpectedly, I must come with him. Trying not to gape in surprise, I watched his face and listened as he, uncharacteristically, pleaded and cajoled: Please, please, drive home with him. His car was in a local garage and, after I spent the night with his family, he would take me back to London. I might have done it because my London commitments were not pressing, and I was curious. This was, however, too strange—an invitation that felt like mischief. I thanked him but no; maybe some other time.

Thinking he, too, might drive off to leave me alone on the train to London, I kissed my mercurial Greek fully, lingeringly on the mouth, something I had wanted to do since I first saw him, while Albert forced a piece of paper into my hand. It bore

the address of his London club where, the note said, he would
be two days hence at teatime. He left, the Greek stayed on the
train, and we laughed our way to London.

The next day I received a note from Albert, reminding me
that he expected me at his club the day after. I would enjoy the
old place, one of the few left with extravagantly painted ceilings
and the teas particularly good during this Christmas season. Please
try to be there at four o'clock. I was on time, wearing my jauntiest
holiday dress. He was already there. I kissed him and sat down
to order a drink and talk. We were together only about fifteen
minutes when a warm voice called to him from the doorway.
The voice became a smiling, red-cheeked, curly-haired woman
dressed in sturdy country clothing and laden with Christmas
packages. This was Mrs. Albert. As he introduced us my misty
illusion of an interesting affair, a now-and-then thing that propelled Albert between Sussex and London when he was on leave,
flew off, up into the pink buttocks of the ceiling cupids. He was
wary, was my friend Albert, of his strong wife and had used this
impromptu arrangement, since I had refused to drive home (with
a stop where?) with him from Southampton, to prove that I was
no American cutie he had bedded on board ship, simply a solid
young woman, independent as herself and not easily taken. She
could judge that his interest in me was hardly pressing, just a
pleasant shipboard friendship he must have mentioned when he
described his trip. He had manipulated me to prove, in his
oblique way, that I was of little importance to him. Wrapped in
his deathless, illusory love, he hadn't much use for either of us,
but it was now expedient to act out the contented father and
husband home on Christmas leave, free of shipboard entanglements. I never returned to the club, gaudy and lively as it was,
nor did I answer two or three notes he sent me. Mercury? I
received an invitation from him to join his family on a yachting
trip among the Greek islands. Suspecting, maybe unfairly, that
he was using me as Albert had, I thanked him, but sorry, I had
other plans. And *that* was *that*—leftover, scrambled bits of our
golden egg.

17

Tom

THE *Mexico: Places and Pleasures* manuscript was swelling but not quite finished. It might be time to cull and to expand with newer matter, should it present itself. I would have to fill out the freezing hours of sitting through the Night of the Dead on the island of Janitzio; describe the ornamented graves to which drink and food and flowers had been brought and often tequila and guitars for dance-stomping. Feed them, sing and dance for them, remind them they are not forgotten, not really dead. I should treat more fully of the cruel fear of the many maids in a friend's large Mexico City apartment house, shunning and cursing her own maids as companions and carriers of death since their employer, my friend's husband, had died. Was there enough of the tall, pround Tarascans? Of the shy, tiny hill people of Yalala, of the *cantini* machos, the solemnity of religious Puebla, of the scholarly dignity of Morelia? How about the encounter with a rural ancient who addressed me as Princesa, who had long ago heard of the rule in Mexico of French aristocrats, didn't know it was over, and felt that she had to address foreign women as French royalty?

Where to take my bundle of papers and work on it away from the distractions of Mexico City, a place that would be new to me and maybe worth a few pages? I had heard of the remote, untouched island village of Cozumel and grew interested in it when I met a woman who ran a small hotel on the island, a worldly, clever woman who found the simple island life smooth and easy and lured me to it. There were, at that time, no direct connections to the island; one had to wait for a plane that, winds and tropical storms permitting, made the flight from Merida two or three times a week. When I finally arrived, looking for the woman in whose hotel I had arranged to stay, two men, both Americans, came toward me and introduced themselves. The young, good-looking (and aware-of-it) man said he did not live at my hotel but made it a habit to see who came off the plane, distracting pauses in the long days he spent writing a book. (Here was one of my favorite Mexican clichés; almost every expatriate I met who was not painting vast social-conscious shrieks of pain in the style of Siqueiros was writing a book, the Great Book.) This man, I imagined, met the plane in the hopes of finding some likely female to share his cabin on the beach. Attractive as he was, I was not tempted nor did I seem to tempt him; he would want someone younger or maybe in time would settle in with one of the local girls, a girl with no father to whip her into marriageable chastity. The other man was older, statelier in his speech. He had the reliable looks of someone in an American history book, Thomas Jefferson or an Adams. He introduced himself as a client of the hotel; he had offered to pick me up because our hostess was busy umpiring a screaming battle between her cook and her laundress. We talked some as we drove. He was there for a light rest cure and a bit of sketching free of the mediocrities imposed on him by his usual work as a commercial artist.

The hotel was a set of airy, colorfully furnished thatch bungalows ranged along the sides of a long garden. The dining and entertaining rooms were at the front end of the garden, giving on to the street. Tom, as he had introduced himself, asked if I would join him for a drink in the front *sala* after I had washed and unpacked. At about seven? No one ate until nine or even later. I met him for the drink and yet another while we listened to the house musicians, boys who were waiters, assistant cooks, and sweepers during the day, rehearsing for the dancing that would follow dinner. They were skillful and inventive, concocting musical confections of bits of rhythm and tunes picked up here and there. Since we were less than one hundred miles from Cuba their music often had the propelling beat of salsa rhythms, often sweetened with the rueful tunes of Haiti; at times the long wail of Mexican ballads often followed by the merry jumpiness of Veracruzana songs, like "La Bamba." (Memory being the diabolical thing it is, I have forgotten many events during those months on the island but still insist on remembering "Señores, que Pachanga" as a fast, heated merengue and "Tiès Oiseaux," sung in execrable Creole, as a subtle dance of insinuation and erotic promise.) After the rehearsal we had a surprisingly fine dinner of venison in the Yucatán style and tropical fruits touched with Grand Marnier. I met the other guests and my host, a restless acerbic man, who, as long as I knew him, held his sharp tongue when he spoke with me, maybe in fear that I might write of his inn unfavorably. I never would or could; it became, for the better part of a year, my tropical Garden of Eden.

After dancing and drinking for hours that night, Tom and I spent the rest of the night in his bungalow. We became intimate friends and lively lovers and stayed friends and lovers during all my time in Cozumel. My resolution to work assiduously on my book, to write and reshape for a few hours every day, began to melt to the point where one page a day was all I could manage; an occasional letter to friends in the States became a major achievement. The only work I did, after a while, was to make notes on trips I took with Tom. Our first excursion took us to a disused old lighthouse where we spent a few days in the company of an old retired keeper who couldn't bear to leave the place, never mind wife, children, and grandchildren. Our diet was crude and tasty, always accompanied by thick, delectable tortillas called *gorditas* ("fatties"). We fished, we loved, we cut our way through the surrounding jungle to examine rare plants and flowers; we watched the bird life that dazzled the air around us. My own private toilet was a small Mayan temple, one of several we stumbled on.

Other times we spent long, radiant days on copra boats, laden with beer and rum—the first priorities—along with Danish cheese and Argentine sausages smuggled from Belize. As we sailed we fished for lobsters we later cooked over palmetto pyres on distant beaches whose coconut palms marched into the sea. When the plane from Mérida could not outride the winds, we picknicked on delectable local fish and turtle steaks, oranges, mangoes, and bananas. We bounded around in the backs of trucks that trundled through beach sands and jungles to fiestas in lost villages whose *jefes* had sent us ceremonious invitations but invariably were thoroughly drunk by the time we got to them; it was the women who fed us and the children who entertained us and found hammocks for us to rest in. Tom and I hunted for lost Mayan ruins and artifacts with a number of bogus archae- ologists for the fun of it and in anticipation of the fanciful books they would write. We snorkeled at a nearby hole of jewellike fish, I so entranced with their color and the susurrus of their whispers that Tom always had to pull me out. We watched our boys kill iguanas and the local fishermen spear the sharks that came threateningly close to our scallops of beach.

Once in a while we donned our city clothing for a few days of sightseeing and souvenir shopping in Mérida. On one of these visits Tom bought me a small Mayan flute, an ancient instrument as delicate and exquisitely proportioned as the Mayan antiquarian who sold it to us. It seemed to me a terrible portent, and probably to Tom as well, that in later taking the flute out of a duffel bag crammed with camera, films and books, we found it crushed. I said I thought we could have it repaired. He said, no it was too badly damaged, almost in bits. Had he wanted really to give me a piece of Mayan antiquity I had coveted or not? Was crushing the flute an oblique denial of fidelity, an act of rejection? Was he proving to a former wife that I didn't really matter? It was for a long time a troubling experience, the unease recalled yesterday, today, whenever I touch a small bundle of shards in my desk drawer.

*   *   *

A healing experience, one of the oddest passages of love and devotion, was a shared, simultaneous attack of Montezuma's revenge. I moved into his cabin because it had the better-equipped bathroom and we spent three or four miserable, hilarious days, moaning, groaning, laughing, in and out of the toilet, comparing symptoms, feeding each other pills and dry toast. David and Sheba, Cleopatra and Antony we were not, but as tightly bound to each other—if not sexually, viscerally.

There were one or two snakes in my Garden. Like a number of Midwesterners of rural background, Tom enjoyed an occasional anti-Semitic quip though he knew few Jews. I quickly warned him that I had never been intimate with an anti-Semite and didn't mean to be. He was a ready learner, and I never detected any hint of anti-Semitism after that. Another snake was his constant references, after he had had several drinks, to former wives with affectionate descriptions of their habits and oddities—how they put on their makeup, what they liked to eat, how they dressed. Some of this was to be expected in the endless hours we spent together, but I grew tired of these women and finally, with a whip of anger, said so. They didn't disappear but took his stage less frequently.

When I returned to New York, my manuscript in some magical way ready for my publishers, he soon followed and settled into a flat borrowed from a traveling friend. Although he missed our former closeness I couldn't have him in my flat; I needed to be alone and undisturbed to work. Besides, he was drinking fairly heavily, depressed because he couldn't find a suitable job and his savings were fleeing at a frightening pace. I invited him to frequent meals and tried to encourage him, not too convincingly, I think. He and I had become other people, grounded in work and money concerns, far from the sea, the sand, the glittering birds, the sparkling fish, the beach picnics, the dancing. He was becoming sadly elderly and I rather stolidly set in a career. The resonance between us was going, gone. He didn't leave sharply, distinctly, but his calls and his visits became widely spaced until they stopped. I heard from him several years later in a letter that made a suggestion about an article or book I might write. The idea offered no practicality for me, and I took it to be an attempt at opening yet another chapter in our lives together. I put the letter aside unanswered, regretting that I hadn't had the anesthetic sense and the wisdom to have broken away completely in Cozumel, the enchanted setting for the last idyll I would have. (True for him too, I suspect.)

18

The Children

ROM the time that I spent hours staring at my baby wondering if she were thinking, could she think without words, or was there a vocabulary that was lost in the agony of being forced through the birth canal or destroyed with the umbilical cord, I've stared at babies in buses and supermarkets, watching their eyes move from object to object, wondering if the color and shape of an orange was pleasing and how that pleasure expressed itself.

Although I am responsive to children and they to me, I have always found them mysterious, their sudden impulses, their unexpected gestures and sounds, the mystery often tinged with respect, sometimes with sorrow for them, sometimes with anger for subtle abuses. When I was, for instance, in China in 1983 or 1984, our group was taken to a model settlement with neat small repetitive apartments. The climax of this show of new prosperity and progress was a performance by a group of three- to five-year-olds. In contrast to the black cotton pants and shirts their mothers and grandmothers wore, the children were dressed in high gaud made by those mothers and grandmothers: knitted yellow caps with red pom-poms, bright green sweaters, and purple pants. They were enchanting, the faces shining with smiles; they knew they were a cute as toys. Young as they were they had clearly been well trained in singing in chorus (the introductory number was "Happy Birthday" sung to the tune of "Clementine"). This was followed by pretty dancing steps and arm movements that imitated birds and butterflies. The *pièce* of this infantile vaudeville was a martial dance of heroic and, when they could manage them, bellicose stances, led on by the waving of red flags. Here I grew angry; this was a political form of child abuse, these delightful little dolls with the endearing faces used as propaganda for a country whose ambition masked its dirt, its poverty, its semislave labor.

In another country, ours, I witnessed an act by a gaggle of children that earned my profound, amused respect. A group of people my husband knew—quasi intellectuals, publishers, writers (I was then on my first book) were invited to a large beach house on Cape Cod. The adults and their various children took picnic baskets down to an isolated section of beach. We were, the adults, all on either edge of middle age, not altogether unattractive but showing a paunch here, floppy breasts there, tensed neck muscles, varicosity's purple stains. One advanced lady, more vain than her realities merited, a flirtatious woman with intellectual ambitions that expressed themselves primarily in searching out artists to engage in conversations about the inner meanings of pop art, suggested that we sun and swim in the nude. There was hesitation, embarrassment, but the assemblage could not confess to being tied to old conservative modes, to bourgeois hang-ups. They took off their bathing suits awkwardly, the pop art lady playing her small towel around her in a sort of striptease that might also have served to hide imperfections. With the first drop of a shoulder strap, the children all scampered away, far away. I would not take off my bathing suit. I had no great pride in my allure, and the gesture seemed an affectation, rather ridiculous; forced. The only other person who did not strip was a cartoonist who paid me the silent compliment of opening a box of watercolors he carried and painting butterflies on my arms and back, one large and spirited butterfly of striped lavender on my neck, spreading iridescent blue wings on my chest.

Came the time for unpacking the baskets for lunch. One mother, Venus turned Mom, said anxiously, "What about the

kids? We have their lunch here. They didn't take their basket."
She waited for a volunteer to take food to the children but everyone lay sun dazed and too self-conscious to move out of their
optimum poses. Finally she poked her husband, who began re-
lucantly to pull on his bathing shorts. Before they were fully on,
a young shout came from the distance into which the children
had disappeared. We turned to the voice and saw two little boys
approaching. As they neared us, they turned their faces away,
then, blindly grabbing the nearest basket, ran swiftly back to their
faraway, carefree place. (The averted faces suggested to me figures
in Greek drama, a ritualistic gesture refusing to witness shame
and guilt.) I admired the whole far-off gang, wearing their bathing
suits, having fun that wasn't faked, sensitive enough to be embarrassed by the foolishness of their parents.

One of the best pantomimes, which told an elaborate story
in childish gestures crammed with mature ploys, took place one
summer at a beach resort not far from New York. Bill's divorce
settlement gave him the right to have his two little girls on Sundays and summer holidays. I was always with them at those
times—cooking their favorite meals, playing games and roller-
skating with them. (Whatever sharp rocks the marriage stumbled
on, there was never any complaint about Bill's efforts for my
daughter and mine for his children.) This particular summer it
was decided between her parents that the older girl, about nine,
was ready for camp. We rented a beach house; I was left in sole
charge—all day until her father returned from work—of the six-
year-old. After a week of sullen, "My mother says you're fat,"
"My mother hates you," "My grandmother hates you," "I hate
you," we gradually became joysome playmates; a dizzying number of merry-go-round rides, a plethora of ice-cream cones, great
cities of sand castles built; a playful life for both of us, the child
delighted and a delight.

The fun had to come to a close at the end of the month; her
father was to take her back to her mother's house. The night
before I had put out her newish, smocked city dress; fresh, be-
ribboned underwear; and formal city shoes. I awoke very early
to get her ready and found that she had been awake for some

time—or maybe the havoc she worked was set in motion during the night while we were asleep. A challenging smile on her face, she emerged from her room wearing her bathing suit; one full side of her longish, blond hair had been cut to the roots, the city dress lying on the chair had been ripped from top to hem. The pretty underwear had disappeared as had one of the homecoming shoes. There was nothing I could do about her hair, nor could I find the underwear or the shoe though she made lazy gestures at opening and closing closet doors and looking under beds as if to help me search. So she went home (her bathing suit as underwear) in the homecoming dress into which I had quickly sewn a seam to gather the ripped sections together; one shining shoe; and one worn sneaker. The fresh underwear and the other shining shoe never appeared, although after her departure I made a meticulous search of the house and the front garden as well as the garbage can. She must have buried them among the backyard bushes during the night.

Why had she done it? To prove to her mother that I had been careless with her, that I had tried to return her as downright ugly as I reputedly was? Was she saying that she didn't want to go home, that she wanted to stay with me and my indulgent ways? A joining of both meanings? I have never asked her.

A couple of years after my sister's death my brother-in-law remarried. To win favor with the new wife and for my own needs, I took the three children into the city from their suburban house on frequent Sundays. The first attempts were nervous and tearful, childish desires and conflicts running between ice cream and merry-go-rounds and for the boy (the eldest), wandering through shining knights in armor of the Metropolitan Museum, not for his young sisters, resistant, protesting. I smoothed matters by taking one child at a time on successive Sundays. The boy, then eight or nine, continued to seek out the mighty glistening knights and their murderous lances—until one time, I, thoroughly bored with armor, lured him to an upper floor with a long corridor where he could run freely. He ran up and down the hall several times and then stopped midway to stare and continue staring at a large, effulgent nude by Courbet, that master of large effulgent nudes. The boy had probably never seen a nude woman before and stood rooted, entranced, before this goddess lying in a leafy dell. Conscious at one moment of my nearby presence, he ran up and down the long hall again, then stopped in front of the woman; continued to run, stopped, stared, ran some more. Of course the encounter was never mentioned, but I suspect a momentous shock and flash of enlightenment in a young boy's life.

The middle girl was easy; she liked window-shopping and could imagine herself in the pearls of Tiffany, the silken swaths at Bergdorf's, Italian shoes as fragile and unattainable as Cinderella's slipper. The youngest preferred the Christmas windows, not only for their animated, cozy animal families out of Beatrix Potter but more particularly for the sophisticated shows that displayed the styles of various cultures, rather knocking me flat when she differentiated unerringly between modern East Indian and older Mogul styles in dress and art. The keen eye and sure judgment never left her, nor did her essential poise. It was from this confident creature when she was three or four that I learned a couple of indelible lessons. One, that sex appeal—not necessarily laced with marked beauty—was a very early acquisition; this child always had a little boy walking and talking with her, offering her lollipops and marbles. (The family legend had it that she was born followed by a minute boyfriend hidden in the birth canal, magically gone when others began to crawl after her before they could walk.) The more impressive, personal lesson she taught me was the message of a stormy, snowy day. As a Christmas present, I had given her parents the use of my city apartment for a week while I took care of the children in the suburbs. One deeply snowy morning meant plowing through cold and wet lashing winds to meet the school bus the seven-year-old-girl was to board. She wept and wailed and complained all the way— "I'm cold, I have a headache, my throat's sore, I want to go home, I have to go to the bathroom"—a battery of hints that she was jealous of the little one, not yet in school, who would have me and my indulgences all to herself. While the wailing and complaining cut through the swirling snow, a dulcet little voice called, "Oh, Kate, here's me; here I am," the snow almost to her neck, the voice sweetly seductive, the baby teeth twinkling. At that moment I thought, "If I had known at thirty-four what you know at four—the appealing, undemanding voice, the delicate calling of attention to oneself with fine tact, what a different life it might have been for me."

As these children grew beyond my guidance and company—into dense adolescent friendships, invitations to many parties, off to colleges, I found myself choosing older lost-daughter substitutes, one a particularly unhappy girl with prosperous, generous parents whom she scorned in fits of sullenness alternating with coarse barking. I invited her to the opera, to foreign movies, to curious little restaurants. She was civilized, polite, and intelligent, and liked to discuss her wispy love life—the rightful property of her mother, I thought—with me. It dawned on me rather slowly, since I was pleased with the tie between us, that I was interfering with her life as it had to be lived out with her parents and probably therapy; that I had no right to use her to fill my emptinesses. On the fortunate excuse of a book that required a long stay abroad, I cut the tie. And never made another; I had several young women friends but never again appointed them my daughters, though some of them sought the role. But this was a matter of their own needs, never again mine. I would all my life look for Lexie but never shape, or help shape, a substitute.

When I was preparing to visit my brother and his family in Jerusalem, I was advised to bring apples and bubble gum for the children. I bought two sacks of apples at the Athens airport, the penultimate stop on a thirty-six-hour (prejet) journey to Tel Aviv, and, having cajoled the local candy shop in my New York neighborhood to sell me all the bubble gum it had on hand, I was ready to be a most welcome visitor. Both nieces were delighted, excited. The older girl stored her gum away to gloat over and use judicially. The younger, then about seven, used her box of bubble gum like an experienced politician. It was a memorable thing to watch her, minute and skinny, bubble gum boxes in hand, standing at the top of her apartment house stairs, a long trail of children lined up below, saying to one supplicant, "You can have a piece because you helped me with my arithmetic last week," "You can't have any because you didn't lend me the jacks your aunt brought you from America." "You may, you may not" emerged from the stern little mouth, a normally pretty little mouth, expressing supreme power, chilling to see and listen to.

The most heartbreaking child I knew was a little girl consumed by a love heavier, greater, than her few years should have had to carry.

Steve, Lexie, Steve's parents, and I lived for a time on the upper story of a large, two-family house. On the street floor there was a family of mother, father, grandmother, and two children, a boy of six and a girl of about nine or ten. I had no great interest in her—another little girl of the many in the neighborhood and in the park we faced. I began, however, to notice that she broke away at about five o'clock each afternoon from playing potsy and jumping rope to sit on the outer street stairs of our house, her skirt pulled down over her knees, her hands folded in her lap, in a posture of patient waiting. I watched her when I could and then more attentively, attracted by what passion, what obsession held her for hours on the stairs, that took her out of her young play world. One day as I passed her on the street, Steve came around the corner. I saw her rise and stand stiffly, staring at him as he approached. He nodded, she said nothing but, as if in a trance, fixed her eyes on him as he searched his pocket for door keys, turned the lock, and went into the house. She didn't return to her playmates but walked into the backyard wrapped in sadness, in solitude.

Because Steve was on a schedule that required spending two or three long evenings and often nights at his hospital, she often waited for fruitless hours. I could hear her father shout at her, "Enough already. You'll catch cold sitting there on the stairs. Come in and eat your supper, right now." And her grandmother cajoling, "Come, I made potato *latkes*, you'll like them. And after supper Papa will buy you ice cream. Come in, *kindele*." As night and cold deepened, she would reluctantly take her taut little body home. I was moved by this child, wanted to know her better, and began to engage her in conversation. She was shy with me, and probably frightened, but she did ultimately respond to the usual questions about school and what books she had last taken from the library. The friendliness slowly kindled until she dared to ask me, eyes downcast, her voice frail and shaky, "Could I come up to your house in the mornings, before I go to school, and watch Doctor Steve shave?" Taken aback, I hesitated. I had to ask his permission, I told her. Maybe he wouldn't mind, maybe he would. I promised to let her know. Steve was amused and a bit disturbed—"That's a hell of a load of adoration for a little kid"—but he said I could invite her to watch him shave. She came three or four times, standing stiffly at the side of the bathroom, totally absorbed, watching him with her whole body. Her father, who once followed her, became angry with us and expressed vehemently his contempt for people who would indulge a child in such a *"meshuggeneh"* impulse. He put a stop to it. She no longer waited on the stairs, nor would she talk to me, and she ran away when she saw Steve.

I don't remember her face, but I shall never forget the patient, folded hands, the motionless waiting of a woman profoundly, hopelessly, in love.

19

Parisians

As most travelers know, August reduces Paris to Pompeii; there are signs of life, work, food, but only as symbols, immobile in a gum of lassitude. Windows on my street, the rue de Grenelle, were tight shut. Several cats had been turned out by August vacationers and were howling of hunger in the hallways and turning savage, spitting and clawing at each other, in the streets. The one drugstore required to stay open was many blocks away, and my favorite cheese shop, the domain of a bitter old crone, was closed; my other bitter crone, my concierge, stayed, as always, taciturn and scowling. The only nearby shop that was open was the small bakery on the street level of my building. I had bought baguettes and an occasional piece of fruit tart there almost every day for about a year, and never yet had the salesgirl, the daughter of the owner, I believe, said *bonjour* or *merci* to me, as she did to the Frenchwomen who came daily to make larger purchases than mine. Those customers were away in their houses in Normandy and just a few of us oddities, very few, were around. The girl remained rude, handing me my baguette and change with her usual sullenness until one day, about Ascension Day, in the middle of August, she greeted me— I recoiled in surprise—with, "Madame, I am so happy to see you! How have you been? Isn't it lonely around here? It frightens me to be alone hour after hour in the shop. What can I serve you? These peach tarts are fresh and delectable. Would you like one?" She thanked me effusively as she wrapped the tart and bade me *bonsoir*. It never happened again. After August she returned to her sullen self and stayed there; no more *mercis*, no more *bonjours*, ever.

I went at café time—about six o'clock—to report this minor August miracle created of fear and loneliness to my friends a few streets away. They were my closest Paris friends, and I saw them most evenings at the café and often took them to restaurants I was visiting for a book on Paris then in the writing. Once in a while I would climb the five steep flights to their clever tiny apartment into which Peter, once an architect, had inserted a narrow box of stall shower and equally narrow toilet, not part of the original apartment they had bought when they escaped troublesome America for the freedoms of Paris. One of the privileges of walking the long flights and their nervous *minuteries*, which left one in the dark groping for the button to relight the stairs for another thirty seconds, was the possibility of passing on the stairs a frog-faced man, unfocused bulging eyes under thick spectacles; it was the great Sartre, my friends told me, visiting one of his several lady friends. He never offered me a greeting or even a look, although we shared the narrow staircases, almost touching, several times.

Peter and Norma were, like expatriates I had before met in Mexico, happy to loathe American capitalist pragmatism; the rigidities, the false moralities, the primitive anti-intellectualism of the United States. Not successful as an architect, bound to a job that bent him endlessly over blueprints for someone else's building, Peter decided to move to Paris and make a brilliant reputation as a designer of interiors, of furniture, of books, of jewelry, of anything innovative and chic. I never knew absolutely, but a sureness grew in me that he was homosexual and trying desperately to hide from the knowledge, mired in the censorious American mind-set that he could not shake off even in the city of Verlaine, Rimbaud, Cocteau, and the decaying berouged Oscar Wilde (as painted mercilessly by Toulouse-Lautrec). He was a large, handsome man, carefully dressed, well informed, and witty, and we had wonderfully high-flown, vehement, and nonsensical arguments when I brought a couple of bottles of wine— which he and I consumed, becoming brighter and brighter and then incoherent as the bottles emptied. He supplied a bottle now and then but couldn't do it often because Paris didn't offer him the glamorous career he had hoped for; he was the calligrapher for a print shop that designed ornate invitations and wedding announcements, and his salary allowed for few luxuries.

Norma did not drink—some vague stories of desperately sick reactions to medicaments, varied with hints of past addiction to some of them, maybe alcohol itself. He and I drank as she listened or read aloud, stressing significant phrases, from *Le Monde* and *Le Canard Enchaîné*. She was singularly homely and made a devoted career of being eccentric. She wore ill-fitting, sloppy clothing; her nails were never quite clean; and, when we went to a restaurant, she ordered dessert first or some strange concoction while Peter and I ploughed lustily through the full menu, course after course. I suspected that she might have been a lesbian and had some proof of that during the celebration of July 14, Bastille Day, in the headiness of drinking, dancing, and singing that went on at the local firehouse. Peter did not dance but drank and looked on with a mixture of pleasure and aristocratic disdain. She insisted on dancing with me. Why not?—everyone was dancing with anyone. She held me tight, leading forcefully, her grasp tighter and tighter as she pulled me toward her. When we were head to head she gasped a low but unmistakable, "I love you. I love you. I truly love you." I pulled away and went to stand with Peter. There was never again so overt a declaration, but her excessive praise of my looks, my style, my swiftness with French, my engaging personality, were uncomfortable to live with. When I created a scenario of their bizarre marriage—a faithful rendering or a piece of imagination, I wasn't quite sure—I leaned to the possibility that they had gotten married to protect themselves and each other from the suppressed desires they had hoped to unleash in Paris but couldn't.

When Peter died after a short illness (Norma blamed it on

inept treatment in a local clinic; I suspected an eagerness for death), I continued to spend mournful time with Norma. She had no other friends but the barmen in the neighborhood café who served her afternoon coffees. I soon became a victim of her anger over her loss; she began to turn on me, to find fault with my looks, my personality, what she called my "high-class" vanity because I dressed presentably while she looked more and more like a *clochard*. Fortunately my work in Paris was about finished, and I left to do a book in London. Living on the limited pittance she had after Peter's death, she spent large sums telephoning a mutual acquaintance in London asking if they had yet seen "that bitch," myself, who owed her money, a lot of money. I didn't; on the contrary, I had been as generous as I could with her, buying her coffee and meals, giving her some of my clothing. The calls stopped after a while, followed by stinging, cursing letters. Neither my London friends nor I answered, and Norma faded from my life—until, on a later visit to Paris, walking on a street far from her rue du Dragon, I thought I saw her and, panic-stricken, afraid to meet the madwoman she must surely then be, dashed into a shop for shelter and a calm that came slowly. A fear of her still exists, and I find myself searching far ahead and on both sides of streets when I am in her *arrondissement*. She has soiled St. Germain forever, and though she may be dead, I cannot forgive her for haunting me.

Another friend I made in Paris, Pierre, was not mad but sick and bitter. He loathed the city and yearned for the freedom and humanity of London where he had served with the Free French. Impelled by he could not remember what, he had married on impulse the sister of a friend. The marriage was contentious and then venomous, although they managed to stay together through the birth and early years of two children. The only reason he could bear it, he said, was that, as an engineer, he had jobs away from Paris quite often, respites from the travesty of a marriage that he continued to endure. Once, when I asked him why he had not left, he answered that he loved his young daughters too much and could never abandon them, no matter what the cost.

She abandoned him; he came home after an absence in Rouen to find his apartment empty, his wife, his children, his possessions gone. He ran from relative to relative, from friend to friend, to learn that she had taken the children, after selling everything in the apartment, to London.

Her flight may have urged him to join the Free French in London, where, in every spare moment, he tried to track her and the children down. It was a long, exhausting search, but he did locate them and made some sort of temporary truce with his wife so that she allowed him to take the older girl off for one Sunday outing. Instead of taking her to the zoo, as he had promised, he rushed with the child to the airport and boarded the first Paris plane. There he located a childless couple, old friends, who were willing to take care of little Monique while he continued to serve in London. He made frequent visits back to Paris to see the girl and, a year or two later, returned to live there with her. She was then a bewildered, shy ten-year-old who soon began to accept life with the father who showered her with solicitude and devotion.

Shortly before I met him, he had been stricken with a severe heart attack and told to be extremely careful, to moderate his life. He couldn't; he had to continue his work journeys and to take meticulous care of his daughter. Living under a cloud of doom, he hated his life, misspent in a peripatetic, unrewarding profession and a poisonous marriage. And he hated Paris, which became a symbol of all that was loathsome. A ride with him was accompanied by mutterings of *"emmerdeur," "vieux con,"* directed at every driver. He took pleasure in showing me the squalid shacks of squatters who dragged their starving, dirty lives in and out of Bidonvilles (public shelters). He took me to the Algerian quarter and warned me that I would see them put a little girl in front of passing cars so that the child might be injured; an uncle, a father, would then come running out of a doorway to demand money from the driver, and get it. What if a child died? They didn't care; girls were expendable.

As we grew to know each other better, he said he wanted very much to go to bed with me but was not too keen on establishing another linkage with a woman; he'd had enough and, in any case, he had been warned that sex might be bad for his heart. I was rather relieved at not having to share a bed or part of my life with this too-troubled man. Our time together was not all bleak, though. When we had dinner together, it was usually in the zesty Tunisian-Jewish section of working-class Belleville. Pierre wasn't Jewish but liked the color, the animation, and the good cheap *bouriques* and *beignets* we ate there. His daughter, Monique, joined us at some of those dinners. She was still shy, awkward, and stolid and, in the beginning, could barely speak with me. But he insisted on bringing us together, and her monosyllabic answers to my questions gradually grew to sentences, still bare but somewhat fuller. I asked her the usual cliché questions— what was she studying in school, did she like practicing the piano, did she have many friends, who was her favorite? And so on. When Pierre saw that we were managing, she and I, some sort of basic sociability, he asked me to take her on one of my walks in Paris—the Marché aux Puces, maybe, or the Marais or the bird market on the Île St. Louis. She would enjoy it, he said. I took her along with me, and she seemed in her restrained way to be contented, never youthfully enthusiastic. I saw her as a child who never ran freely or played or cried or shrieked with surprise and delight.

She was very pleased, Pierre told me, to know and be taken about by me. He was leading up to something—obviously not a marriage proposal, out of the question—but where and how did it involve Monique? He laid out his plan with some embarrass-ment. Since he might pop off any day, would I take her in my charge? It was of course impossible, I was very sorry to say. I was leaving Paris within the year and then going on to London to work there. In any case he could see, I said, that I could not afford an apartment large enough for both of us, or supervise her schooling, or entertain her friends and maybe later boyfriends. I liked her very well, I was flattered by his trust, I would like to relieve him of his worry. But. What about his old friends, the childless couple; wouldn't they be more suitable? No, they were separated and each had left Paris. In spite of my deep concern and sympathy, I couldn't take on Monique's care, I repeated. Surely he understood why. He did, he said. Our dates became less and less frequent, although Monique telephoned me and visited several times. Then they both left my life altogether, something of a relief. I later heard from mutual friends that Pierre had died of a heart attack and that Monique had been taken to the farm of relatives near Avignon. I wondered for a time why she hadn't returned to her mother in London—surely Pierre would have left enough money for that—but assumed that her life had been so confused and troubling that she found a farm—an easy-cadenced, uneventful place—the safest place to be.

One of the delights of my Paris was elderly Marthe, the last of a distinguished family, now mayor of a suburban village. She had once run a finishing school in her large, handsome house on the outskirts of Paris. She continued the school under the sharp scrutiny of the Nazis when they took over the city. After a few suggestions that she improve the history classes with greater concentration on the noble past and present of Germany, they left her unmolested. Through the Jewish grapevine that reported nuns who would shelter Jewish children, by way of information from expert creators of false passports, it became known that passionately anti-Nazi Marthe would keep in her house treasures that fleeing Jews could not take with them, to be claimed at some later time. She thus became the guardian of a cache of valuable paintings, of Stradivarius violins, of numerous rare books and boxfuls of carefully tagged fine jewelry.

When I knew her, the school was closed, the Jewish possessions redistributed, but old and ill as she then was, she still had the zest and courage to fight vigorously for the welfare of her villagers. She enjoyed the disputes and the politicking as she enjoyed a good meal in a fine restaurant, as I enjoyed being her hostess: to watch her settle herself with a contented sigh among the pink and lacy whites of Le Doyen, then a restaurant of fine manners and courtly service, an aristocrat to honor with its skills a fellow aristocrat of the blood and the spirit.

20

❖

Roads Not Taken

EUROPE made wearisome, dark travel in 1949. There were a few London restaurants that found mediocre food for tourists, but the general supply was meager. To see what English office workers ate, I followed a lunchtime group of girls—typists, stenographers, file clerks, I imagined—into a cafeteria that offered one dish and a cup of tea. We were served a slice off a loaf that was mainly congealed porridge flavored with bits of sausage and enlivened by one bit of hard-boiled egg per portion. It is still depressing to taste that dreary flavor crawling across the years. Driving through rural France we were disturbed, saddened, by the clatter of crudely carved wooden shoes, leather still lacking. Genoa's once-mighty harbor was a drowning place for immense, gaunt metal fingers, shards of sunken ships.

We stopped in Madrid only long enough to explore the then poorly lit and neglected Prado, where I became newly acquainted with Zurbarán and Ribera and the stunning antique "Woman of Elche." We headed south where the Civil War remained as simmering fury between Loyalist and Falangist houses. In Córdoba we met a young man exploring, as we were, the staggering play of pillars and Moorish arches in the great ancient mosque. In the course of a conversation (he had some English and I a fair supply of Mexican Spanish) he told us that he was visiting a friend who was a poet but earned his living as a teacher. The friend, now on vacation, would very probably enjoy taking us to local places; born in Córdoba, he knew the environs well. That afternoon we met him, a courtly man in his thirties, luminous, all gold. His hair was brown gold, his eyes golden, his skin tanned gold, the tone echoed in his gold tan shirt, his trousers and shoes. This was, I assumed, not casual dressing but in so self-assured a hidalgo, enhancements he required and deserved. After a short exchange of *mucho gustos* and *que gran placer*, we arranged to go together the next day to a bullfight about an hour's drive through barren hills from the city. Since Bill spoke no Spanish, the conversation remained between the lustrous poet and myself, becoming less impersonal as the kilometers rolled away. His clear voice softened into ardent murmurs of praise: my white, round arms (it was a hot, sleeveless day), like the arms of the women in Ingres paintings, arms one wanted to stroke and lick and nibble; my high, wide cheekbones come from some exotic, far kingdom; my crest of blond hair, the crown of a *reina*, his queen. (He addressed me as his *reina* for the rest of the day.)

As we neared the bull ring, he asked that Bill stop the car. He dashed into a roadside shop to return with a large bullfight poster of a torero, his body a taut, graceful curve flowing into a flourish of *banderillas*. The Cordobese offered it to me with a gallant phrase of admiration. My husband, who had naturally grown sullen in the course of the ride, brusquely offered the golden man money for the poster. It was refused with aristocratic disdain, and I asked Bill not to insist. I added a few words of apology for excluding him from our conversation as we later looked for our seats in the stands. The bull ring was small and crowded with locals who had come to see one of their boys conquer a bull. As far as I could see there was only one woman in the stands, I, sleeveless in a province where most women covered their arms. I had attended many bullfights in Mexico and was on the way to becoming a lightweight *aficionada*—not yet enough for sure expertise at judging the quality of bulls and toreros—but it was obvious to me that not one of this group was capable of pacing the death duet in what can be an awesome ritual.

The last torero was the boy from the nearby town, vociferously greeted by his many *compadres* and sponsors. His capework was unimpressive, and his retreat from the not-quite-dizzied bull lacked the arch-backed arrogance of the seasoned, confident bullfighter. However, he placed the *banderillas* neatly, and the kill escaped the butchery that too often betrays—and humiliates—the young matador. Because of the fairly decent kill and because the officials were his friends, if not his relatives, the boy was granted the honor of taking not one but two ears as his prize for gallantry and expertise. Head bared, smiling in glory, arms raised, hands holding the bloody ears, he paraded slowly around the ring to look for a recipient for one of the ears. He circled once, then began again and stopped in front of our seats. He bowed and gestured toward us—me, I realized. My mind and emotions raced between yearning for this extraordinary souvenir from the heart and guts of Spain and at the same time repelled by the imagined feel of the bloody piece of flesh of an animal I had seen killed—cleanly but with no great dignity. I chose to take the ear. As I began to stand to receive it, the golden man gently pushed me down and stepping in front of me, waved his arms and shook his head in gestures of rejection: No! No! The torero went on to throw the ear to one of the officials.

Back in the car I asked the Cordobese why he had refused the ear meant for me. He answered that it had not been a distinguished *corrida*, that the young man had not deserved the ears, not even one, and he didn't want me desecrated by an ignoble gesture rotten with falsities. (This was a memorable gift, this hidalgo gesture of Spanish honor bowing in high esteem to a *reina*.)

We arrived in Córdoba in time to have a drink at the street café attached to our hotel. Bill and I ate *tapas* of shrimp, while our friend ate little naked birds, his strong teeth making crackling sounds as they bit into the tiny beaks. I expected to be appalled at the sight and sound of someone eating thrushes, sparrows, possibly canaries, but I wasn't. In a youth that had been peppered with the words *crazy, very odd,* I had learned to accept the bizarre

in accents, in costumes, as in eating habits (a tolerance essential
to the travel writer I was later to become). Back to the *tapas* and
my Spanish admirer: Bill invited him to have dinner with us,
not very enthusiastically; it was the polite thing to do with a man
who would accept no fee for acting as our guide to the bullfight.
The man bowed his thanks and refused. Turning to me, he said,
"Leave him here. Come to my house. I'll fix you a wonderful
dinner with bottles of good, red Spanish wine. I'll teach you to
pour it into your mouth from a skin bag as we all do. Come.
Come. I implore you." He actually used the word *suplicar* which
suggested, of course, *supplicate*. I was moved by the soaring of
his words from earlier politeness to seductive flattery to avowals
of humility, enslavement. I refused his invitation; I couldn't do
this to anyone in my company, especially my husband, who had
already been humiliated enough that day.

As we shook hands and exchanged thanks and good-nights,
the Spaniard whispered that he would wait outside my hotel all
night, that I was to come down to meet him whenever I thought
Bill was fully asleep. Dinner was as usual in Spain, very late.
Bill, who was tired and still raw with insult, drank half a bottle
of wine and was fast asleep almost immediately after he got into
bed. I did not undress but sat for a while reading, or appearing
to read, waiting to be sure that he was actually sunk deeply in
sleep. After an hour or so I opened the door quietly and ran
swiftly down the carpeted corridor into the street. There he was,
waiting. As I approached him, he ran toward me. We did not
embrace but stood close together, he kissing my hands in a meld-
ing of deference and pleading. He was in love and I almost,
wrapped in flames and perfumes that revived half-forgotten, distant days. He begged me to return for a few essential bits of
clothing and to go with him to his house. He would make me
happy, joyously happy. He earned enough to keep us both mod-
estly. But I didn't want more, did I, when there was so much
love? And we could travel; he knew I liked that. Second-class
train fares were cheap, and we could visit his sister in Sevilla and
his father in Cádiz; we could stay with his old school friends in

Barcelona, a jewel of a city full of bright, talented, witty Cata-
lans—the city of young Picasso, of Miró, of Gaudi. I would ruin
not only his but my own life if I didn't stay.

I couldn't stay. I couldn't, I told him, leave Bill so abruptly,
without a word of warning or apology. Nor could I do this—
never—to my daughter whose only memory of a father was that
of a frighteningly sick man who died when she was eight and
who now basked in the pleasures of having a more privileged life
than she had had with me alone as a working mother. Though
he countered my excuses and urgently resisted them, he ultimately agreed they were reasonable. (I thought it best not to speak
of something I had observed about Latins: After three or four
steamy weeks of hyperbole and the twisting, coiling balletics of
sex, the lights that shone on me would move on to dazzle someone else, a piece of tall, blond exotica, perhaps from Sweden.
And what would I do? Where would I go? I might cable a friend
for fare home, but how would Lexie, as highly moral as many
youngsters are, greet me, if she would at all?)

I broke away from him, speaking thanks, many thanks, and
affection, and put in his hand a small Mexican rain god I had
been wearing as an amulet. Then up the stairs to our room,
where I spent a sleepless night sitting in an armchair, approving
and disapproving of myself. Of course, my primary obligation
was toward my daughter, and though my marriage was not of
stellar quality, I did enjoy the prosperity that gave me a roomy
apartment, charge accounts, an occasional designer dress, household help, and, most important, leisure. I had been working
since I was thirteen, and had never until my marriage with Bill
had the pleasure of playing with money, no longer a deadly
serious preoccupation as it had been all my life before. Should
I be pleased or not that the curiosity that had lured me toward
trouble in my adolescence was dulled? Not too dulled to wonder
if his body was as golden as his face, and were his mating gestures
as graceful as his words?

I'm no longer sure of his name—Carlos? Manuel? Then why
does the little Victrola that sings half-forgotten themes in my
mind now intone, "Go 'way from my window; go 'way from my

door. Go 'way, 'way, 'way from my bedside and bother me no more"?

My friend Eva, whose husband was then working in North Africa to help in the relocation of elderly threatened Jews, met me at the Tunis airport on my arrival from Rome. Her house, one of the most entertaining I had ever seen, was livable only because Eva had improvised its spaces and uses as she had done in the several countries in which they had worked and lived. This was a small, decayed beach palace still bearing faded spreads of its original Moslem-blue paint and sinking into the sands. In my several days there I never learned the geography of sudden nooks, the unexpectedly placed kitchen and toilets, nor could I identify the considerable number of children, except for hers, who ran in and out of the crooked, arched doors. Energetic, restless, and eager to explore everything about her and share it with friends, Eva dragged me soon after my arrival to the main souk, to examine its hammered metals, Berber rugs, gaudy cloth, and oversweet sweets. After several cups of mint tea and gossip about friends in Rome the next morning, we started out for a Jewish fete that, she told me, was particular to Tunis. Just where it took place I cannot remember, but we did stop on the way at the house of a friend who was busy digging up Roman tiles in her back garden and fitting them into the gaps of an already half-shaped handsome mosaic of fish and animals bordered by grapevines, resembling many I knew in and around Rome. Our friend was obviously living over a Carthaginian palace, or a set of baths or a theater—an enviably antique ruin that time and successive owners had shaped into an elderly, loosely designed Arab house.

After a lunch of flatbread and hummus (garlicked sesame–chick-pea mash) we went on to a village that seemed to be almost all synagogue, surrounded by a few low houses and a vivacious crowd eating at outdoor tables, running in and out of the synagogue (used as casually and companionably as medieval village churches once were), inviting us to sit, to come, to see. In the merry confusion I tried to push my way toward synagogue rituals, unsuccessfully; they were obviously limited to men. I wandered

about in the crowd, introduced by Eva to some of her friends—
she seemed to know everyone in the community—and being
accosted by women in long, hand-embroidered gowns I coveted
while they examined and envied my loose Western cotton dress
and light Italian sandals. With their admiration they offered
dishes of couscous, mounds of black and green olives, and layers
of honeyed cakes. While I nibbled, admiring and admired, now
without Eva whom I had left in an animated conversation—in
Arabic—with yet another friend, I noticed a man in a Western
suit and tie, pleasant looking and in early middle age, following
me at a tactful distance. When Eva reappeared she had the man
in tow and introduced him as a physician who served that community and several others, also head internist in a Tunis hospital.
His English was good, and as Eva slipped away to greet other
friends, I began to question him about his practice and the problems he coped with in these poor, dissolving Jewish villages that
had lost their youth to France, to Israel, and some to the States.
As we spoke he conducted me to a bench under a tree, signaling
politely to a young girl in a tinkling headdress to ask if she would
bring us tea. While we sipped we examined each other as tactfully
as we could. After an initial uneasy pause, he said, "I'd like to
ask you a question that I hope won't offend you. I am a widower
without children, and although I have busy days and a good
number of friends, I am, as you might imagine, frequently lonely.
I have been looking for a wife, a wife who would understand my
life and sympathize with my work, a woman I could talk with.
I have a large library and an extensive collection of records, and
I know that you, as a friend of Eva and her husband, must be
interested in books and music. It would be a wonderful thing for
me if you would consider marrying me; it would bring life to the
rest of my years. I am not religious but do enjoy some of the
ancient rituals, which—I can tell by your presence here—you
enjoy too. Your first response quite probably might be that it
would be impossible to leave your friends in New York, in London, in Rome, your life of concerts, museums, your wide traveling, your writing. I can promise that I will travel with you
frequently; I can arrange that with associates. We can go to New

York, Paris, London, anywhere you like for concerts, theater, friends, anything that would please you." Eva had apparently told him more about me than I knew about him, although the interests he revealed, his eager offers, his speech and appearance were promising.

I could not accept; the proposal was too sudden, and though he was willing to take on someone who was, in spite of superficial display and hearsay, basically a cypher, I could not. I was not eager for marriage—rather, I suspect, eager to avoid it. Too many people had left my life and he might too. And all over again I would have to—carefully, cell by cell, vein by vein, effort on effort—rebuild. I thanked him kindly; I was flattered by his offer, I assured him. I might have considered it seriously under different circumstances. And here I spoke one of my favorite lies, a useful lie that saved face all around—I had a man in Rome whom Eva did not know; we were talking of marriage and settling in the States. Truly, I was sorry about his loneliness, I knew how it felt, and hoped he would find a lovely, lively companion very soon. I then left him wrapped in his aloneness in the middle of that noisy, darting-here-and-there crowd. And I wondered for a few days how I might have done as the wife of a doctor in Tunis. Not too well, I thought; I know.

Among my assortment of friends were two Catholics, Betsy and George, torn between searing love and fear of church opprobium. George had been married and divorced, and already lived in a threatening cloud of hellfire. Betsy had never been married and had consented eagerly to the acts of adultery the church thundered about. Although they worked in different cities, they managed to meet frequently in storms of passion and guilt. Submitting to dogma, they stopped going to confession and mass. I stayed with Betsy in New York between voyages abroad. These were times when George could comfortably visit, letting it be known that he had come to see me, a beloved relative. This was mainly for the building superintendent, a zealot of many eyes and ears and unforgiving moral judgments. I also acted the duenna in a country house of an aristocratic beach town, an ancient cottage

Betsy had inherited from a spinster aunt who had lived there into the years of aged New England eccentricity and held in awe by the townspeople as such. (Later, cooler judgments would have put on her the less distinguished stamp of "Alzheimer's" when she chose to run her dry little body naked through winter snows.) The legend in this house was that George was my lover, Betsy a generous victim of the questionable friendship.

When George retired from a job he had long found onerous and Betsy inherited substantial sums of money from a collection of spinster aunts who died almost simultaneously, they were married in the chapel of an obscure rural church and began to travel widely, luxuriating in freedom from the jobs that had separated them and from the judgmental mutterings of Catholic acquaintances. They no longer needed a duenna but we all enjoyed a shadow of repetition of my role when I met them for the Christmas–New Year's holidays wherever they happened to be. One year it was Tangiers where they met me hung with golf clubs, symbols of a new enthusiasm and the leisure to cultivate it. After a few days in Tangier we headed southward, toward Marrakech, in spite of our knowledge that accommodations would be almost impossible to find during the holiday season. Unworried, carefree, we lingered for a few days in Meknes and a week in Fez— which held us—unable to leave the dyers stirring their pools of henna, dark rose, royal blue. And George had to watch for hours the shapers of brass ewers, as they brought them to form and shine. At night we hung around the storytellers and fire eaters with hundreds of others in a huge square that never slept.

We reached Marrakech on the night before Christmas. Like caricatures of the Holy Family we went from inn to inn, apartment to apartment, finally shop to shop, to find a place for our heads. Our first stop was, of course, the extravagant, sybaritic Mamounia Hotel, which looked at us sadly and shrugged its French shoulders in regret and helplessness although George exerted all his persuasive Irish charm and offered to pay handsomely above the ordinary price for any space. "Sorry, monsieur, there is absolutely nothing, and not for some days, until the holidays are over." After our hegira through almost every street in Marrakech we drove back to the Mamounia to sleep in our tiny hired Fiat—Betsy a full-bodied Ceres, George a slight leprechaun, and I somewhere between both in size, tucked tightly into our Topolino (Mickey Mouse Fiat) in the full, safe light of the hotel. At about three in the morning, a tap on the window. "Monsieur, monsieur, we have a room for you and the ladies. Please come right away." We unfolded ourselves and ran with this heaven-sent messenger to a magnificence of space in satins, velvets, ornate chairs and languid lounges. In one corner there stood a high silken screen and behind it a bed. This was to be mine while George and Betsy used the luxuriant bed, a silken altar to love, that filled the middle of the big room. We settled ourselves in for three or four joyous days, one of our many pleasures the discovery of a system by which Betsy and I were addressed as two members of a ménage à trois. How it was arranged we never understood; we conjectured that there were staff meetings every morning when it was decided who was to be wife and who mistress and how we were to be addressed that day. So, on the first day the men at the desk, the waiters, the doormen, the bellboys, addressed Betsy as "Madame" and myself as "Mademoiselle." The next day, without one slip, the whole crew greeted Betsy as "Mademoiselle" while I became "Madame." We tested the telephone operators, the concierges, everyone. Not one mistake in the meticulous French arrangement.

The merriment began to fade as we tore back, having made a late start, to catch a plane at Casablanca for a flight to Algiers, where I was to meet a friend who was on a committee, as Eva's husband was, of a Jewish rescue mission. We drove through early morning mists, skimming past goats, children, women carrying loads to market, none of them expecting swift little cars, frightening bulletlike cars, that ripped up the dust of their roads. As George sped along Betsy said nothing but I could see her usually open, candid face tighten. I couldn't say a word but sat stiff-backed and tense, so tense that my fingers stayed clenched for an hour or more, taut, bunched, immobile. When we reached the airport at Casablanca we were told that the Algiers plane had taken off and that there wouldn't be another for some hours. For a minute I didn't know whether I was relieved or not. I did have a firm appointment with the friend in Algiers; we were to take off from the airport directly to Djerba, a place I very much wanted to visit. While I stood regretting my friend's wasted time and my possible loss of Djerba, a thick black dread began to consume my body and mind. Terror imprisoned me; I could not, would not, go to Algiers; something dreadful was about to happen there. I pleaded with George to go on without me. He said not to be silly, this irrational behavior was not like me; I would soon get over it. Besides, we wanted to see more of North Africa, didn't we, and taking the next Algiers plane—we could have lunch as we waited—was the next logical step. I begged that we go on to Marseilles, instead; there was a half-empty plane leaving soon. It was a carefree, raffish city, I said, famous for its hospitable New Year's celebrations. Later they could go on to Algiers, not too long a trip, while I stayed in France. Please. George continued to look and talk skeptically about this aberration I was suffering but Betsy had been staring at my clenched hands and distorted face. She said, "Let's go to Marseilles."

We did, into rain and rain, cold rain that beat at the windows of our sailors' inn. We tried to entertain ourselves and each other in a small room; basic and tight, a sad contrast to the luxuriant glow and the sophisticated politeness of the Mamounia in Marrakech. During our semi-imprisonment, broken only by swift, wet forays to local shops for baguettes and pâté and wine, George began to show signs of a cold that soon turned into a fevered flu.

It was, finally, New Year's Eve. The rain had stopped and sounds of revelry were coming through our icy windows. While we women hovered between caution and courage, George insisted, absolutely, adamantly, on going out. We poured whiskey into him to enhance the panaceas sold us by a local pharmacist and were off to the waterfront and its beckoning calls and songs. We stopped into one or two places for a glass of wine and exchanges of New Year's greetings and then on to a third, where everyone kissed us as we entered. And continued kissing us while Madame cleared space for us among a few of her cronies who shoved at us a huge iron vat of bouillabaisse and the *aioli* sauce that heightened its fishy wonders. Madame kept insisting that we eat more and more of the gorgeous fish stew, scolding us for looking so peaked and George almost a death's-head. We obeyed, stuffing to bursting, kissed intermittently by Madame and her *copains*. When we were finally about to stagger out, awash with bouillabaisse and wine, every one of our new chums lined up to hug and kiss us and send us off to a bleary, very Happy New Year, an exultant experience for me, who had sat through cool, formal New Year's eves in Paris.

George and Betsy went on, I don't remember where, but I stopped in Nice to pick up mail at a hotel whose proprietor was an old acquaintance. There I found a letter, written a week or two before, pleading with me, warning me, that I not, under any circumstances, go to Algiers. My friend there had been imprisoned for trying to export Jewish money and goods to relatives in France, an illegal act for Jews. Had I looked for him I would undoubtedly have been arrested and imprisoned as an accomplice.

He was released, I learned later, after some months in a stinking cell, rescued by an international human rights organization. His story is now old and almost forgotten, but my one experience of prophecy, of seeing across great distances, of being a sibyl, an intimate of future disaster, left me frightened of the secrets, suddenly to reveal themselves, in the being I thought I knew.

I had met both of the friends with whom I later traveled in Europe at first in Mexico City shortly after my arrival there to write the allures and mysteries, the magnificences of Mexico's past and the haplessness of its present. I had been asked in New York to search out a young rabbi I had once met, a dreamer fired by two missions: to reform traditional liturgical practices and to deliver Mexican peasants from their dour, hungry lives (an impossible program on both counts; he didn't stay long). I, having been traduced by the Mexican sunshine, was not yet prepared for the cold nights and sat blue and folded in on myself, shivering—no coat, no sweater, no rebozo—in the large, unheated synagogue. At the end of the service, an attractive, well-dressed woman approached me, saying, "Come home with me; I live nearby and I'll lend you a sweater. The sweater developed into a friendship that gave me a home in a large, airy apartment where I could scrub the dust off my skin, the stains off my clothing, after weeks of exploring primitive hinterlands. There I could change my diet of bananas, peanuts, and mangoes for Mexican-European delights prepared by two gentle, gifted maids. (Through vicissitudes and long separations, Fanny and I stay linked to each other.)

Stella was someone I met at a party in Mexico City. We made no mark on each other. It was some time later, in New York, that I received a call from her asking if we might meet for lunch. She had phoned me—why me, hardly an acquaintance?—to discuss a family problem she could not handle. Out of the lessons my analysis had taught me, I made a few tentative suggestions that seemed to ease her. The amateur-therapist and eager-patient roles burgeoned as a lively, talkative connection. She had never had a sister, I had lost mine, and we tacitly appointed each other the missing sisters. She was the only friend with whom I fought long, hard, loud battles—one shrieking match winging us from Ninety-sixth Street at Madison Avenue all the way to Thirty-fourth Street at a furious pace, bumping into passersby, disregarding traffic, catching comments and warning from every side. We didn't care; it was, though not admitted, one of our methods of release from controlled lives and basically, thoroughly pleasurable. Our arguments never involved small matters (we had no objections to each other's tastes and habits); they concentrated on how we designed our lives. Why was I schlepping around Mexico and Europe alone when I could find an attractive prosperous man to marry in the States and settle down to safeties and comforts? Why didn't she, with grown children and a husband frequently away on long business trips, try some of the freedoms, pleasures, and enlightenments I was living? We fought over these questions like sisters: intimately, insultingly, shrilly, with never the threat of profound anger or of separation.

It was in Stella's house that I lived when I made my annual trip back to renew my ties in New York, which was, in spite of

rewarding, happy substitutes—Morelia, Rome, Paris, London—
home. We talked, we shopped, we ate, we visited with friends,
went to the movies, all the ordinary, easy pleasures that I sometimes missed living alone. One New York–Stella day leaps up
vividly. It was a rainy, cold day and Stella suggested an unusual
entertainment, that we smoke some grass. Although I had pulled
on the rare marijuana cigarette from the time I was an adolescent
(when the word was *reefer*), she never had. One of her friends
who had a backyard garden had raised a few bushes from which
she had given Stella a bunch of dried leaves. We made two
bundles of the leaves, as fat as the cigars smoked by old-time
movie gangsters, and puffed and choked on them. As we pulled,
swallowed, and coughed, we began to laugh uproariously, finding
each other excruciatingly witty. Soon, ravenously hungry, we
raided the refrigerator, gorging on everything we could find in
it, stuffing and swallowing—fast, fast—including the boneless
slices of chicken put aside daily for the Siamese cat who was
spoiled as prayerfully as if she were an Egyptian cat goddess. After
the huge, shapeless feast we slept for hours, waking up at some
odd hour, giggling and weaving about, ready to order up a
Chinese feast from a local restaurant. The next day was not so
good; we were misty, dull, swollen with bellyaches.

After much cajoling I convinced Stella to join me in Europe,
to accompany me on one of my work trips. I introduced her to
neat little almshouses in obscure parts of London, to the decrepit
charms of Shakespeare's Southwark, to Saint Helen's Church in
the very old city, to the Bermondsey market at the first icy hours
of the winter dawn. I dragged her on foot—she always pleaded
for taxis—to my favorite mosaics in Santa Prassede's church in
Rome and down the narrow *salita* that ran from the Aventine to
the Tiber and the medieval ghetto. Our most memorable day
was her birthday. We were, Fanny along with us, in Florence,
where I catapulted them from Masaccio to Donatello to Fra
Angelico to Michelangelo; more slowly through the Uffizi and
the Bargello and the Pitti and, and, and (Stella moaning for taxis).
Then back to the straw market, where I bought Stella a shawl,
telling her that it wasn't the important present. I led them to

Giotto's tower and there stopped to dedicate it to her as the real birthday gift. She knew how much I treasured its joyous lift and laughing colors and was moved, staring at it with pleasure for several minutes. (She, too, in spite of life's stumbling blocks and pitfalls, pleases me and I her.)

Our first meeting place had been Siena, as sacred a city to many—I among them—as Jerusalem. We worshipped before the smooth, ample, contented *Peace* and the gurgling colored pools of the skirts of girls dancing in Ambrogio Lorenzetti's "Good Government" city; stood awed by Simone Martini's great *condottiero* and Duccio's panels and fell in love with the plump, golden saints in the museum. We then pushed on (it is always too soon) to Florence.

On then, with stops at friendly, third-class hotels and *mamma-e-pappa trattorie* to Ravenna, to stand in the shimmer of myriad mosaics and their play of light on superb hieratic figures. We waited for them to speak, to command, especially the Empress Theodora, crowned and garlanded with jewels, her face imperious, the queen of her Byzantine world as Cleopatra was the supreme power of her Egypt. She had the power, as she stood in her glowing light, not only to rule us from her canopied room in the Church of San Vitale but to make of *us* Theodora, proud necked, solemn eyed. We were still empresses, bejeweled, tall and proud, as we later made our slow, noble way to the railroad station and the train that was to take us northward to Venice.

Theodora left us almost completely, a faintly shining shadow, on the train; we became American travelers, hungry for our lunch of several thick porchetta sandwiches, paper cornucopias of olives, and bags of peaches that poured Italian sun onto our chins and hands. Neither Fanny nor Stella had ever been in Italy and had, like most tourists, become happily manic with the art; the good-natured Italian anarchy; the earthy skepticisms; the beauties of cypresses, olive groves, and vineyards gathered together as masterly compositions. Throughout the train ride we called to each other pointing out the vines clinging to old olive trees, the little girls dragging wheeled boxes of babies, the smooth purple jewels of eggplants heaped in a yellow market basket, the flapping, squalling chicken swinging from the hand of a black-shawled old lady. And we ate and ate with the raw gusto we had borrowed from our Italian fellow passengers, particularly a gaggle of young nuns feeding rapaciously out of paper bundles wrapped in white cloth.

Stupefied with food, tired with the effort to see all the churches in Ravenna, we allowed our heads to droop; our arms fell idly into our laps, our eyes closed. A light tap on my shoulder awakened me. My eyes rose to a royal face like that of the Emperor Justinian in the mosaics, touched with the smile of Mastroianni and rakishly topped by a conductor's cap. I handed him our tickets. He stared at me for a long moment and then moved on to the little nuns. About a half hour later, while my friends were fully asleep, he returned and sat himself in a seat across from me. I was accustomed to the frank leer, the pinch on the bottom, the mutter of invitations to love and bed, but not to a long, solemn look that did not wander to my body but stayed with my face. "*Lei parla Italiano, non è vero?*" "*Si.*" Slowly, without an effort to charm, without a note of flirtatiousness, he began to tell me that—he was almost sure—he loved me. He had been watching me from the end of the car; I had struck him with the force of a bolt of lightning. I laughed, entertained and flattered, and using a common response to Italian declarations, said somewhat coyly, "Thank you very much, but unfortunately I don't feel the same way for you." Looking more and more like Mastroianni, he bent over me, his voice appealing, importunate. He had a wife and children—he would not lie to me—but the irregular hours of his work gave him considerable freedoms. He could arrange with union mates to take sections of his run so that we might meet in Rimini soon, maybe tomorrow. Or, since I probably felt responsible for them, I might settle my friends in Venice. He would meet me there and take me to his sister's house in Padua, a nice house near Giotto's murals. She was an older sister, like a mother to him; she did not like his wife and always kept a room for him alone although the rest of her apartment was a *pensione* and I might enjoy its liveliness and the sights of the city on the days he could not be with me. He bent lower and lower over me, whispering, his back a begging arch, his face urging, pleading. What was happening? Who was this creature of swift, immortal love, like a maddened knight out of a chivalric romance, like Tristan, like Orlando? The blows of sudden love—Romeo and Juliet, Mimi and Rodolfo, Paolo and Francesca, and a populace of love-mad literary characters—still attracted my grown self as they had my adolescent one. Consent? And why not? He would probably leave me stranded in Padua at one time or another. So what? I would hurt and heal. There was no one to judge me whose judgment mattered. I had had no binding attachment since Tom in Mexico. But what if his sister disliked me as much as she did his wife? What if the wife tracked me down and, like any furious Italian wife, tried to tear my hair out or went for my eyes? Suddenly a vivid, grotesque scene from *Rosenkavalier:* a black-clad woman leading a chorus of wailing children asking for pity and alms. That did it: the pitiful woman and the shrieking children in an ironic scene that filled my eyes and ears. I explained to Orlando that an affair as he designed it would be lovely but impossible; I had to travel for my work and must soon leave his Adriatic route. Sorry, so very sorry, and *mille grazie.* No regrets; a swift light like that of a glowworm, a bit magical, a bit laughable, as I found my head singing Strauss as background music to Alec Guinness in *The Captain's Paradise,* a 1950s film.

21

Italians

To the skeptical surprise of my friends (and, to a degree, my own) I had no affairs in my many months in Italy—the land of soaring operatic love duets, of impassioned painting as religion and eroticism, ceaseless chanting in song, story, and conversation, about *amore*. After I had been not-too-surreptitiously grabbed and pinched by friends of friends; after thwarting countless pickups in the street and cajoling voices from cars; after yelling *"Va te ne"* to old crocks whose gimpy legs, gallant as they were, could not always keep up with my quickened stride; after lingering in shops and cafés to wear out the patience of the persistent middle-aged (all certainly married with a girl on the side), my mind and taste—an actual physical taste, as if I had been feeding on too much oily and garlicky pasta—recoiled. No! No! No more! Short, sad lives with men I had known before, elsewhere, left me a little cautious, but mainly empty of interest.

Three possible entanglements offered themselves, none of stirring quality. A bisexual friend, who had once said to a group on the beach at Fregene that he would sleep with anyone reasonably clean and minimally attractive, offered himself to me, the most pallid of invitations. Going to bed with me would mean going to bed with anyone, everyone, no one. I shrank from the anonymity, from being one of an infinity of depositories. And there was the Yugoslav I had met in New York who had mysterious businesses that called him to Italy frequently. It was his habit to take me to dinner, come home with me and—stretched out on my bed, arms folded under his head—talk and talk in fairly good English, erasing slow hours until the singing little idiot I carried in my head began to chant, "If you don't like my cherries why do you shake my tree?" With this I would tell him to go, kiss him in a motherly style on the cheek and forehead, and then close the door on him. His supposed ploy was to wait for me to pounce, to seduce, to rape him. I'd had enough of that a long time before. During my teenage years, with their confusion of conflicting self-portraits, I would occasionally decide to take aggressive steps in a courtship. That approach never served me; I felt like an Amazon butcher readying to knock out the brains of a lamb while I really wanted to be a wood nymph, ribbons flying coquettishly, almost within reach of a faun with witty, salacious lips.

The third Rome Lothario (only joking, one had to understand) would grab my breasts in his large hands, usually in a corner of a hallway and, pushing his body against mine, prove what I was able to do to him; lucky, sexy me. My amulets against these assaults were the romantic pulses and hearts lent me by Keats and Schubert, whom I would never betray so coarsely. So, no Italian love affairs, no one to whom I could say, "Thou art the grave where buried love doth live, / Hung with the trophies of my lovers gone." Instead, a clear, broad, and free horizon, un-hampered freshness, and undiluted attention for my Italian work, which gave me other modes of falling in love and staying, with no complications, forever in love. (I know and love Siena more deeply and indelibly than men with whom I've had tentative little amorous passages; Todi is clearer and bound in richer affection than a face that once tried to share my pillow. Gubbio is my Don Quixote and Rome my Don Giovanni, I his besotted, never-to-be-cured Elvira.)

He was an architect, meagerly employed and thus often free to show me the dignity and musicality of the mosaics in the Church of Santa Prassede, the setting for one of Robert Browning's poems.

It was he who helped me and my quaking body stand on the pinnacle platform of Saint Peter's, wrapping my arms tightly in his. It was he who took me to the Colosseum one midnight to observe a gathering of "queens," gorgeous grotesques worshipped like deities by their adoring subjects, the scene a quirky Walpurgisnacht as the adherents of one majestic figure shrieked insults at the cohorts of another. My architect directed me, informative and entertaining, through the paleo-Christian museums of the Vatican and through the bright rags of the flea market at the Porta Portese. He was of medium height and slender, his face not handsome but impressive, with the resolute, sharply carved features of a Memling portrait. Like many architects he dressed with a certain distinction—an unusual scarf, a jaunty beret, never too much but enough to distinguish him as an artist, a scholar, a man of independent tastes.

One spring afternoon—I remember that I was trying to write the ancient sadness of the marble columns at the edge of Rome's ghetto—my phone rang. It was my architect friend, Guido, weeping, barely coherent. I could understand that he was in the railroad station. Where was he going? He didn't know. Why was he at the railroad station? He didn't know. "Come to my house, right away," suddenly the strong Jewish (or Italian) mother. "Get on the bus and come here directly!" I spent a nervous hour looking out the window, up and down the street, and then ran out to stand at the nearest bus stop. I found him wandering close by as if he didn't know which direction to take to my house. He was still weeping, the tears coursing down his cheeks. The distinguished scarf and beret were gone; he looked depleted, poor, not the quick, graceful man I knew and admired. I led him to my house where I put before him wine and cheese and the country bread we both liked. When his face had gathered itself together I asked him what had happened, what had so hurt him that he had to run blindly to anywhere, nowhere.

I knew Guido lived with a man, Riccardo, whom I had met only once. I had no sure knowledge of their relationship: lovers probably, but to what degree? Was this convenient rent sharing with a bit of sex now and then or was it total immersion in one radiant being? If Riccardo was that being, it appeared that his shining image had turned to dross this insupportable day. Guido had told Ric that he would be home at five but returned at three for some sketches he had forgotten. In the kitchen he found a quartet of louts who greeted him with, "Come, *bello*, eat," as their fingers pulled strands of spaghetti out of a communal bowl. Two other boys were making love on his bed. Ric himself was on the living room floor playing steambath games with a squirming boy. Sickened by Ric's use of their house as a bordello, by this testament of Ric's wide-ranging infidelity, disgusted by the spill of semen on his Oriental carpet and the steamy coiling of bodies on the fine lace coverlet his mother had made, his life and its neat shapes a garbage heap, he had to run. Where? The railroad station would decide, but he had little money with him and was incapable of making a choice between nearby towns— Viterbo, Orvieto, Narni, Terni—and in his rage and powerlessness began to cry.

I was his closest heterosexual friend, he truly loved me, he said. Although he was one of them, he loathed *"frosci,"* homosexuals; he didn't trust them, a heedless, perfidious race, a tribe of vicious infants. Even if he had to become a monk, a silent, mystical Carmelite, no more of *them*. I broke into his tirade to ask where his hat and scarf had gone. He had thrown them away as he ran to the station. His humiliated house, Ric's disgusting taste for rough trade, made him feel like a liar, a fraud too, so he tore off the affectations and dropped them, wherever. I suggested that he not try to return to his apartment for a while; he could use my guest room for as long as he chose, and we did pleasant, calming things in the next two or three days. We shopped for fruit and vegetables in the small market under the building that bore witness to the residency of the Brownings there, Robert's famous avowal of love for Italy carved into the walls as *Aprendo il mio cuore vi trovaste inciso Italia.* We spent one long gray day (good weather and color for ruins, Guido said) exploring the Forum and Michelangelo's Campidoglio; another day among the gardens and Greco-Roman antiquities in the museum of the Baths of Diocletian, closing that day with a long walk across the

city to the Tiber and a café called Bianca Neve (Snow White)
for its unique confection, a *mela stregata* (poisoned apple).

After the days with me, Guido went to live with relatives in
the suburbs. I continued to see him frequently, delighted with
the sounder mood that induced him to borrow money from his
brother for a trip abroad, probably America, where they seemed
to use architects and paid them well. I saw him some years later
in New York. He was thriving, speaking impeccable English,
sporting a broad, multicolored cravat and a hat that was a close
copy of that once worn by Frank Lloyd Wright.

While I was still in Rome I ran into Ric on the Piazza di Spagna,
had a capuccino with him at a local café, and, in spite of myself,
began to like him and his strong Roman head, his robust, good-
humored manner. We became friendly enough for him to invite
me to spend a day or two at the country house of an absent cousin
near Arezzo. I arrived early on a Sunday. The kitchen was already
full of young men preparing soups and vegetables, exclaiming
over their lovely color and the perfection of their shapes. Look
at the shine on that eggplant! Look at the form and perky stem
of this tomato! They might have been sculptors admiring a fine
piece of stone, painters pleased with a newly ground color, or
their own grandmothers wondering at the beauty of their market
purchases.

After a large midday meal of pasta, chicken, country bread,
heavy wine, and fruit, I took a nap. I awoke to see the boys
spreading blankets and sheets under the olive trees on the rise
across from the front doorway. There must certainly have been
more efficient ways to pick ripe olives, but the boys were using
a technique, or lack of one, that went back to the Caesars and
before—shaking and beating at the trees, knocking off the high
fruits with long sticks and rakes. As the bags of olives were stacked
under the porch eaves, the birds began their evening twittering.
Ric said that soon the nightingales would sing their mating songs.
We sat waiting silently as the air became still and pale, as the
shadows of the trees lengthened. A lacework of trills came to
embroider the dusk; the delicate patterns of nightingale tunes first

from the right of our valley and then, after a pause, as if there were a thoughtful message to return, light glittering trills from the left. It stayed a short and lovely time, this filigreed skyful of myriad tunes.

That day—the joy in the forms of the earth's yield, the crusty country bread, the hearty wine, the succulent fruit, the shimmering of silver gray olive leaves, and the songs of nightingales—remains one of the happiest and most Italian of rural days in my memory. It all must have affected the boys as well. I heard no obscenities, saw no salacious gestures; the sense of being in a pure, graceful place and time must have touched them, too.

One weekend of another visit to Ric's borrowed country house, Sunday turned raw and gusty, pulling leaves and branches off the trees, dashing them against the windows. It was a fine day for gossip and big bowls of hot soup and reminiscing. "Remember when?" brought forth laughter and stories that gave me a few new pictures of "gay" life in Italy. Remember when Gino had been thrown out of a café not because he had decided to dance on a table but because the table was frail and broke under his thick, heavy flesh? This called, naturally, for emptying a carafe of wine over the innkeeper's head and shoulders. Remember when Enrico was picked up near the Uffizi in Florence by a rich Swede in a stunning white car, driving with the supercilious bearing of a movie star? Enrico, the Swede, and the car were stopped on the Appian Way by a couple of motorcycle cops who put them through tough questioning that proved the shining white car did not belong to the glittering blond gentleman with the heavy gold chains on his wrists. He was simply a thief, and poor Aldo had to explain that he was a pickup, "one of those" (*"finocchio,"* one of the cops spat out) trying to earn a few lire and had nothing to do with the theft. Followed by a string of insults, he slinked away while his gentleman stayed. Probably, one of the boys added, to be imprisoned for a long time; Italian justice, we know, crawls at a cruel pace, further slowed by not a whit of sympathy for foreign thieves.

"Remember," someone shouted laughingly, "Franco's courtship and wedding?" One courteous young man filled in the background of the story for me. Franco had lived as servant and lover with a German professor whose home was a baroque palace near Asolo. He was studying and writing an interminable book on Piero della Francesca, frequently visiting, with Franco as companion, the paintings in Arezzo, in Sansepolcro, and Urbino. It wasn't a bad life, they all agreed, interesting and well paid, and the German (*"disfortunatamente,"* someone commented) was a rock of fidelity. Background set for me, our narrator went on: In the course of a visit to a local farmer to buy eggs, Franco took one drowning look at a newly hired hand and fell desperately in love with the boy. He found a fertility of excuses to return to the farm: He needed more chickens for Sunday's big dinner; maybe the farmer would take five baskets of grapes from their vineyard in exchange for a bagful of his choice tomatoes; he needed a bicycle pump, maybe he could borrow it from the farmer. The professor became infuriated as his suppers were, more and more, yesterday's scraps, his coffee cold and stale, his bed hastily arranged in big lumps—cuts that grew to knife wounds of suspicion. Franco could not give up his exceedingly lucrative position nor would he relinquish the surreptitious pleasures in which the boy joined him: behind a hayrick, in a toolshed, hidden in a dense clump of bushes. Pragmatic and resourceful as most Italians are, Franco worked out a solution to his dilemma: He would marry the farmer's puffy spinster daughter if her father would release the boy (who, it was said, he also enjoyed) so that Franco might hire him as gardener and handyman for the professor's estate. It was arranged (the Italian word *combinato* says it better), the spinster swinging between bewilderment and joy as Franco bought her bangles and colored combs for her matted hair, kissing her laundry-reddened hands and addressing her as *"tesoro."* The boy liked the possibility of improving his status and his love life. Everyone was happy but the professor, who promised Franco all sorts of expensive presents, maybe even a new motorbike, if he would drop the crazy scheme. Franco held fast and won out.

There was a wedding, a tripartite wedding, attended by curious relatives and friends who came considerable distances to observe and enjoy the German's hospitality, reluctantly offered but nevertheless generous. The Communists, who would not attend a Catholic ceremony, devised their own rites based on love and revolution. The agnostics sat with the anarchists for a session of extolling the joys of love and sex in a totally unfettered society. A few Catholic guests and the wedding couple were finally released to the patient local priest for a swift set of gestures and words and a quick, disgruntled departure. (The story was beautifully told, with lively pantomime and voice changes that made of it a *commedia del arte* performance.)

The storytelling continued with several such revealing stories; clearly, the homosexual life was as full of weird turns, bad jokes, and jolts as that of heterosexuals. In city walks with these new acquaintances I refined the knowledge I had had from Guido. I learned to watch and enjoy the music of eye duets; the tentative, cautious approaches; the relief of agreements. Along the riverbank, in the corridors and ticket lines of the railroad station, in the cafés of certain quarters, I learned to tell the transvestites from the authentically female prostitutes and envied the skill of the transformed boys in the draping of seductive hairpieces and their masterly use of makeup. I tried to copy them when I was bored with myself and once, more elaborately, when I was invited to a gay party. My transformed self was not a success. Among the handsome women and pretty men—a number of them casually bisexual, my hostess friend pointed out—I walked a tightrope, rehearsing in my head just how to say, "No, thank you. You're truly enchanting, but I'm seriously attached to someone else. No. She—he?—isn't here tonight." All I could actually manage was a stupid face spread in a foolish grin. I couldn't hide in ignorance of Italian because at that time I had it fairly glibly. Idiocy was the solution and stinginess an added protection when I refused to chip in for a deck of cocaine that could be bought around the corner from the newsdealer's son. I wouldn't make the contribution because, I said—and it was true—that cocaine smelled like medicine and hurt my nose; sorry, count me out. I was, I'm sure, criticized later for my lack of team spirit and courage. Enough money was collected, without my tithe,

though. The contents of the small white envelope were carefully
poured onto a mirror and, with the edge of a playing card, cut
into fifteen narrow paths, a snort for each contributor. The talk
grew more voluble, the laughter louder. I doubted whether this
was the effect of the drug, more likely a self-induced conviction
that it should be. The boy around the corner was a well-known
corrupter of cocaine, adding substantial quantities of flour and
talc to his mix; the merry sniffers had been gypped, and yet not.
I slipped out early, with no good-byes, no thank-yous.

I had, shortly after the party, the last of my encounters with
cocaine. During one particularly broke month, my advance
money wearing thin, my meager alimony slow and further held
up by a common feature of life in Rome—a sudden, unan-
nounced postal strike—I decided to sublet my choice apartment
and live as cheaply as possible for two or three months. I inquired
among my friends who might know of cheap *pensione*. It appeared
that the newsvendor's wife, the mother of the local supplier, had
two or three small rooms to rent; she was a pretty good cook,
too, I was told. I moved in and stayed quite contentedly, counting
my improved moneys, until two incidents urged me out. At about
two o'clock one morning I was awakened by harried whispers
coming from the kitchen. When I looked in I saw the newsvendor, his wife, and his son frantically wiping the table, sweeping
the floor, peering deeply into drawers and cupboards. They were
pouring the pale dust they collected into a bowl covered with a
fine linen handkerchief; the powder sifted through the linen, then
poured into a dark wine bottle. The son, both distraught and
amused, explained that he had put his cocaine supply in a thermos bottle at the top of a closet, never realizing that it stood too
close to a hot water pipe. The steady heat finally exploded the
thermos, which spread its fine, expensive mist all over the kitchen
and the careful dusting, the linen sieve, were designed to gather
as much cocaine as could be rescued. The dark wine bottle came
to rest inside the small clothes washer Mrs. Newsvendor never
used; she preferred her more trustworthy scrubbing board and the
sociability of clotheslines that crossed her backyard.

My second adventure in the house awakened me with a fright-

ening start, again very early one morning. There was a loud
banging at the door punctuated with several voices shouting,
"Police! Open up!" Before I could jump out of bed, I found a
heavy-booted young Che Guevara with wild beard, wild hair,
and malevolent eyes standing over me, his machine gun pointed
at my throat. My landlady yelled at him from my doorway,
"*Americana, ammalata* [sick]," as a neat man in normal clothing
and hair grabbed Che, pulled his machine gun from him, and
pointed him out the door. It appeared that someone had directed
a finger at the dealer and the police, a number of them a new
contingent of hell-bent-for-heroic-deeds boys, came to make a
bust. Sending a few more of the Ches out to wait in the wagon
below, two older, calmer men looked into several closets and
chests, tasted of the jars of rice and flour, then left.

And so did I, that very day, almost immediately after the
polite plainclothesmen and their new Sicilian recruits (whose life
choices, incidentally, were limited to unemployment, soldiering,
and joining the police force or a thieves' gang) left. I was ready
for a Sicilian who might steal my purse or tear an earring from
my flesh if he thought it was gold, but close confrontation with
a machine gun? The mothers and sisters of these young Sicilians
had approached me at bus stops in Palermo with, "Watcha you
beg, leddy," and I hugged my pocketbook to me as if it were a
sick child. Three men at a card stand near one of Palermo's
graceful moresque churches gave me the lesson supreme: Don't
carry a bag at all, but put your money in your bra, and they
demonstrated, bra and its contents stroked by sets of rough, fun-
loving fingers. It was a memorable lesson that I couldn't help
finding amusing when, perhaps, I should have felt assaulted. In
any case I met only female solicitude and rough, male playfulness
but never, never a gun of any kind in the hands of a Sicilian—
except as a Roman police recruit.

22

Russians and Other Slavs

WE—a couple who were close friends and I—were on the first yachting trip organized by the Yugoslav tourist authorities (whether there were others later I never could ascertain). It was not a lordly vessel but reasonably usable and had the distinction of a crew of three to see to three passengers. There was a captain—a square bundle of Sicilian muscles, deep-grained wrinkles cut into his leather face and an indigenously Italian confidence in his allure though he was well past sixty. Since I was somewhat older than my friends and single, he was entitled to select me as his particular companion and was happy to do me the honor. Besides the charms of the old dance of his amiability melded with my persistent gentle rejection—a mild pleasure for all—he had substantial value as a friend of every bootlegger along the coast—someone who claimed he made wine only for himself and his friends and never enough to submit to the local cooperative, or whatever the uncertain socialist state required of him.

Yugoslav rules were wavery things, and we managed to sail into many tiny harbors, find a friend, and, for a small exchange of coins and bottles, stock up on the local blood-red rough and the more feminine imitations of Hungarian Tokay.

The second member of our crew was the cook, of whom we still speak with nostalgic affection. About forty years old, he had a newborn face, a naive face full of wonderment at our language, our clothing, our pleasures, as if he were observing the lives of gods from a foreign planet. As a conscientious cook, he made heroic efforts to shop for the most delectable and fresh fish he could find on the local docks, furious that the Mediterranean was losing all the fishy wonders he had known in his youth, and, loving us with a springtime passion, wanting us to enjoy them. He tried desperately, searching among fishing cronies for the best and most unusual to serve us, and fell into hours of depression if he thought a meal was not quite the Lucullan feast he had hoped. Generous, affectionate, delicate within his disordered bulk, he was a delight.

Less lovable was our cabin boy, an eighteen-year-old with a long, supple diver's body. He was disagreeably slouchy as he made the beds or cleared the table but came to resplendent life when he postured at the mast as we approached a port, posed in compositions of muscles that were imitations of strongmen in physical culture magazines, pictures often suggested by Greek sculptures. The boy's poses were carefully prepared, rehearsed, and reenacted each time a port drew near. The women selling fish, the women mending nets, and especially the girls of the village were thus apprised of the treat in store for them. There must have been a special girl or girls in Korcula, who deserved a classic pose that was difficult to hold, clearly a strain on the tan satin ropes of flesh but obviously worth the effort.

Once in a while the cook, the captain, and we Americans went dancing in some village square or another. Sporting a be-plumed Bersagliere hat, as coquettish as a boa on a woman's shoulders, the captain spoke of himself as the Lupo del Mare—Wolf of the Sea—and wore a wolfish leer throughout the evening. The cook clumped around happily with us and with some of the girls who otherwise sat around on park benches or danced dully with each other (their boys often choosing to play cards with their cronies). The cabin boy never came with us; he had other entertainments, possibly inspired by his gorgeous acrobatics on the mast.

Sunning, drinking, eating; watching the rehearsals of our Adonis; loving our cook; talking, talking, often into the realms of fantasy. (I thought, for instance, that Colette and I should write each other's autobiographies, a writing fancy I still find attractive.) Leaving the boat, we traveled inland for a while and then turned to Dubrovnik, whose polished old cobbles I can still feel as satin under my feet. (There was something Isadora Duncanish about my walking barefoot in Dubrovnik, and I found it fun to posture like her while other tourists stared.) The city was joyfully frenetic with entertainment; concerts of chamber music in antique palace salons, folk dancing and more folk dancing in any and every bare broad space. The men's dances, as in many countries, were daring, wild with macho swordplay and high athleticism, much more imaginative than those of the women, whose role was to twirl their plump, colorful skirts, their faces passive but for an occasional smile, a winsome simper. In one of the parks we saw a superb performance of *Twelfth Night* performed by actors who were skilled acrobats and dancers. A clump of trees and a large rock served as sets. Shakespeare sang and laughed as merrily in Serbo-Croatian as he did in English.

Freed of the rudimentary shower on the yacht, we swam and wallowed in the pool of our Dubrovnik hotel—until a subterranean rope swung maliciously to the surface and slashed across George's eye. His vision never especially sharp and a constant cause for concern, George rose from the water trembling and crying for help. He could not open either eye; both teared profusely. We pulled him out and, seating him in a poolside chair, ran to the desk to ask for the address of an eye doctor and a taxi to take us to him. The offices we were driven to were small, basic enclosures. We were conducted to one of these boxes to wait, George terrified and shaking, both his eyes tight shut and tearing heavily. The doctor appeared within fifteen minutes, which anxiety had stretched to hours. She was a large woman, sturdy as a rock, with the strong voice and face of the tractor-driving women of early Russian films. She forced George's eyes open, poured some drops into them, and dismissed him with, "What are you making such a fuss about? You still have one good eye. Next patient."

The next day Colette and George took off for the States while I remained, accompanied by a driver and a guide-translator, a pretty college student with understandable if eccentric English. I had many questions for her, serious questions: What sort of socialism encompassed variations that touched on minor capitalistic enterprises that vaguely resembled the *kibbutzim* of Israel, quite another form of socialism. Was there more cooperation or still some of the old hostilities between provinces? She, however, had no interest in politics and queried me about the husbands Elizabeth Taylor had accumulated. Was there a new picture being made by Cary Grant? She could hardly wait to see it—she adored him—if it ever came to Yugoslavia.

My indifference to and ignorance of the lives of Elizabeth Taylor and Cary Grant established her in the serious job of guide. In some time-stricken little hut that might have been a chapel, she introduced me to a tall, cadaverous, thinly bearded man with wild eyes wrapped in a dirty worn cloak that might once have been a monk's habit. They seemed to know each other well, and on a word from her, he took from the wall a one-stringed lutelike instrument and, strumming it tunelessly and incessantly, droned out, she explained to me, details of his ancestry back and back to a revered abbot who lived in a sacred monastery on a high, difficult hill, a hill only the most devout would or could climb— an unbearably dull story, and the hut stank.

In her fervor of guiding—interspersed with flirting to collect partners at village dances—she took me to a small church where, she said, Cyrillic writing had been invented by its monks. On the shores of Lake Ohrid, in a meshwork of drying nets and women showing off the prizes of their catch, she helped me buy— almost wrest—one woman's earrings made of old coins and a hair ornament to match; clanging, gypsylike, large, and bold, waiting to be given to Colette's daugher—not yet born—on her twentieth birthday. The one act of provincial wariness I had heard about and finally witnessed was a meeting between my blond guide and a woman at the border of Macedonia. The woman, dark, with high cheekbones and eyebrows that seemed to meet as one—common in the area and reminiscent of the figures in Persian prints—drew herself up flat and straight and spat out the one word, *"Makedonski."* My girl, too, became tall, flat, and straight and spurted out loudly, defiantly, *"Srbirski."*

I left the girl and the driver in Zagreb to fly on to Belgrade, a dull city of row on row of square, state buildings in the Stalin-Mussolini style and there encountered a man whose eyes I had earlier felt as I helped a sick girl who sat next to me on the plane. My short time with him, painful and ultimately pointless, was so peculiar that I have appointed it the story of someone else, not me. I refuse it.

Should I ever be struck with a total loss of memory, no images or words to utter them, there will remain, I am certain, the one Greek word, *melteme,* and the blows of its malevolence. We met in Athens—Colette, George, Marie, Ed, and myself—planning to sail among the Greek islands. The only boat we could find in Piraeus was a tired thing that might sleep four but not five. It was agreed that we were to take turns, one of us sleeping on deck each appointed night. The sailing was fairly smooth to Hydra, where we spent most of a day on sharp-boned donkeys. Starved and stupid as they appeared, they were sure-footed in spite of the fact that they were hung with saddlebags that swelled with their own manure carefully shoveled by the guides each time a new supply was emitted. (The dry islands needed the fertilizer, the guides explained.) My donkey was a show-off with a taste for daring himself and me on the outermost edges of paths which were always a breath away from a precipice.

We grew accustomed to the daredevil Greek donkeys but never to the *melteme* that struck the Aegean shortly after we left Hydra. The sun shone, kept on shining, while the wind whipped the sea into sharp, dark teeth that threatened to devour us, ship and all (a surviving agent of the old Teutonic Lorelei?). Nor was our skipper skillful or reassuring; he reminded us at least once an hour of the heart attack he had recently suffered and would undoubtedly succumb to soon. Nor was it comforting to be greeted at several islands with anxious questions about a French party—had we perhaps seen them?—that might have been eaten by the waves. We spent several days, each in our own way, trying to cope with the storm. George took the most sensible measure to ride it out; he slept and slept throughout the day and night. Ed, who could not stay below, tormented by the memory of weeks in the hold of a merchant marine ship years before, sat on the deck, tied by ropes to his seat and sections of railing, his eyes growing red and brighter red as the waters lashed his face. Marie ran around merrily, vomiting often and lightly, as if she were spitting flowers, like a Botticelli girl. Colette and I lay on my bunk, head to foot, trying to talk the time away. Afraid to make the perilous journey, I pushed away the need to go to the head until I absolutely had to. Hanging on to anything that wasn't swinging, shaking, shuddering, I made it. After urinating in several directions, I began my unsteady return, to bang into the refrigerator. The door flew open and with it flew a bottle of ketchup. It splashed me with dark red stains, many. Colette lifted her head, saw a ghastly red me, and screamed, "Kate has committed suicide!" some measure of how terrifying the storm was, how long it lasted, and how crazy it made us.

Calmer days did finally come, and we stopped at several islands for a while: strangely evocative Santorini and self-conscious Mykonos among them. But Poseidon grew bored and went back to his favorite toy. He wound it up, baring its black teeth on my night for being strapped to the deck. Having become accustomed to the rolling, the rocking, the howling wind—and very tired—I was able to fall asleep, to be awakened before dawn by shouting voices and thumpings and creakings from two boats that flanked ours. Both were laden with and busy delivering tables, chests, credenzas, waking the whole island, which rushed down to the waterfront to claim its deliveries. Why before the crack of dawn? Why in this hellish storm? The Greeks were, it seemed, as unpredictable, as mad as the *melteme* and, my sleepy anger said, they deserved each other. (Now, in 1989, in reading about their eccentric, screaming politics—something like the disputes among their founding gods and heroes—I wonder if the *melteme*, howling or waiting, is not their basic native atmosphere.)

One advance into Eastern Europe was slowly paced, beginning in Amsterdam where I was to meet a group of journalists, invited like myself to join a cruise on a luxury yacht, truly luxurious, to several northern ports. Arriving from London, where I was then living, I spent a few days with the city's Rembrandts and Van Goghs and in the pearl of Dutch museums, the Mauritshuis in The Hague. Pacing the streets of Amsterdam, staring into sex shops, expecting the blatancies of Times Square, I was surprised and charmed by the neat, matter-of-fact displays similar to those of ordinary shops; like jars of mayonnaise, boxes of cornflakes, bundles of Brillo pads, lacking murmurs of arcane pleasures except for an occasional odd object like a menorah whose candlesticks were penises. And, as if I were examining Vermeers, I studied the illuminated one-story-up windows to stare at the well- and respectably dressed women for sale on display, hair carefully arranged, a clean, white blouse over a neatly pressed skirt—your sister, my kindergarten teacher—in an atmosphere of comfortable domesticity: a red velvet bench, a well-shaped table, a cut glass flower vase. A couple of the women sat at their tables reading (or feigning?); one or two preened in front of long mirrors, showing a twist of waist, a swell of breast, a generosity of rump as they turned slowly, with small smiles.

After the orderly, dignified pleasures of the Scandinavian cities, we sailed on to Hamburg. I had, in college, stopped all contact with the German language, with Goethe, Schiller, Lessing (even Heine, though he was born a Jew), when I learned of the Nazi "final solution." I had no wish to speak the language— which I could still manage—especially not in Hamburg, our next stop, whose lures, except for the night life of the Reeperbahn, did not attract me at all. I joined, instead, a bus tour that rode through dull, flat country bare of crops and studded with gun emplacements—Russian, I was told, and the first I had ever seen except in films—each one an assault. My goal was Lübeck, the town in which Thomas Mann was born; a visit to his house would be the only act of homage I would offer Germany. As we approached the town where I expected to find a monument or at least a large commemorative plaque, I was met by gaudy stands and signs announcing that Lübeck was the marzipan capital of the world. I loathe marzipan, and the endless display of little pink piggies and dead red strawberries and darling bunnies swelled my distaste. I escaped the cuties and waited for my bus group near the museum that displayed Lübeck as the major member of the medieval Hanseatic League, which controlled the northern seas. On to the heavy, dour cathedral, that visit followed by a large German meal of the expected schnitzel, potatoes, and mounds of sauerkraut.

After lunch, with time to spare before the tour group left for the return to Hamburg, I went on my quest for Thomas Mann. I asked our driver, I asked the hosts at the restaurant, I asked people on the street. Not one of them knew the house. As I wandered and questioned, the word *Mengstrasse* suddenly burst into my mind. Could it have been mentioned in *Buddenbrooks*? I found the street and examined each door and lintel. On one house, considerably modernized to accommodate the offices of a periodical and other modest enterprises, I saw scratched into the lintel, pale, the color of fading old plaster, "Here is where the Mann family lived and *Buddenbrooks* was written." No mention by name of the Nobel Prize winner, of the writer of *The Magic Mountain*, of the refugee from Nazism still given short shrift by his very German town living in its sticky marzipan gemütlichkeit and fading memories of Hanseatic might. (Collections of Mann memorabilia were later displayed elsewhere in the town.)

Hamburg made amends for Lübeck's chilliness by being polite and solicitous to a group of us who spent that night on and around the Reeperbahn, in the notorious red-light sailor's-delight district—now theatricalized with too many Lili Marlenes leaning against lampposts—pit of the most obscene, mordantly contemptuous, and wildly funny demonstrations of how ludicrous the flesh can be. (On leaving one night spot, we had to kiss some

of the entertainers good-night; they insisted. When I was embraced by one fat genius of lubricity I felt engulfed in a large
mass of sweet, pink chewing gum.)

As our ship approached Leningrad I summoned my accustomed
anachronistic literary pictures of Russia: dour, gray, full of consumptive psychotics and ragged, freezing peasants; dissidents driv-
en to madness in Siberian cells, my collage held together by the
ugly, worn face of Tolstoi as he finished his raging life. And
there would be impassioned anti-Americanism. But no such
thing. Without Gorbachev, without glasnost, without highly
praised exchanges of information, Intourist, eager to impress
American journalists, made our way smooth and pleasant with
comparatively few restraints. We descended to the pier into a file
of Russian soldiers in ankle-length woolen coats. They took our
passports—not a word—gave us receipt slips and marched us
toward the city past large photo portraits of honored workers who
had accomplished singular things in their factories. At the end
of the portraits and the pier we were met by an attractive young
blond who greeted us in startlingly good American, college-bred
English although, she told us, she had never been out of Russia.
She had a program designed especially for us journalists—a walk
through the enchanting and slightly demented Baroque palaces
in bassinet colors, the summer playgrounds full of practical jokes,
the villas and tricks ordered by the Russian giant, Peter the Great.
Of course the tourist shop and the Hermitage Museum and a
performance of the ballet and, for us journalists, meetings with
members of Intourist, the seducers to Russian travel. They were
memorable meetings. The first took place in a square, cold,
official building. We were ushered by our guide, Manya, into a
large room whose center was filled with a long, wide table covered
with green felt—very much like the table in the famous Joos
ballet, and it chilled me to the bone—and a distribution of vodka,
cigarettes, matches, meticulously spaced, a precisely, coldly
measured placing of objects that were normally meant to suggest
hospitality and relaxed conversation. There was no conversation;
we were lectured by a short, trim man who gave us a glowing

picture of Russian tourism as it would be the very next year: From the borders with Finland and Poland, across thousands of miles to the border with Outer Mongolia and quite possibly beyond, the Union of Soviet Socialist Republics would provide every convenience for visitors, especially those traveling in hired Russian cars, stopping here and there, wherever it suited them. They would find many gas stations; auto repair shops; inexpensive, comfortable *dachas* in which to lodge; pleasant conveniently placed restaurants; and playgrounds along the roads for the children to enjoy. We sat there, stunned with wonder and admiration at such a soaring pipe dream. (No one, incidentally, touched the vodka or took a cigarette; the feeling among us was that these were part of an immutable, fantasy stage set, not to be disturbed, ever.)

Our last encounter with Intourist was a farewell dinner given in our honor. It was a fine dinner, generously bewined and bevodkaed, accompanied by balalaika-strumming men in high-necked Russian blouses and tall boots; sad songs by ladies in long silken robes and tall headdresses, rather like the gentlewomen in the Polish scene of *Boris Godunov*. Our host was a tiny gentleman with a crinkly face gathered around pearly dentures that twinkled as he talked and smiled and smiled. No one saw how it happened, but we noticed suddenly that he was without the vodka bottle that had stood near his plate and in whose companionship he had been quite happy. He must also have been given a signal to close the revelry. He rose unsteadily from his chair and, with the last drops of vodka in his glass, toasted, arm held high, the *Amerikanski narod* (American people). We had no interpreter, Manya had gone out, and we sat foolish and tongue-tied. Either because I knew the meaning of *narod*, gleaned from early Russian movies, or I had more vodka in me than the others, I stood up, glass in hand, and toasted the *Russky narod*, rolling the *r*'s in the local fashion. Applause and cheers all around except from Manya who had returned and came quickly to me, saying, "You *do* speak Russian, don't you? I was pretty sure you did." I denied that I knew more than ten words of the language, learned in a few lessons long ago. My accent? It was the gift of my early childhood, when I learned to mimic the sounds of several languages. She looked skeptical yet said nothing more about my knowledge of Russian. I knew she would keep her bright blue eyes on me.

The next day, our last in Leningrad, was devoted to several hours in the Hermitage. Our group was dropped at a front entrance, and I dashed in alone, not because I didn't like my companions but because I had selected the galleries I most wanted to visit in our limited time (the Watteaus, the Impressionists, the Dutch), and I didn't want to be distracted by anyone else's tastes. When the time approached for meeting our tour bus, I wandered a circuitous route out of the staggering complex, finding my way to broom closets, locked doors, an antique toilet redolent of use and time, and finally, a small, obscure back door. As I expected, there, at this unused exit, stood Manya. She said, "Are you lost, Mrs. Simon?" "No, not at all." We walked around the building to join the others. When we parted for the last time later that day, I left her a few small American gifts, since money as a tip was unacceptable. As we shook hands warmly, she said to me, "I'll write you a note sometime—in Russian." Had she been a zealot and not the intelligent, admirable girl she was, I might have been questioned as a spy, one of my friends suggested during the outward journey. At this safe distance it appears as yet another titillating experience I missed.

23

❖

Once More: Flight

LAST night's exhausted confetti winked from the gangplank, faded paper ribbons slid across damp wood. I said good-bye to him, a deep kiss that I hoped might express affection and regret: The best we had been able to summon out of the three-day journey from New York to Puerto Rico was a bed rolling on sea and liquor, the touchings and meetings without bud or scent. It seems to have been tainted by defiance, by militancy, war with an ill-fitting marriage. He stayed on board; I went on to what I hoped would be profounder, less frustrating adventures. I caught a last gleam, as I waved from the dock, of his funny crooked tooth, an appealing young thing in a middle-aged face, and wondered whether he would ever find, keep, or return the ivory earring I had lost in his bed.

I was escorted off the ship at Ciudad Trujillo (now Santo Domingo) by someone in the universal Latin-American lower-echelon uniform of baggy khaki, a bright button or two, and a visored hat, who conducted me to a tall, vast room empty except for three young men in fatigues, with bushy hair and large machetes in hand. They opened my valises and launched into a unique customs search whose logic eluded me. I had a book on the area written by a liberal writer whose name they were just able to decipher. They seized it, leafing through the pages they clearly couldn't read. Coming to their rescue, I assured them

220

that the material on the Caribbean ended in 1880; it was an old history and had nothing about present politics in it, certainly not about President Trujillo, not a word. The next item of suspicion was a book of double crostics. I explained that it was a word game like crossword puzzles. Ah, but no, Señora, they had seen crosswords, said one whose curly bursts of hair pushed his cap up to make a foolish ornament at the top of his head. He gave me a wise, slanting glance and pointed out that crossword puzzles had patterns. This so-called game book contained none and must therefore be a book of codes. Something about my laughter, the fact that he had nothing more to say about codes, no proofs to spit at me, made him return the puzzles reluctantly to my bag. His friend then picked out a box of tampons and, with a machete designed for the thickest of sugarcane, began to shred, skillfully wielding the point of his great knife, the absorbent cotton wrapped on cord. "This is the way you American women carry drugs, very clever." I said nothing as he searched among the fluff of cotton and thread to find whatever he was looking for. Nothing to say or do about the white mess on the counter. Another young, eager official removed cartons of cigarettes from my valise and with the fine shining edge of his machete began to rip into packs and then single cigarettes in fury and frustration. What to say or do now with an Americana, alone, under their power in this huge vaulted stall? I said it for them. "Clearly, sirs, you saw no drugs, nor codes, and why destroy the cigarettes you might take home and share with your families?" In a show of pride my inquisitor of the forest of hair (I had heard him called Pablo) shoved the cigarettes aside disdainfully, undoubtedly to divide among his mates later. What next in this highly important protection of the country from foreign contamination?

We stood and stared at one another while they probably thought of additional ways to annoy me. The stalemate was ripped into by a slight man who came in carrying on his head an enormous box, a grotesquely large box as long as he was tall, lightly balanced and seemingly empty, a box of air, but as carefully held as if it enclosed treasure. Before Pablo could get to him, Chuchu of the thick sideburns ran at the man with his machete at the ready. With one swift blow he cut the string that held the box closed. The top swung upward, releasing a thousand, a million, a quadrillion, colored Ping-Pong balls in high flight, soaring to the ceiling, rebounding off the walls, meeting, clacking, kissing— an enchanted moment in a life of too many rough, rude customs sheds.

I was on my way to Port-au-Prince in Haiti, and this seemed a convenient, possibly interesting short stop. Haiti, as shelter for at least a while, was partially inspired by the strict, literal shapes and explosive flowers of primitive paintings I had admired and by reading about voodoo practices, an alluring subject. I was also impelled toward Haiti by the most complex and yet simplest of reasons: I was escaping from the insulting banalities of a marriage as it dragged on from year to year. So here I was, ready for a shiftless, maybe dissolute Caribbean life, often both eager and afraid.

Released by the officials still aghast at the Ping-Pong explosion, I dragged my bags out to find a taxi driver who almost immediately explained to me that the son of Columbus had lived here but I mustn't take pictures of the place. Why not? *Quien sabe*, it was the law. He left me at a hotel draped in purple bougainvillea, the doorway flanked by red flamboyant blossoms; hot, tropical, a place promising Somerset Maugham adventures. After I had washed and put on a loose, flowing dress, I went down to a source of sound that suggested a restaurant. It turned out to be a long, curved companionable bar surrounding a few dining tables. I sat down at the bar, next to a man with a hard-boned face. "Hello," he said. "Did you just get in?" The voice, too, was hard-angled; I seemed to hear the skull of a horse speaking. "Yes, I'm spending the night here and then picking up the plane for Port-au-Prince." "Why so fast?" "Why not? What's here that Haiti doesn't have?" Unsmiling, the harsh face challenged, "Why don't you stick around and find out? We could," he began to smile narrowly, "start with a drink—rum and fruit juices—and more rum and more rum." I consented to have a drink with him. We had two or three of the rum mixes, making desultory conversation until the alcohol began to move the words more nimbly. Suddenly, my companion, Joe, called to a man at the end of the bar. He came quickly, at an obedient slant. "What can I do for you, Joe?" "You can sit right here and talk to this lady and order her another drink or two. I have some business to take care of right now but I'll be back. And you be nice and polite." "Okay, sure." As Joe slid off his seat, I caught the glint of a gun in a holster under his jacket. Adventure with this sort of man, who played his sorts of games, I hadn't counted on. The old excited curiosity and terror charged back, the terror strongest. I tried to escape my guardian, who had introduced himself as Raoul, by asking to be pointed to the ladies' room. He insisted on accompanying me and waiting until I emerged, then propelled me, his hand guiding my elbow, back to the bar. An hour and another drink had passed when Joe returned and gestured Raoul to slip away, with no thanks from the boss or from me.

A marimba band struck up a clatter of sticks, rattles, and drums, and Joe pulled me off my bar stool and, holding me very close, began to pull me through unaccustomed, reluctant steps, bending me back painfully—in reminiscence of other dances in other places. But that was a long time ago, and why should it come back? Coming back was what life did, it seemed; nothing was ever quite finished, always the misshapen shadow, the distorted whisper of a half-forgotten tune.

I thought I could feel the gun as he held me close, his arm tightening and tightening, his excited rum breath bathing my face. I pulled away and ran off the floor. He followed me, dragged me up the stairs to the bedroom floor and shoved me into one of the rooms, signaling the maid at the door to leave. She did, quickly. He shut the door and came at me (cowering in a corner), reaching to rip off my floating, flirtatious dress. I fought him, pulling the cloth back around me, trying to circle back to the door, to open it and run. The grotesque contest stopped almost instantly. He opened the door and, filling it with his thick limbs and a burst of derisive laughter, called at me, "You cockteaser, who needs you? The bar is full of your kind who need me more than I need them. That's why you're here, to get fucked in a stranger's bed. Maybe you'll find another bed; I don't want you in mine." With a sharp snap of the lock, the door closed.

I didn't want to know, certainly not understand, what had happened and, with a couple of sleeping pills floating on the rum, banished myself for the night.

The next morning, on the plane for Port-au-Prince, I heard a familiar voice behind me. "Hello, missus, remember me, Raoul?" I acknowledged him sourly as he slid into the seat next to mine. This was a different Raoul, a flash of big gold tooth at the corner of his mouth, a rakish slope of Panama hat on his shining hair, a big ring on his finger, *muy macho*. He spoke to me familiarly, almost as an old friend, telling me about the casino–dance halls in Port-au-Prince and the gambling. The odds were usually good, he had friends there, and why didn't he and I meet for a drink, a dance or two, and some gambling? The stakes didn't have to be high, although he was in pretty good shape financially and could stake me. He had done the boss a big favor and the boss was grateful and always generous, especially when you let him know what was going on in rival circles—who was also dealing in guns, the boss's specialty, for instance.

That night, having settled into a light airy room in a pension in Petionville above Port-au-Prince, I took a taxi that plummeted down the hills to leave me at the brightly lit casino where Raoul said he would be. It provided a wide collection of pleasures including an attractive show of Haitian dancing, a mix of African hop-and-belly swing modified by reminiscences of gavotte and minuet that remained from earlier French days. Raoul and I danced, not too differently from the professionals, except that the gavotte was replaced by a step that seemed to imitate the burdened market women, baskets on their heads, walking in a rhythmic limp down the steep hills from the high fields they worked. This was the favored merengue, the peasant limp-step refined with smooth, subtle undulations, rarely abrupt, always erotic. Having danced and drunk some of the choice local rum—not for export,

I was told—we went to the gaming tables. Raoul chose the dice channel and, declaring that I felt lucky to him, asked me to roll the dice. I did, and time after time he collected, sometimes much, sometimes less; always he won. His white linen suit was wrinkling, his Panama had slid to a caricature angle, the gold tooth in his broadly smiling mouth shone like a small lighthouse. He was a happy man, in control of fortune. To share his luck, he turned to me and shoved a hundred-dollar bill down the low, ruffled front of my dress. I was Zola's Nana, a Toulouse entertainer, all the whores I had read about, not a nice—not-so-nice— Jewish girl from the Bronx, a winner of the high school English medal, a graduate of sedate Hunter College. At first I laughed a languid Odette laugh, pulling the bill out of my bodice and coolly putting it in my purse. Then, burned by a stomach pain and nausea, I ran to the bathroom and vomited. I don't remember how or who was involved—not Raoul, I think—but I was taken back to a room in Petionville.

I lay on a bed, not talking, not eating, not responding to anything or anyone for a couple of days. On the morning of the third day I was aware of the beaded strings at the doorway parting. A black woman stood there, as I felt she had several times before, offering a cup of soup, a dish of bread, the doorway beads a mantle over her shoulders, her extended black arms urging, "C'est bon. Mangez, mangez." She didn't approach me but after a few moments of urging left the food on a table near the doorway. I got out of the bed with dragging difficulty to try the soup but couldn't eat it. I wasn't physically sick. I wasn't dead. I wasn't alive, just gutted and waiting to disappear. I would wait, without food or fresh air, until I turned to thin shreds and floated like daffodil seeds into the air; no substance, no direction, no memory. This was not only the face of guilt, the misery that makes soured layers of the flesh, that mutters mea culpa in myriad languages, that trails through slow time like a twisted leg. It was also shame, very like the shames of childhood. My mother won't talk to me if she finds out where I've been and what I've done. My father will kill me. They'll both lock me out of the house with nothing to eat and nowhere to sleep. My brother will shout my terribleness all along both sides of the street. It was too much to bear; I had to crawl into disappearance.

The brown proferring arms and the cooing Creole voice changed in one aware moment to slender white arms and words in an unexpected accent. Crisp words: *up, get up, dress, eat,* snapped out in English with a trace of European cadences from a tanned face crowned by a coil of white hair. "My name is Mrs. Wegener and I'll explain my looks and name and accent after you get up, eat and talk, talk about what happened to you and why you want this passive suicide you don't even have the will to perform efficiently. But later. Now, get up. I'll show you to the shower and then take you to the dining room." She was forceful, I must have been ready. I got up, showered, dressed and followed her.

The cottage that was the dining room had the expected red-and-white checked tablecloths and small vases of exultant tropical flowers. At one side of the room, seemingly unsupervised and free to everyone, a refrigerator that revealed heaps of fruit and on its top, like a crown jewel, a noisy, shaking mixer. Mrs. Wegener introduced me to no one but pushed some sliced pineapple and papaya onto my dish, poured me a cup of coffee, and charged, "Eat. You can have eggs and toast, too, but I don't think you're ready for them just yet after days of starvation." She sat down at my side, watched me eat, examined me for a while, and then said, "You wonder about me here, an elderly German-ish woman. I live next door in a set of houses like these. They were once a pension too until I inherited some money and stopped catering to crazies who found themselves on the alluring road to Haiti and its magics. I'm not one of those; my story is less personal; history left me here. In the middle of the nineteenth century, I've been told, the German government dragged all the Jewish boys they could find into the army. As you can imagine, the more desperate and adventuresome found their way through the woods, usually stripping their telltale sidelocks and sometimes disguising themselves as women, until they reached the coast of France and vessels carrying French goods to Haiti. There were about twenty-five or thirty of them that made it here. They let their religion go and married French Catholic girls. The only part of their heritage they wouldn't part with were their names, and so we still have a few families, no longer Jewish but with Jewish names and although they are officially Catholic, the families form a small aristocracy, proud of their names. I think you're Jewish, aren't you? I could tell by the way, dull and flat as you are and probably feel, you gave me a lively look when I said 'Jewish.' "

Although the dining cottage began to fill up with couples and trios, people I later came to know, Mrs. Wegener insisted I come back to spend the day in her house; I was not ready for company but maybe for a little private talk, she said. Her house was of light latticework and bamboo, the walls hung with Haitian paintings: the superrealism of a marching band painted in Jacmel, minute red houses hiding behind huge purple-and-white pansies threatening as gaping vulvae. She followed my eyes to the paintings and smilingly said, "It all looks very innocent at first, the processions, the landscapes, the houses, and out creeps the sex— like, I suppose, in a lot of art. Look at your own Georgia O'Keeffe. Lie down, rest, and let's talk. Or let me talk. I heard about you; every new arrival is the subject of much gossip or keen guessing, which travels fast on this island. You probably tore out of a fairly respectable life, you wanted a fuller, more courageous one. But your view of the unconventional life was conventional—things from books, from movies, from your not-uncommon fears and fascinations: the man with the gun (I know him) and a reputation as a gunrunner and killer, a man who didn't prize you enough to rape you. And his little friend the messenger-spy (I know him too), the nothing who treated you like a whore because you treated yourself like a whore. Too many drinks, too much slithery, snaky dancing, shooting craps like you saw in a Las Vegas movie. The greedy movie vivacity you wanted to imitate, and finally the money stuffed into your whorish bra. You had, for a time, almost made it as a whore but hated her and began to search desperately for the woman you had been although you did not like *her* much, either. But you couldn't find her and so you were nobody, lying in a strange bed in a strange room, strange to yourself and hoping to fade altogether into a total blank." I said nothing.

The next day we went back to my official pension, the home of the rattling mixer. My introduction to the place was startling, soon to become a familiar leitmotiv. A beautiful Fury, wild-haired and gardenia-skinned, shrieked into the air as she opened the door. "Can't you smell it? He smells, always he smells, of women, of cheap perfume, of sweaty, dirty skin and dirty country cunts. Always he stinks of them and brings me the stink. I don't want him to touch me with his dirty fingers, and so he says it is my fault I won't sleep with him, I force him to other women." She tore back into the house and we retired to the garden where we saw the offender, the husband, golden-skinned and lissome, smiling and, as if continuing the dialogue with his wife, saying, with no interruption for an introduction, "Of course she's wrong and if I go to other women—rarely, you understand—it's because she drives me to them. But you heard her and her hysterics—." He continued to smile cordially as if this durable domestic crisis were no great matter. Surveying me at lightning speed (I could almost feel his fingers on my arms and tracing the curve of my waist), he then introduced himself, Robert Herzberg, another of the elite once-Jewish society.

Returning, first slowly, then more speedily, to curiosity, I looked forward to more entertainment from this couple and richer knowledge of other guests I saw in the lush garden. I can't say that any particular tablemates and neighbors provided the pages of a new primer from which I learned telling lessons, but they all produced questions that widened my sack of life's myriad patterns. That nice dumb little sailor who had jumped ship, how was he living at the pension? Who was supporting his contented life? Was it Madame Herzberg? The taciturn, very American agronomist, where did he get his kicks in this *louche* atmosphere? How did an elderly Italian, cheery and pasta-paunched, come away with a creamy blond Viennese hausfrau and settle with her in Haiti, both gigglingly happy and both formidable masters at dominoes, their victories a generous source of extra drinks? Why was Jim, a long way from Oregon, working at the not-too-busy harbor, checking cruise ship documents? Because, he told me, he was a Catholic and couldn't be divorced from that goddamned bitch and so let her father take care of her and their children. And whom did shy Mel talk with except a friend in California, connected to him by ham radio? And Mr. Post, who would attract conversation from his porch by repeatedly complaining about the grotesque size, like blankets, of the postage stamps. Why, when Jim and I, after becoming quite friendly, locked arms and legs on the ride in the pension car down to the waterfront, did we find Mr. Post's leg mingled with ours? It was hard to know from a man with such limited conversation whom he actually wanted, but from the worshipful looks and forced encounters I assumed that it was Clark-Gableish Joe he wanted and would never, even to the point of polite conversation, ever have.

Mr. Dubois, a landed neighbor friend of the Herzbergs, prided himself, among other feats, on the rich banana-pineapple-rum-mango confection that he whipped up on our whining mixer. He was also proud of the French he spoke, the French of Tours, not the ugly tongue taught by Canadian nuns (an important social distinction), and would converse only with inferiors in the patois, unlike many of his elite friends who seemed to prefer the light bird song of Creole for informal conversation. He was, in short, a snob and dressed like one—in subtle shades of gray with a gray pearl in his cravat—his crisp gray head meticulously neat and shapely. It was Mr. Dubois who presented me one Sunday afternoon with a novel Haitian gift, a piece of social knowledge that throbbed with earthy realities. He ushered me into his well-dusted car, placing a basket on the back seat. The car began to climb the hills north of Petionville, passing stands of the peculiar, slender papaya tree, heavy with fruit, and large orange pearls of mangoes dropping from among glistening green leaves. The air was sweet and cool in the hills, perfumed with fruits and flowers. We rode in silence until Mr. Dubois turned to me and said, "I want to tell you something about what you're going to see. Some years ago there was a massacre here, our men killed off by murderers on the other side of this island that was Hispaniola. We had only women left and some children. Who was to take care of these hill women who had nothing and knew nothing about preserving their lives? The rest of us men, of course, those who had found safety in the towns or had fled to France for a while. We decided to take care of them—in our own way—creating a system we call *plaçage*, related, I suppose, to the 'placing' we arranged for some of these women."

With the last word he turned his car toward a tiny garden with a slatted fence against which a pig was rubbing its back. The garden was a version of a Haitian painting of unabashed high colors and unexpected perspectives: fat melons sending great creepers and leaves up the frail fence posts, a papaya tree sheltering under a banana palm, above them all, like a god, a huge coconut palm. Inside this Eden sat a bandannaed woman stripping vegetables, her palm shining pink against the long, agile black of her fingers. A large red rooster was picking at the greens she dropped, trying to chase the rooster were her two little boys, two or three years old, round cheeked, round buttocked, sleekly black and shining. Mr. Dubois greeted the woman with a handshake and then picked up each of the little boys in turn, stroking them affectionately. He then concentrated on the business of examining them carefully: first the mouth and throat and, with the ivory toothpick he always carried, the insides of their nostrils. He then examined their genitals, scrutinizing each fold, and then, turning them over, spread and explored as far as he could each anus. "Worms. I don't want them to have worms," he muttered. After the examinations, he patted the heads of the wailing, insulted children and from his basket pulled bunches of lollipops as peacemakers. He gave the woman some money, nodded and waved at the assembled family, and left with me in tow.

We made several such stops in the hills: gardens, children, women, pigs, and chickens replicas of each other and the scenario the same, except in one place where I was left with a baby girl. She was frightened by my pale skin and whimpered when her mother and father entered the small hut adjoining the garden to stay for an hour or so and reappeared, expressionless and wordless. There was no gesture of farewell to child or woman; money must have been passed to the woman in the hut. We went on, soon plummeting down the hills, back to the lighter bewilderments of the pension, I never to be free of the thought that elements of *plaçage* entered the lives of many women, including the immigrant women among whom I was brought up. This version was brightly flowered, hung with festoons of birds and fruit, but the cool man interested mainly in his progeny and only casually in the women who bore and cared for them was my father and the fathers of my childhood friends.

It was Mr. Dubois who took me to what he called an "inside" voodoo ceremony, one that was not staged for tourists but for a group from local villages. He was a friend of the *mamaloi* who was to conduct an initiation of novices; she had invited him and a friend, if he liked, to observe. We went earlier than the actual time of the ceremony and were conducted through the several rooms of a large ramshackle house. In one small room there was an altar area, actually a table on which were propped pictures of Jesus, Mary and, to my astonishment, Lenin. (Any saint might be of help if sufficiently revered?) Before the personages hung the bead gourds that were the rattles used during the ceremony; a number of black, repellent little figures, probably of voodoo gods; several bottles of *tafia* (raw rum); and three drums, one small, one larger, one huge. In an adjoining room sat six girls in white dresses, the novitiates, unsteady and wild eyed, with uncomprehending faces, seemingly incapable of speech. Mr. Dubois explained that these girls, ready to be initiated as members of what appeared to be a closed society of the especially chosen, were starved for several days, given rum in considerable quantities, and sent into trances by their imaginings, their fear and pride, their sensations dizzied by the rhythmic pounding of the drums, the incessant harsh rustle of beaded gourds.

We were called into a large area where a number of spectators, neighbors and families of the initiates, were already gathered. The drummers appeared and four men with rattling gourds took their places and waited for the *mamaloi*, who soon appeared, a large, broad presence, confident, mighty, unsmiling, like a black Minerva, her dark gold, silken skin shining under her red kerchief tied in a high commanding knot. She approached a bowl on a stand as the magicians began their beat and, taking a handful of maize from it, began to draw a design on the earth floor. Slowly but without hesitation she allowed her hand to complete a figure that was recognized by the spectators as the symbol that dedicated the ceremony to the god of love. Chanting in words that were incomprehensible to me, less Creole than African, the people on the floor, their leader among them, began to dance to the drumbeats, bending, shaking, stretching, breasts astir, hips quivering and trembling (one middle-aged woman smilingly showed the assembled guests the control she had over one obedient buttock, the rest of her body held still). The drums pounded louder and faster and the whirling, contorted bodies (now including the white-clothed, blank-eyed novices) circled faster and faster, the chants growing louder and now and then ripped by a shriek. Two women fell to the floor, convulsed bodies coiling and uncoiling like snakes. These women, I was told, had been overcome and subject to the god with whom they were in close communication. They were carefully carried into another room.

The pause in the dancing opened a path for a tall man in white trousers, a jaunty white straw hat, and a gauzy, transparent blue shirt that revealed his strongly muscled arms and chest. He was carrying a live chicken that he proceeded to whirl about his head as he chanted to the god, obviously making him an offering. (I suddenly remembered a description I had heard in my childhood of a religious ceremony that required a chicken to be whirled over someone's head to banish evil and sin. Mysticism and superstition seem to cover all parts of the world, from a small town in Poland to Haiti and places beyond.) The drumming, the dancing, and droning continued as he chanted and whirled the chicken. The drummers and dancers grew wilder and wilder as he poured rum into the beak of the chicken and then, with a sharp blade, swiftly cut its neck. With a shout of triumph in which the dancers joined, he held the chicken, dripping blood, high over his head. As if this were an orgasm, the crowd sighed and murmured, slowly stopped dancing, the drums dropping to a slow whisper.

*   *   *

A worldly Italian friend transferred by his diplomatic service to São Paulo in Brazil once told me of the compelling fascination and the growing yielding to the rituals of *candomble* on Bahia. I would not have known what he meant by "yielding" and "almost believing" had I not tottered out of the voodoo ceremony lost, stupefied, clinging to the reality of Mr. Dubois's arm.

24

Hallway to Exit

Like a parent slowly walking a young child into cold ocean water, one pace at a time, the Bone Man was leading me with slow, unhurried steps toward the place where all my lost people were. My small stomach, feebly kicking, mewling, and vomiting into my intestines over any insult—hot food, sweets, cold food, anything it chose to hate—was certainly not yet happy with me, as was however the gleeful irrationality of the fates who have a taste for the excesses no self-respecting soap opera would accept. ("God has no taste" says Alan Bennett in one of his plays.)

Rushing from my telephone in loose slippers, I was caught, pulled by loops of wire, and flung violently to the floor. A friend who was visiting (I wonder how I would have managed if I were, as often, alone) came running when she heard my crash, and I said to her, "I think I broke my arm and maybe my leg; I can't move either; the pain is dreadful. Call nine-one-one." Two young cops quickly arrived, a black girl and a fresh-faced young blond boy, followed by medics who put me on a stretcher and carried me down to a waiting ambulance that rushed us to a hospital in my neighborhood. The mobbed emergency room was frantic with tears and calls, with wheelchairs and twisted bodies, with flying stretchers and wringing hands. Reasonably soon I was put into a small room where a thin, middle-aged Hispanic couple sat, wearing the fatalistic flat mask for pain that I had known in Mexico, undistracted from their private agony by the portable X-ray machine that was brought into the room to search out my injuries. I had called them correctly; there was a crack in my upper arm and a break in my right thigh. (Had I been twenty, I thought angrily, I would have had colorful bruises, but now, my bones polished to delicacy by the sculptor Age, were fine, to be shattered by any harsh blow.)

X-rays done and the machine removed, I was taken to a nearby hospital that concentrated on my sort of injury and lifted into a bed. The room was small, a tight space for two patients, a wheelchair, two television screens, several chairs, and although there was a curtain that could be drawn between the two beds, we two patients were in each other's eyes and bodies to a disconcerting, often repellent degree. Because we were so bound together in pain and space we became at times one body, one will. My roommate was a large woman who had fallen like a great tree, breaking her limbs in several places. She was seen to by a slight, courtly little husband, pale and very thin, with the obsequious manners and accent that made me think of him as the last man alive in Auschwitz. The nurses intimidated him, the mysterious system of communicating and not communicating information— a villainous game—bewildered and frightened him. I came to his rescue when anyone would listen to me, to insist that he be allowed to stay beyond the usual hours, nervously awaiting his wife's return from a testing or treatment room.

She and I frequently bellowed a duet for bedpans. When she had fruitlessly rung and called for half an hour, I took up the cry, which sometimes produced a pan, often not. (I devised a scheme that worked only a couple of times: lying in bed, awake at five-thirty in the morning before the six o'clock nurses' shift came on, I found my bladder yearning for relief. No one answered the light that was meant to signal nurses; the night shift, about to depart, was taking on no more duties. I lay there wondering if I should let go and wet the bed. They would be punished— one becomes childishly vengeful in helplessness—by having to remake the wet bed. However, lying in my own urine for God knows how long was hardly a triumph. So, I called down to the main phone station as if I were not a patient but rather a doctor or a social worker and asked for the nurses' station on my floor, got an immediate answer and my Holy Grail, a bedpan.)

Since I broke my arm and leg on a Friday (the thirteenth) and was an unscheduled patient, my leg could not be operated on until some open time the next week. Trussed up like a chicken ready for the oven, I had several days for learning something of the nurses who ran in and out taking blood pressures and temperatures and drawing tiny rivulets of blood. Many of them were young women from the Philippines, a few of them tired and homesick, the rest helpful and good-natured. One member of the early morning shift was an aristocratic black gentleman who walked at a steady, stately pace, his neat head high, arms stiff, as if on parade. He was distant, prompt, polite, impeccably correct, and efficient. Another, younger black man was more responsive and friendly—to a degree. I had never been attended to, bedpan and all, by a man, much less a black man, and wondered how these men felt about their white patients. I never found out. How does one ask? And these men, no chatterers, would find some way to ignore the question if it were asked. One plump black nurse was friendly and cheery one day and a virago the next; yesterday's amiable fat quivering with rage today. Another black nurse walked into her rooms scolding into the air and then directly at anyone who addressed her. The nurses who actually frightened me were tall, broad, elderly black women in carefully starched white who never said an unnecessary word but looked unremittingly disdainful, contemptuous, permanently insulted and insulting. This latter group clearly represented reverse racism: We were broken, sick, and totally dependent, and they seemed, by their harsh voices, their short, sharp commands and stony eyes, to enjoy our feebleness. The young black aides who had not yet accumulated such anger were bright and merry, especially one loose-limbed clown who shouted on her arrival early one morning, "Up! Up, everybody! All out of bed! Get dressed and into the streets!" I thought her act was amusing, but my neighbors, suspecting it might be the call to a nurses' revolution or at least a strike, were frightened and protested. Watching, watching, I saw young Philippine women dash from patient to patient all day, some of them dragging their tired legs through extra-duty hours. Between the much-publicized nursing shortage and antiwhite stances there were deep gaps in the service to patients and yet considerable care and forbearance from a few of the dedicated.

Mrs. What's-Her-Name of the timid, obedient husband was a voluble woman who introduced herself to me as a schmoozer (talker), "and are you?" I answered, "Not much," reluctant to be rude but hoping to avert dull question-and-answer sessions: "What happened to you? Where do you come from? What do you do? Are you married?" questions I found entertaining on foreign trains but not from hospital beds. Mrs. X was loudly uninhibited about her many discomforts. After hearing constantly about the pain a catheter caused her, I began to feel the choking discomfort of the instrument within myself, her flow of urine inside my bladder too. Her complaints of constipation hurt my intestines. When she inquired anxiously each day about the level of her blood pressure I felt mine rising, and when she moaned and begged for cold compresses to diminish an imaginary fever, my brow grew warm and sweaty. We were becoming Siamese twins, the big, noisy lady and I, and I was deliriously happy to leave her, the nurses, the hospital and to be my own single maimed self. After a stay of three weeks that had included skillful beginnings of physiotherapy and follow-up therapy at home, I began to lead a timid, soon less-timid, imitation of my customary life: friends, concerts, work, and the essential humdrum et ceteras. As I had told a young psychologist studying the moods of older patients—depressed? optimistic?—I was still interested.

Here I sit typing after years of fighting with typewriters, pounding as haphazardly as, or worse than, I ever did, still working, insistent on working. The room in which I work faces, on one side, an apartment wall hung with small iron-fenced balconies that startle themselves with flowering bushes in the spring. The other side gives me the openness of a long stretch of low buildings brightly punctuated by a Korean fruit-and-flower stall, then running on to the dash and stutter of Fifth Avenue traffic. At night my sky is a corner of Xanadu. My window gives me a close neighborliness with the Empire State tower adorned in various seasonal brilliances. To its left, the golden-crested cap of an insurance building and, surrounding that, ornaments that blink gaudy colors through the night. From my bus stop on Third Avenue I see, always with delight, the art deco jewels that crown the Chrysler building and, fronting the video shop and the cut-rate drugstore, a black water tower whose night shape is formidably large and threatening, become an Aztec goddess of death.

At seventeen I was so enamored of life, of its vagaries, its soaring flights and precipitous depths, that I promised myself I would experience everything, stipulating no qualities good or bad, and it has pretty much all happened. Little more than I knew at seventeen do I surely know who I am at seventy-five. At five o'clock on a gray winter morning I am alone in the world, its oldest orphan, singing with Leadbelly, "Good morning, blues. Blues, how do you do?" Parts of me seem to want to retire— teeth, bones, innards—and when will they call a halt, entirely, to the stubbornness that sustains me? Where do I go when I become afraid of slipping in the bathtub, when I fear a stroke and no one to find me for days? I might for some limited time be sheltered or supported by friends who gather a charity pot when I can no longer work, but who will free me of humiliating pain before I die, who will help me die quickly? When the morning light brightens the window I grow younger; seven years old as I feel myself neglected by a friend who was to call several days ago and didn't; she hurt my self-esteen, as tough Rosie did on La Fontaine Avenue in the Bronx decades ago. When the day lengthens I am forty again, hating an unknown woman trailing three young children while I have none. I return to several young ages at other times, when my heart lifts with a ballerina who becomes a silken breeze before my entranced eyes, when I am mesmerized by the audacity of Vuillard's designs and their

murmuring colors; when I fall once again in love with Ambrogio
Lorenzetti's dancing women of happy Siena as I remember them;
when I hear Lotte Lehmann sing the Marschallin in the *Rosen-*
kavalier on an old recording. I am back in Hunter College when
I read Shakespeare sonnets, as if for the first astonished time;
when I reread *The Brothers Karamazov*, finding new shock of
recognition in those endless mazes of the human condition. (And
since I have no saving religion, no protective saints, no promise
of heaven or hell, no progeny, I must content myself with the
possibility that my shadowy immortality will come with the love
of my immortals.)

The late evenings are often as haunted as the early mornings,
a little voice in my head singing an appropriate tune to name
the mood. Frequently it is Schubert's "Auf dem Wasser zu
Singen" with its rueful refrain, *"Wieder wie gestern und heute*
die Zeit." Sometimes it is as direct a blow as, "I hate to see the
evening sun go down." Another day gone, irretrievable, lost forever in the hideous cavern that is the mouth of Cronus. I have
been, am, a pretty good—if cowardly and silent—hater, but there
is nothing I loathe so much now as time, slippery, uncontrollable,
irresponsible, answerable to no one and nothing, the most powerful of nature's dirty tricks. Time has arranged to leave me on
the dock while the others, the younger, take off on my favorite
adventures; to make me furious and vindictive with those who
reflect my slouching descents. The man I haven't seen for a
number of years who now bends his head toward mine, repeating,
"What did you say? What did you say?" as I speak to him. I hate
it and in some terrible way enjoy seeing him shuffle away as I
measure his creeping hairlessness. And what does he think of
decaying me?

The encounters bring back an old English song, "Oh, once
I had thyme of my own and in my own garden it grew. But now
it is covered with rue, with rue. But now it is covered with rue."
I can sometimes dispel rue by remembering Paul Claudel's astonishment at getting along well despite frail eyes, ears, teeth,
bones. Or darken my mood thinking of tubercular young Keats

whose "spirit is too weak," on whom "mortality weighs heavily." Or move again into the light with a gleeful Renaissance nonagenarian on whom the sun shone steadily.

One of those months, these years, I will close book, sights, voices, pains, pleasures. How will I actually meet death? Might I be the center of a common African tableau, as much of the landscape as thornbush trees? A weak, slow zebra, left behind in the speeding migration toward water, dazzling the landscape with their lightning of stripes, has been pounced on by a lioness. She is now feeding off him lustily. Watching her from a distance, fixed, concentrated, is a hyena with the mottled coloring of disease. Not far from him stands a jackal, motionless, waiting his turn at the leftovers. In the branch of a tree, also fixed and waiting, a vulture. Would vulture, jackal, hyena be my funeral cortege?

Would I be the enormous fish a few friends and I caught and hauled in off the coast of Zihuataneho, near Ixtapa, in Mexico? As he lay on the deck, gasping and struggling, he took on magnificent coloring—iridescent blues and golds, scarlet patches near his fins, the colors flowing and melting into each other. He meant to be superb in death and he was, until the color faded from him and he lay gray and still. Just before his last gasp he raised one broad sail of fin, pointed it stiffly up into the sky and there held it for a long minute. It was an awesome act of defiance or denial, or a salute to powerful death. Maybe I will not be a frail, foolish zebra, but raise my arm, stiff, straight, into the sky in defiance and homage.

Or possibly I will wait with the calm and grace of my hospital companions, the blind regal Catholic, the godly old Orthodox Jew.

If I'm to be cremated (in spite of Robert Frost's recommendation for destructive ice), OK. If I'm to be buried, though, I should like to be accompanied by handfuls of beaming, fat-thighed, ornately coiffed Mexican fertility goddesses.